PELICAN BOOKS
A404
ANCIENT VOYAGERS IN THE PACIFIC
ANDREW SHARP

# ANCIENT VOYAGERS IN THE PACIFIC

*

*Andrew Sharp*

PENGUIN BOOKS

Penguin Books Ltd, Harmondsworth, Middlesex
U.S.A.: Penguin Books Inc., 3300 Clipper Mill Road, Baltimore 11, Md
AUSTRALIA: Penguin Books Pty Ltd, 762 Whitehorse Road,
Mitcham, Victoria

—

First published by the Polynesian Society 1956
Published in Penguin Books 1957

Made and printed in Great Britain
by The Whitefriars Press Ltd, London and Tonbridge
Collogravure plates by Harrison & Sons Ltd

# Contents

# List of Plates

# Maps

# Foreword

The numbers in the text refer to the Sources and Bibliography (pages 213–28). They do not include additional subject matter or comment.

'Western Polynesia' means the Tonga-Samoa-Ellice-Rotuma area, and 'Eastern Polynesia' the Cook-Tahiti-Tuamotu-Mangareva-Marquesas area. The word 'Maori' is restricted to signify the pre-European inhabitants of New Zealand and their descendants and language.

I am indebted to Mr A. P. Vayda of Columbia University for invaluable detailed criticism of my earlier drafts, to Dr W. R. Geddes, Mr J. B. Palmer, Mr B. Biggs, Mr J. Golson, and Mr C. R. H. Taylor for further helpful comment, and to the Polynesian Society for providing an initial forum for my views. Mr J. Pascoe assisted me greatly with the illustrations.

ANDREW SHARP

# CHAPTER ONE

# Captain Cook's Forgotten Theory

*

EVERYONE has heard of the 'Polynesian problem' – of how people with brown skins and black hair, speaking dialects of the same language, were found by the European discoverers on all the inhabited islands in the east and south of the Pacific Ocean. Some of these islands – Hawaii, New Zealand, Easter Island – are 1,000 to 1,800 miles from the nearest other inhabited land. How did the Polynesians and other Pacific Islanders get to their distant islands? For 200 years men have propounded their solutions. Some have thought that they must have passed through chains of islands or continents which have since sunk beneath the waves. Most writers, both scholarly and popular, over the past eighty years have imagined that the farther islands were colonized by deliberate voyaging. Yet the key to the truth was left at the beginning by the greatest of Pacific explorers before death suddenly claimed him.

The natural groupings of the Polynesian Islands can be summed up in a few words.

The western area, comprising Samoa, Tonga, Rotuma, and the Ellice Islands, together with Fiji, forms a large group, in which the longest gaps without intervening islands are of 200 to 300 miles.

On the eastern side of this archipelago, at a distance of 1,000 miles from Samoa, is the Tahiti or Society Group, usually called Tahiti from the largest island. To the east of the Tahiti Group, at a distance of 170 to 230 miles, are the Tuamotu Islands, comprising a great number of low atolls at no great distance from one another. The Tahiti-Tuamotu islands together form another large archipelago, in which the longest gaps without intervening islands are these same distances of 170 to 230 miles.

Outside these two main areas are a large number of scattered islands. A few of them form minor natural couplings separated by no great distance from one another. The islands of Hawaii and of the Marquesas are examples. All these scattered islands, and the minor couplings which exist here and there among them, are at least 300 miles distant from either of the main areas, or from one another.

It can be demonstrated beyond doubt, from what the Polynesians told the early Europeans in the Polynesian islands, as well as by much supporting evidence from other sources, that the deliberate long voyages of the Polynesians were confined within each of the two main areas, namely Western Polynesia-Fiji and the Tahiti-Tuamotu archipelago. No deliberate contact occurred over the gap separating the two main areas. Within these two areas, the longest off-shore voyages that were made without intervening islands were over the distances of up to 300 miles which separate Tonga, Fiji, Samoa, Rotuma, and the Ellice Islands, and the 230 miles which separate Tahiti from those Tuamotu Islands which lie to the north-east of Tahiti. No deliberate colonization even of the central groups of islands – Fiji, Tonga, Samoa, Tahiti, the Tuamotus, the Marquesas – took place, much less of New Zealand, Hawaii and Easter Island.

The sole manner in which each of the groups, and of the manifold isolated islands, was separately peopled in the first place was tentatively deduced by Captain James Cook. His view was fully proved, unconsciously and independently, by the combined evidence of every other early discoverer and observer in the Pacific, as well as by a great deal of modern evidence.

We now embark with Captain Cook[1] as he leaves the shores of New Zealand for the last time on 25 February 1777, and sails east. After Cook had run up into the tropics for some time, the look-out shouted that land was in sight. This was the island of Mangaia in the Cook Group. From Mangaia Cook's two ships moved on, and 140 miles north Atiu came into view. No European eyes had previously seen Mangaia or Atiu.

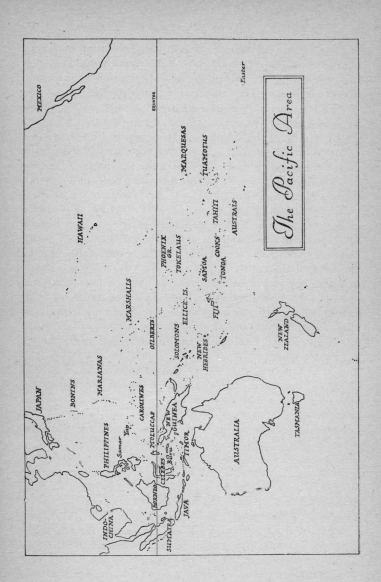

The Pacific Area

MEXICO

EQUATOR.

Easter

JAPAN

BONINS

MARIANAS

HAWAII

MARQUESAS

PHILIPPINES

Yap

CAROLINES

MARSHALLS

PHOENIX GR.

TOKELAUS

TUAMOTUS

TAHITI

Samar

Borneo

CELEBES

NEW GUINEA

MOLUCCAS

POLYNESIA

GILBERTS

SOLOMONS

ELLICE IS.

SAMOA

COOKS

TONGA

AUSTRALS

INDO-CHINA

SUMATRA

JAVA

TIMOR

NEW HEBRIDES

FIJI

NEW ZEALAND

AUSTRALIA

TASMANIA

13

(The reader is requested to glance at the map on pages 16 and 17 when an unfamiliar island is mentioned. The map has been simplified by showing only the names of the groups and of those islands which are mentioned in the text.)

The islanders of Atiu proved friendly, and some interesting information was exchanged through Omai, Cook's Tahitian interpreter. Omai was surprised to find that three of his countrymen from Tahiti, over 600 miles to the northeast, were on the island. They were the survivors of a canoe containing about twenty people who had been blown away in a sudden gale while passing from Tahiti to Raiatea, an important island about 100 miles west of Tahiti. For many days they continued to be exposed to the elements, during which time most of them died. The canoe turned over, and the four remaining men were left in the water, hanging onto the sides of the canoe. After a day or two more the canoe and the four survivors clinging to it were cast on Atiu, and the islanders brought them ashore. This had happened long before, and in the meantime they had settled happily in their new home. Apparently no visitors from Tahiti to Atiu, nor from Atiu to Tahiti, had in the meantime given them a lift home.

After making contact with the people of other islands nearby, Cook decided to sail west to familiar haunts in the Tonga Group, which he had visited on his previous voyage, and where he knew he could get supplies. He therefore came west to Palmerston Atoll, on the way to Tonga. Palmerston is a low atoll, and like most of the atolls is not very fertile. The high islands of the Pacific are formed from solidified basaltic lava for the most part, overlaid with fertile volcanic dust, and have therefore been the main regions of population. On uninhabited Palmerston, Cook's boats secured coconuts, sea-birds, crabs and fish. They also found the remains of a canoe which Cook judged to have been cast there in a storm, and several brown rats which he thought might have come as stowaways.

From Palmerston Cook ran west to Tonga, a distance of 700 miles, with only one small island, Niue or Savage

Island, in between. The winds were variable, frequently from the north and west.

By this time Cook had traversed the Pacific three times. He had the first-hand evidence of the accidental one-way voyage of the Tahitians to Atiu. Furthermore Cook was familiar with de Brosses's accounts of Pacific voyages, in which is told the story of a more significant involuntary migration. In 1696 a large canoe came on an accidental journey from the Carolines in the North Pacific to the Philippines, having been lost at sea in a storm while passing between two local islands. After seventy days, it arrived on the Philippines island of Samar, 1,000 miles away, with a number of men, women, children, and babies, none of whom had any idea where they were.[2]

When therefore Cook came to write up his thoughts in his journal, which he prepared for publication from time to time on the voyage, he gave a tentative explanation of the peopling of the farther islands in the following memorable words. Speaking of the accidental journey to Atiu, he said that this *will serve to explain, better than a thousand conjectures of speculative reasoners, how the detached parts of the earth, and, in particular, how the South Seas, may have been peopled; especially those that lie remote from any inhabited continent, or from each other.*

In the Tonga Group Cook and his men spent five pleasant months. The main object of their visit to the Pacific was to try to find a navigable passage round the top of North America from the Pacific to the Atlantic. If this were successful, vessels could have come from England to Asia by that route, instead of round the Cape of Good Hope or Cape Horn. They could not make this attempt until the following year, and therefore spent ten months in the Tonga and Tahiti Groups before going north.

At this time the Tongans ranged far and wide over the adjacent islands. Their trips extended to the Samoa Group; Poulaho, a Tongan chief, told Cook that he resided occasionally in Samoa. To the west of the Tongans were the formidable Fijians, whom the more daring Tongan chiefs

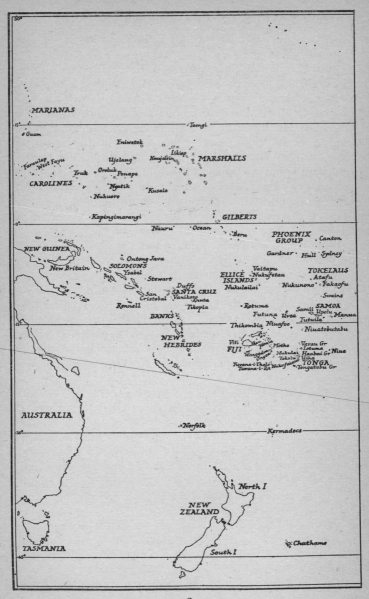

MARIANAS

ₒ Guam

Taongi

Eniwetok

Ikiep
Ujelang    Kwajalein
Faraulep                           MARSHALLS
West Fayu
Truk    Oroluk    Ponape
CAROLINES
Ngatik    Kusaie
Nukuoro

Kapingimarangi    GILBERTS

Nauru    Ocean    Beru
PHOENIX
GROUP    Canton
Gardner    Hull    Sydney
NEW GUINEA    Ontong Java
New Britain    SOLOMONS
Ysabel    Vaitapu    TOKELAUS
Stewart    ELLICE    Nukufetau    Atafu
ISLANDS    Nukunono    Fakaofu
Duffs    Nukulailai
San    SANTA CRUZ    Swains
Cristobal    Vanikoro    Anuta    Rotuma    Samoa
Rennell    Tikopia    Futuna    Uvea    Upolu    Manua
Tutuila
BANKS    Thikombia    Niuafoo
Niuatobutabu
NEW    Viti    Vavau Gr
HEBRIDES    FIJI    Motho    Lotuma    Niue
Wangava    Nukulai    Haabai Gr
Ongea    Tokelu    Uiha    TONGA
Fuvana·Thela    Tongatabu Gr
AUSTRALIA    Turana·i·Ra Mbatsa

Norfolk    Kermadecs

North I

NEW
ZEALAND

TASMANIA    Chathams
South I

16

The Pacific Islands

30°

Necker
•Nihoa

HAWAII     ◇Hawaii

15°

Palmyra
•Washington
•Fanning
◦ Christmas

Jarvis                                                    0°

• Canton

Hull  •Sydney              •Malden
                           •Starbuck

TOKELAUS
•Atafu        NORTHERN  COOKS            MARQUESAS
◦•Fakaofu   Rakahanga   •Tongareva    Nukuhiva•
•Swains    ◦Pukapuka  •Manihiki              ◦Hiva Oa
           Nassau
SAMOA
◦Upolu •Manua                        Manihi
Tutuila°                             ◦•Takaroa          15°
•Niuatobutabu                    TAHITI
                      Fenua-Ara•  •Borabora    TUAMOTUS
                      Mopihaa• Raiatea•Tahiti
            •Palmerston  •Aitutaki    Maitia•  Anaa•   •Hao
  •Niue     Manuae• •Mitiaro
            COOKS Atiu• Mauke
       Rarotonga•
         Mangaia•
         Rimatara•    •Rurutu
                    •Tubuai            •Mangareva
              AUSTRALS Raivivae                    Ducie
                                                 Pitcairn
                    •Rapa
                                                          30°

                    The Pacific Islands

                    Scale of Miles

occasionally visited. Cook and his friend William Anderson took advantage of the long stay to find out from the Tongans the extent of their geographical knowledge.[3]

Anderson is many times commended by Cook for his patient research and acute conclusions. He had accompanied Cook on his previous voyage, and had earned his master's respect. On this final voyage he was officially in charge of natural history observations, as well as being ship's surgeon. He suffered from consumption, and it was partly in hope of finding a cure that he had joined Cook once more. He died before the journey was over.

The Tongans gave Cook a list of 156 islands which were known to them. As the Tongans named them they were counted off by leaves, and Anderson, says Cook, wrote every one of them down. This Tongan list is an excellent one. Most of the names can be identified beyond reasonable doubt. They account for the great majority of the manifold islands of Tonga, and all the main islands of Samoa. Viti, the chief island of the Fiji Group, appears in its famous rendering of ' Feejee,' from which the Group derives its name. Viti is on the other side of the Fiji Group from Tonga, and since the Tongans told Cook they occasionally visited it, it is not unnatural that some of the islands in between are identifiable. Tuvana-i-Ra, Tuvana-i-Tholo, Ongea, Driti, Mothe, Wanggava and Moala are there, all of them lying between Tonga and Viti. Numbers of others which are obviously echoes of Fijian names are also in the list. That accords with Cook's own expectation, for a Tongan voyager told him that thirty or forty islands lay to the northwest.

Names occur which are phonetic spellings of Nukulai and Nukufaiau in the Tongan islands, or may be Nukulaelae or Nukufetau in the Ellice Group. 'Vytooboo' is no doubt Vaitupu, another of the Ellice Islands.

Some quickening of the pulse may occur when 'Toggelao' is noticed. The Tokelaus are 300 miles north of Samoa. But Tokolu is a Tongan island which, if robbed of this obvious equivalent, would be left out of this Tongan list.

The list contains no sign of any of the Cooks or Tahitian islands to the east, nor even of Niue, the island discovered by Cook 280 miles east of Tonga.

The voyages of the Tongans which Cook picks out for special mention are those to Viti and Samoa. On these journeys, each of 360 miles, the farthest gaps without intervening islands are that of 220 miles from Tonga to Ongea, on the way to Viti, and that of 150 miles from Vavau to Niuatobutabu on the way to Samoa.

The evidence of Mariner and Dillon, two later Europeans who knew the western area at the time of early European contact in the first quarter of the nineteenth century, shows that the Tongans and Rotumans occasionally exchanged visits. Rotuma is a largish island 300 miles to the north-west of the main archipelago. Dillon's evidence also shows that the Rotumans were in contact with the southern Ellice Islands as far as Vaitupu. The nearest of these islands to Rotuma is 200 miles away. On the other hand Hudson and Hale, of the United States Exploring Expedition of 1838–42, who questioned the Tokelau and southern Ellice Islanders closely on their geographical knowledge, found no evidence that they knew of islands to the north. Dillon furthermore states that the Fijians and Samoans visited Tonga only as passengers in Tongan canoes. The Tongans were thus the main voyagers. Dillon also says: 'Thubow (chief of Tonga) inquired of me this morning at breakfast where Mannicolo lay, for that, in all of the voyages of the Tonga people among the islands, they had never heard of the Mannicolos. I informed him that it was close to Tikopia, an island of which he also expressed his ignorance.' Tikopia and Vanikoro (Dillon's 'Mannicolo') are islands between 500 and 600 miles west of Rotuma.[4]

Later evidence of the voyaging in the western area shows that it fell off rapidly as the result of the introduction of European-style vessels and methods.

No final conclusion on the range of voyaging of the Western Polynesians and Fijians at the time of European contact can be derived from this evidence alone. It cannot fail to create the impression, however, that it did not extend beyond the Western Polynesian groups and Fiji.

The Tongan voyages, made without navigation instruments, were among the greatest that man ever made, as the evidence will show.

Some accounts of traditional voyages over long distances were recorded by Europeans in late times. The character and value of this late traditional evidence will be examined in later chapters in the light of the authenticated evidence of journeys that were actually made in native vessels without navigation instruments.

From Tonga Cook sailed back east to Tahiti, taking about three weeks. During this time squalls from the north and west were frequent. In Tahiti Cook was again on familiar ground, having traversed most of the islands on his two previous voyages. He was not the first to visit Tahiti, for the Englishman Captain Wallis discovered it in 1767, and the Frenchman de Bougainville came upon it again in 1768. But from 1769 on, until he left Tahiti finally in 1777 after the visits we are discussing, Cook spent over a year there in all.

Cook found from the Tahitians that a Spanish expedition had come from Lima in Peru and left on Tahiti some priests and retainers, taking back with them four Tahitians when they left; that later they returned with two of the Tahitians, the other two having died, and withdrew their people. Obviously two-way contact between Polynesia and the rest of the world was under way.

Omai himself, who had spent two years in England since the previous voyage, was settled by Cook on an island near Tahiti, together with two Maori lads who had come with Cook from New Zealand. 'Oedidee,' a Tahitian who had visited Tonga, New Zealand, Easter Island and the Marquesas with Cook on a previous voyage, was still living in Tahiti, and Cook went ashore and had dinner with him. These things are mentioned because there will be occasion later to point out that, from 1770 on, many of the islanders visited other places in the Pacific in European ships, and spread knowledge of them on their return.

During the five months which Cook's ships spent in the Tahitian islands before going north, Anderson took advantage of the opportunity for some more fact-finding inquiries.[5] Prominent among them were interviews with the Tahitian voyagers, to see what islands they knew of, which they themselves had actually visited, and who of the islanders farther afield came to visit them. He found that the canoemen of Anaa and the other nearer islands of the Tuamotu Group, 170 to 230 miles east of the Tahitians, exchanged visits with them. That was the farthest extent of the Tahitian voyaging. The Tahitians knew of Mopihaa, an uninhabited island 120 miles west of the inhabited Tahitian islands. They also appeared to know of other islands at a distance without ever having visited them, and the source of their information was a matter on which Anderson reached his own conclusions.

Let Anderson summarize his inquiries in his own words, which Cook does the compliment of including verbatim in his journal, which was written for publication. After saying that Tahiti (Otaheite) was visited by the people of the nearer Tuamotu islands, which were 170 to 230 miles to the east and north-east of the Tahitian islands, Anderson says of these nearer Tuamotus:

These low isles are, *doubtless, the farthest navigation which those of Otaheite, and the Society Islands, perform at present.* It seems to be a groundless supposition, made by Mons. de Bougainville, that they made voyages of the prodigious extent he mentions; for I found, that it is reckoned a sort of prodigy that a canoe, once driven by a storm from Otaheite, should have fallen in with Mopeeha, or Howe's Island, though so near, and directly to leeward. *The knowledge they have of other islands is, no doubt, traditional; and has been communicated to them by the natives of those islands, driven accidentally upon their coasts,* who, besides giving them the names, could easily inform them of the direction in which the places lie from whence they came, and of the number of days they had upon the sea. In this manner, it may be supposed, that the natives of Wateeo (Atiu) have increased their catalogue by the addition of Otaheite and its neighbouring isles, from the people they met with there, and also of the other islands these had heard of. We may thus account for the extensive knowledge attributed, by the gentlemen of the *Endeavour*, to Tupia in such matters. And, with all due deference to his veracity, I presume it was, by the same means of information, that he was able to direct the ship to Oheteroa, without having been there himself, as he pretended; which, on many accounts, is improbable.

The reference to the *Endeavour* and Tupia is to Cook's first visit to Tahiti in 1769. The true extent of the geographical knowledge of Tupia and the Tahitians will be established from Tupia's own data. In the meantime two things may be noted. The first is that the objective evidence collected by Anderson established to his satisfaction that in that day and age deliberate voyages in the Tahiti-Tuamotu area did not span gaps involving great distances without intervening islands, and accords with the previous impression that the same applied in the Tonga-Samoa area. The second is that the clues assembled by Anderson are now confidently taken by him to confirm the view that accidental voyages were the sole means whereby people and knowledge were distributed to and from the more distant islands at that time.

When Cook visited Tahiti in the *Endeavour* in 1769, he met Tupia, a chief of the Tahitian island of Raiatea, who had been defeated and driven to Tahiti. Tupia claimed a considerable knowledge of the surrounding islands, and was taken by Cook as guide and interpreter. Tupia with his own hands, says Cook, drew a chart showing seventy-four islands known to the Tahitians. Cook listed the names of these in his journal, together with their compass directions from Tahiti. Cook marked those which Tupia claimed he himself had visited.[6] Further light on Tupia's data is given by John Forster, Cook's naturalist on the second voyage. Forster was given two charts derived from Tupia's information by two of Cook's associates on the first voyage, as well as two lists of names from Cook himself. Forster also collected some names on his own account on the second voyage. He prepared a chart embodying his interpretations of these data, which he published in 1778 with accompanying notes, some of which embody comments by Tupia and other Tahitians.[7]

One of the claims made by Tupia to Cook was that he had paid a ten-day visit to islands to the west of Tahiti, taking thirty days to get back. At that time Cook knew nothing of the islands to the west, except that Tasman and Wallis had discovered some of the Tongan islands 1,200 miles west of Tahiti. Cook conjectured that those were the islands Tupia had visited. But the farthest recognizable islands to the west which Tupia named to Cook as visited by him were Fenua-ara and Mopihaa, both of which are uninhabited detached islands in the far west of the Tahiti Group itself. A deliberate voyage by Tupia to Fenua-ara would be a wonderful achievement in itself, for Anderson, as we have seen, found that the Tahitians regarded it as a prodigy that a canoe should have come on the nearer island of Mopihaa by accident and got back again.

The only other islands to the west which Tupia claimed he had visited were 'Moenatayo', 'Oatea', and 'Ourio'. The first is obviously the Ocean (Moana) of Tiaio, the Mangaian shark-god whose blood poured into the ocean. But Mangaia is in Tupia's data under its old name of Ahuahu, and yet was not claimed as one of the islands Tupia himself had visited.[8] Anderson's view would be that the name and the legend came with accidental voyagers from Mangaia, which does not impugn Tupia's claim to have been on the waters in between. 'Oatea' is presumably the Adeeha of Forster's chart, which was described as an uninhabited island where fishing was occasionally done. Only the unrecognizable 'Ourio' remains. The thought that Tupia had visited distant islands was Cook's, not Tupia's. In due course Cook found out the true geography of the islands to the west, as well as the character of the Polynesian voyaging. When therefore he included in his journal of the third voyage Anderson's refutation of the surmises of the time of the first voyage, it was highly significant, particularly since these conjectures had been published in the meantime.

Anderson thus considered that the Tahitian voyages were confined to the Tahiti-Tuamotu area, and that such names of islands as Tupia and the other Tahitians knew of outside that area had been brought by accidental voyagers. He says that it was improbable that Tupia had visited a certain island 'Oheteroa', as he had claimed to have done. (This island was in fact Rurutu, some 320 miles south of the Tahiti Group, although this name was not known until after Cook and Anderson were long dead. In the list of islands which Cook got from Tupia, Rurutu is shown as a separate island from Ohetiroa, and Rurutu, as well as Ohetiroa, are marked as islands Tupia claimed to have visited. Cook's associate Banks says that Tupia stated that there were a number of islands in the area whose names began with 'Ohete'. William Ellis stated fifty years later that 'Ohetetoa' was an alternative name for Rurutu, but the name had then been on the maps for many years.[9] Another island which Tupia thought was in the same quarter and claimed to have visited was 'Manua', but no island corresponding to it has ever been found there. Since in Cook's list it is shown in the same direction from Tahiti as other Samoan islands, it may be the Samoan Manua.)

It is obvious that Tupia had a good knowledge of the Tahiti Group. He knew the names of a number of islands to the south and west of the Tahitian islands without knowing quite where they were. Tupia's evidence, examined critically in the light of later knowledge of the geography and the native names, confirms Anderson's conclusions so far as the indirect character of Tupia's own knowledge of farther islands was concerned.

What islands outside the Tahiti-Tuamotu area actually appear in Forster's chart, which is, as it were, a summation of the pre-European knowledge of the Tahitians, including the information gathered by Cook? There are a number of names which were unknown to the Europeans at that time, and which therefore are authentic pre-European Tahitian data. (See reproduction of chart on p. 121.)

The only island outside the Tahiti-Tuamotu area on the eastern side which was definitely unknown to the Europeans at that time, and which can be identified with reasonable certainty, is Nukuhiva (Neeo-heeva) in the Marquesas

Group. (Forster himself had direct knowledge of the correct names of several of the Marquesan islands, and had visited the southern islands of the group with Cook on the second voyage, as his accompanying notes show. He and the other Europeans also made some identifications of the native names given to them by Tupia and the other Tahitians with Marquesan islands known to the Europeans. Not one of these identifications accords with the true native names as they were found to be later. Nukuhiva itself is incorrectly placed in relation to the other Marquesan islands, being to the south-west instead of the north.)

It would be surprising if the Tahitians had not had fragmentary knowledge of one or two Marquesan islands from accidental voyagers, since the prevailing winds and currents come from the east. Cook's list from Tupia, which was published in 1893, shows that Tupia made no claim to have visited any of the Marquesan islands. In the meantime, on the basis of the supposed detailed knowledge of the area shown in Forster's chart – miscalled Tupia's chart – the nineteenth century theorists had taken the Tahitians to every part of the Pacific on deliberate voyages.[10]

When we come to the other side of Tahiti, Forster's chart becomes the most significant piece of information on pre-European Polynesia that we have. Here the Europeans at the time of publication of the chart had little direct geographical knowledge to go on. Eight islands not then known to the Europeans can be certainly identified. They comprise the three main Samoan islands of Savaii (Oheavai), Upolu (Ouporroo) and Tutuila (Tootoo-erre), to the north-west of Tahiti, and Rurutu, Raivivae, Rimatara, Mangaia or Ahuahu, and Tumutevarovaro (the modern Rarotonga), which are the nearest islands to the south-west of the Tahiti Group. Oheavai was described, according to Forster's notes, as the 'father of all the islands'. (It should be mentioned that the Samoan 'l' and the Tahitian 'r' are equivalent forms, and that 'o' before a Tahitian proper name is merely introductory.)

Anderson was told by the Tahitians that while the prevailing winds were from the east, in certain months wester-lies blew, while on occasions violent winds came from the south-west. These are the directions in which all the eight islands named above lie from Tahiti.

Now when the location of these eight islands on the chart is compared with their true position, a curious thing becomes immediately apparent. The Samoan islands are correctly disposed in relation to one another, but the group itself is placed south-west of Tahiti instead of north-west. On the other hand Rurutu, Raivivae, Rimatara and Mangaia are placed north-west of Tahiti instead of south-west. It was realized by the nineteenth-century scholars that this arose from the fact that the Europeans who handed on the data to Forster had misunderstood the native names for north and south as given by Tupia, getting them the wrong way round. Thus 'opa toa' meant the quarter toward which, not from which, the south wind blew.[11]

This means in its turn that the names of other islands which are displaced from north to south must have been derived from the data given by Tupia at the time of the first voyage. Vavau (Wouwou), the northern Tonga island from which the Tongans used to sail for Samoa, then becomes identifiable, while 'Rotuma', 'o-Weeha', and 'Ouowhea' may be taken for the Tongan islands of Lotuma and Uiha, or the isolated islands of Rotuma and Uvea to the west of Samoa.

In the area of these dozen identifiable pre-European names, many instances of knowledge of other islands from accidental voyagers are on record in historical times. The people of Atiu, as narrated by Cook, had knowledge of Tahiti in this manner. John Williams, an early missionary, found that the islanders of Rarotonga knew about Cook's visits to Tahiti from accidental voyagers.[12] He also found that the people of Aitutaki knew about Manihiki, 600 miles to the north-west, in the same way,[13] although contact was not made with Manihiki until nearly thirty years later.[14] In Williams's time a chief of Rurutu was blown to Raiatea, bringing an up-to-date picture of his little-known home.[15]

William Ellis and other early missionaries give accounts of two separate lots of accidental migrants on Tubuai, 400 miles south of Tahiti, not to mention a canoe with a skeleton.[16] William Wyatt Gill, another missionary, recorded an accidental voyage from Fakaofo, 300 miles north of Samoa, to Mangaia.[17] The people who survived these journeys were a living embodiment to their hosts of the islands whence they came, and a source of traditional knowledge of them, as Anderson suggested.

Cook, it will be remembered, found that a Spanish expedition had visited Tahiti. The commander of one of the ships, Andia y Varela, has left an interesting account. He says that the Tahitians had pilots who sailed by the stars, winds and seas, visiting the Raiatea area, and covering distances of forty to fifty leagues or more. His colleagues found they visited the nearer Tuamotus. This is the same picture that Anderson gave, and James Morrison, one of the *Bounty* mutineers, confirmed it again in Tahiti in 1788 to 1791.[18]

Andia collected a number of names of islands from the Tahitians. In addition to those in Tupia's information, they include Atiu.[19]

When the Spaniards returned home, they chanced on Raivivae, 430 miles south. This was by accident, and not as the result of information from their Tahitian pilot Puhoro.[20] Tupia's data contained the name, but he did not claim to have visited it.

George Turner, one of the first missionaries in Samoa, after testifying to the excellent craft and seamanship of the Samoans, says they did not go outside their own islands.[21]

In 1768 the Frenchman Antoine de Bougainville had discovered the eastern islands of Samoa. Autourou, his Tahitian interpreter, was just as surprised at the discovery as de Bougainville himself, and could not understand the language. De Bougainville therefore concluded that there were no exchanges of visits between these islands and Tahiti, and that they were different people.[22]

De Bougainville, who spent ten days in Tahiti, conjec-

tured that the Tahitians made voyages of 900 miles, during
which they lost sight of land for lengthy periods, sailing by
the sun and stars. Autourou told him that their voyages
sometimes lasted fifteen days.[23] These statements are not
claims that off-shore voyages of such a length were made.
De Bougainville himself had just come through a string of
islands stretching over 700 miles, and heard of the Raiatea
area from Autourou. Furthermore, the Tahitian voyages
to Raiatea and the nearer Tuamotus were round trips
depending on convenient winds. When Anderson established that the Tahitians did not in fact go beyond the
nearer Tuamotus, and discounted de Bougainville's opinion,
he no doubt had the last word, but the issue was really one
of how far in the vast Tahiti-Tuamotu archipelago the
Tahitians went. The fact that contact even within the archipelago was limited and occasional was amply confirmed in
early historical times. Mangareva and its nearby islands on
the southern fringe of the Tuamotus were discovered by
accident and were comparatively isolated. William Ellis
said that a number of the place names there were unknown
to the Tahitians.[24]

Positive evidence on the range of Polynesian cruising in
the accounts of the first European contacts with the main
island groups, even in the central belt of islands, does not
support the view that deliberate long voyages occurred. The
evidence on the main groups virtually ends with Cook, for
after Cook the groups were known to each other through the
Europeans, and increasing numbers of islanders visited the
other groups in European ships, so that never again could it
be said that their knowledge was pre-European. Many
scattered islands remained to be discovered piecemeal in
later times, and the same invariable picture of isolation and
confinement of deliberate contact to such few islands as were
close to them, relieved only by occasional accidental voyages, was found in every case.

It is evident that Cook, so far from being an authority for
Polynesian long voyages, is precisely the opposite. On the
third voyage, having traversed most of the Pacific several

times, Cook quotes Anderson in indirect refutation of his own surmises about such voyages; cites concrete proof that accidental voyages conveyed people and knowledge between distant islands; and suggests that the dispersal of man in general, and the Polynesians in particular, to distant islands was occasioned solely by accidental voyages.

Within a short time of giving their mature conclusions in a few pregnant paragraphs here and there in the journal of the third voyage, Cook and Anderson were both dead.

Who shall gainsay Cook's and Anderson's evidence? Anderson was a man who had proved himself as a patient and objective investigator, and was accordingly appointed by the British Government as the official natural historian on the third voyage. He questions the Tahitians on the extent of their voyaging and satisfies himself that it was confined to their own islands and the nearer Tuamotus. He finds that they know of a few islands at a distance without having visited them. He has direct evidence that accidental voyages occurred over such greater distances and thereby spread knowledge of farther islands. He has the courage of his convictions to the extent of refuting the previous surmises of Cook and his companions on the first voyage. Cook includes Anderson's refutation in his journal which is intended for publication. Cook gives accidental voyages as an explanation of the peopling of the farther islands.

It cannot be said that Cook put forward his explanation as a final conclusion. He and Anderson did not have the detailed geographical knowledge which showed how correct their views of the voyaging were even in their own day. They did not express a firm view that in earlier times deliberate long off-shore voyages did not occur. The thought that that had happened in some remote period did not become a dogma until long after their time, when the late European interpretations of Polynesian traditions were worked up into the theory that deliberate colonization had taken place.[25] Cook and Anderson would no doubt have been surprised to know that what did not occur after cen-

turies of local maritime experience should have been supposed to have happened at the beginning and have stopped
later.

Later chapters will give evidence of the truth of Cook's
theory, not merely in that day and age, but in any that preceded it. Polynesia comprised a number of little worlds,
inaccessible except by accidental migration. The limit of
effective navigability was the distance that could be
achieved in off-shore voyages of several days between islands
where the conditions of wind and current were convenient
for such journeys. The only islands which were in deliberate
contact with others at a distance of more than 100 miles
without intervening islands were Rotuma and the Ellice
Islands (200 miles), the main western archipelago and
Rotuma (300 miles), Fiji and Tonga (220 miles), Tonga and
Samoa (150 miles to the Niuatobutabu cluster in between,
and 140 miles thence to Savaii), Tahiti and the Tuamotus
(170 to 230 miles), and Rarotonga and Atiu (116 miles). It
was the circumstances of wind and current that determined
the maritime achievement, rather than the gross distance.
Areas in which lesser contacts occurred were Hawaii, the
Marquesas, the Tokelaus, Manihiki-Rakahanga, and probably Rimatara-Rurutu. These journeys were the product
of a long evolution and were highly impressive.

All these separate worlds were settled by one-way voyages
of isolated canoes. They should not be described as drift
voyages, as the evidence will show. Within each area settlement was for the most part the result of accidental contacts
in the first place. The development of the contact areas was
the result of later deliberate voyaging within the range of
effective navigation.

The same fundamental facts applied to all isolated ocean
islands throughout the world, including the Carolines and
other North Pacific groups, and those in the Atlantic and
Indian Oceans. Many mysteries disappear when examined
in the light of accidental settlement.

Later evidence[26] will show good reason for believing that
on occasion voluntary exiles, or exiles driven out to sea, were

conveyed to other islands on one-way voyages in which precise navigation played no part. The term accidental settlement is a convenient one for migration by voyages arising
either from storms or exile.

# CHAPTER TWO

# Primitive Navigation

*

IN view of the powerful evidence that in Cook's day Polynesian deliberate off-shore voyages were limited to the local islands, one would suspect that there were some fundamental reasons for this. These are found in abundance in the difficulties of navigation without precision instruments. They apply not merely in Cook's day, but at any time. The difficulties are many and varied, but two are pre-eminent. These are unknown set and drift, meaning the displacement of a vessel with a current, and deviation off course with winds. The palpable effects of gales in inducing such divergences are obvious enough, but the influence of set and drift is not confined to storms or bad visibility. If in unknown waters a vessel encounters a cross-current it will be displaced off course without knowing it, even though it may continue to be aligned in what appears to be the right direction. The same effects will occur when a wind is misjudged. When a sailing vessel is caught in an unknown cross-current without a wind, it will go with the current. Such effects are undetectable within the margin of error of the navigation.

Nor is any knowledge of astronomy necessary to establish what the margin of error in navigation to small islands was in bad visibility when the winds and currents were misjudged or unknown. While Cook was spending those five months with the Tongans he secured information about their navigation. He recorded that 'the sun is their guide by day and the stars at night. When these are obscured, they have recourse to the points from which the winds and waves come upon the vessel. If during the obscuration the winds and waves should shift ... they are then bewildered, frequently miss their intended port and are never heard of more.'[1]

If such difficulties occurred in waters with w
Tongans were familiar, what would have happened t
thetical sea-rovers in unknown seas, since on long vo
good visibility is not assured? What would have happe
to them in calms combined with strong cross-curren
What would have happened to them in storms, when
unknown set and drift were combined with bad visibility in
their worst forms?

Centuries of navigation by the highly sophisticated
system of latitude and longitude, which took 5,000 years to
evolve, have made us forget the limitations of off-shore navigation without instruments, as well as its romance and
achievements. There is no more fascinating subject than the
history of man's going down to the sea in ships and then out
across it. It is the story of maritime peoples everywhere.

Crude methods of navigation by the sun, stars, winds
and currents were good enough for voyages of no great
distance between extended coast-lines, where a landfall
somewhere or other was assured even if the destination were
missed. Man originated as a land animal and presumably
graduated through river craft to coastal vessels. The early
off-shore voyages were in the land-locked seas of the Old
World to extended coast-lines on the other side. When the
ancient voyagers made these traverses out of sight of land,
they took their course from the relationship of their directions to the sun and stars. The early Phoenicians, Greeks,
Romans, and northern peoples travelled in this manner
across the Mediterranean, the Black Sea, the Baltic and the
North Sea. The Arabs and Indians did the same across the
Arabian Gulf, where they were aided by the monsoons
which blow steadily in one direction at one part of the year
and in the reverse direction at the other. For these journeys
in the land-locked seas and gulfs, navigation by the sun,
stars, winds, and currents was good enough, for when the
voyagers came in sight of the coast, which they could not
miss, they could pick their way along it.

The islands which were within the land-locked seas,
including the North Sea and the Arabian Gulf, and the

chains of islands which were within easy distance of the continents, did not involve any great difficulty. They include the West Indian islands off Central America, the East Indian islands from Singapore to Australia and the Philippines, and the Asiatic islands including Formosa and Japan. None of these are separated from the continents or one another by more than 100 miles or so, and in very early times there is reason to believe that the gaps were less. We will leave the ancient peoples of the Andaman Islands off the coast of Burma out of account, for the land formations off the mouth of the Irrawaddy may have been different when they came into their islands.

Ocean islands which were more than 300 miles from the continents, or from chains of islands extending from the continents, were in an entirely different class. In their case there was no way of finding they existed by crossing between coast-lines, as in the land-locked seas. The idea of deliberate discovery involves the presumption that the explorers were prepared to go twice as far as any island they hoped to find, and do so many times without success, for an explorer cannot hope to find new land more than very occasionally if at all. Above all, unless one can fix the position of the island one finds, and plot the course of subsequent journeys to it, two-way contact cannot be established, and the discovery means nothing. For the same reason, if a voyager were blown on such an island by accident, the difficulties of getting home again and finding the island a second time were still insuperable, since there was no way of fixing the position of the new island or plotting courses to or from it.

Stories of distant islands before the days of large sailing ships and instruments were recounted in the Middle Ages. They excited interest for centuries because no one was able to prove them or disprove them by looking for them. An Irish monk named Brendan was supposed to have visited a far island in early times, and St Brendan's Island became a stock subject of romance for centuries. By Columbus's day the oceans were replete with imagined islands. The fact

34

that most of them were in locations where no islands were later found has not restrained later identifications of the few that happened to be coincident, although the further fact that differing identifications of these legendary islands have been offered may be considered to detract somewhat from their persuasiveness. In somewhat later times the Sieur de Gonneville was reputed to have been cast upon some island in the Atlantic or Indian Ocean, and to have brought back a native to prove it. But because he did not give the position of the island it has never been satisfactorily identified.[2]

The Atlantic coast-line of Spain, Portugal, and Northern Africa was a great deal more suitable as a base for ocean exploration than were islands, for the voyager could regain the coast-line somewhere or other if he had to retreat. In later times the Canaries near this coast-line showed that islands might exist farther from the shore. If legend is supposed to be a fit basis for a theory of discovery, there were legends enough. The western European coast was for 2,000 years the haunt of a long succession of maritime peoples – Romans, Gauls, Moors, Italians, Spaniards, and Portuguese. If anywhere in the world there was a region where voyagers before the days of instruments might have deliberately settled farther islands if such were possible, it might be here. Yet what do we find?[3]

The Atlantic islands of Madeira are among the fairest known to man. They lie only 330 miles from the coast of Africa, and 530 miles from Lisbon, which have been areas of maritime enterprise since Carthaginian and Roman days. When they were discovered in 1418 by a Portuguese sailing ship which had been blown there in a storm, they were uninhabited. Today their population is a quarter of a million.

The Azores, a group of sunny and romantic islands about 800 miles west of Portugal, were unsettled until the Europeans came upon them in the fifteenth century. Incidentally the finding of a number of Carthaginian coins on Corvo, one of the Azores, has been supposed to be evidence of deliberate contact. If so why did these hard-headed Semitic people leave their money behind? It would be simpler to think that a vessel was carried away from the Spanish coast during the Carthaginian occupation onto Corvo, where everything rotted away except the well-night indestructible bronze of the coins.

The Cape Verde Islands lie about 400 miles off the west coast of Africa. When discovered by a Portuguese ship in 1456, they were uninhabited. They were among the few oceanic islands which were found by systematic exploration, at a period when their positions could be fixed by navigation instruments.

The farther Atlantic islands of Bermuda, St Helena, Ascension and Tristan da Cunha were all uninhabited when discovered in comparatively late times by accident.

On the Indian side of Africa, Arab voyagers ranged up and down the coast and across the Arabian Gulf to India from early times. Aided by the monsoons, they went farther off-shore across the Gulf, and developed better ships, than their European contemporaries until the time of the larger Portuguese and Spanish sailing ships. Here again then were conditions convenient for off-shore colonization of farther islands if such had been possible before the days of instruments. Yet no Arab settlers got to the farther islands in the Indian Ocean – Mauritius, Reunion, the Chagos. They did not in fact get to the nearer Seychelles. When the Portuguese came upon the farther Indian Ocean islands by chance in the sixteenth century they were uninhabited. They are all well suited to human occupation and today sustain quite considerable populations.

Madagascar, several hundred miles off the African coast, was inhabited by an ancient people. The ethnologists are agreed that they must have come from the East Indian islands far to the east across the Indian Ocean. Their ancestors have therefore been pictured as plying back and forth in earlier times. If so they apparently did not stop at the intervening Indian Ocean islands, on which no sign of early visitors has been found. The prevailing winds and currents from the East Indies to Madagascar are among the most constant in the world, which makes them propitious for accidental voyages, but not for two-way ones, and Madagascar is a big island which might be expected to catch such voyagers though none ever came on the smaller Indian Ocean islands. But not all the latter escaped them, for the Nicobars, a group of isolated islands to the west of the East Indies, also had East Indian cultural elements.

The farther Pacific Islands, Madagascar and the Nicobars, are the only islands in the world outside the land-locked seas and gulfs which were more than 300 miles from the continents and chains of islands extending from them and were inhabited at the time of later discovery. All the others in the world were uninhabited – the Falklands, Juan Fernandez, and scores of others besides the nearer and more desirable ones which remained unsettled for so long near the ancient maritime haunts of man.

We find then that our mystery of the first peopling of the farther islands is a mystery of the Pacific and a few islands in the Indian Ocean. They lie on either side of the East Indian archipelago, which is unique in the world in that it has oceans dotted with islands on either side of it. The other great archipelago of the West Indies is hard against the American coast-line, with only a few small islands at a great distance on the windward side.

The fact that so many oceanic islands throughout the world were uninhabited before the days of advanced navigation gives us a powerful clue in favour of the theory of accidental settlement of those that were peopled, for though many of them were desirable and near at hand, they had not come to be settled either by accident or intent.

The inability to hold a course in storms, and the absence of any method of fixing positions or plotting courses precisely without instruments, explains why the range of deliberate settlement was so short while that of accidental settlement was so long.

All primitive vessels, whether outrigger canoes, or large double canoes, or Roman and Viking galleys, or the early conventional sailing ships of the Arabs and Europeans, were liable to be swept off course by gales. Those which were blown off continental coast-lines had some chance of getting back if they survived long enough, since the navigators would know whether they were east or west, and that they could not miss the coast-line somewhere. Those who were blown off islands had no way of re-orienting themselves with the precision that was required, until the fourteenth and fifteenth centuries brought compasses, astrolabes and large sailing ships into the picture. Still less could either continental or island voyagers fix the positions of any islands they found either by intent or accident, outside their limited range of deliberate navigation.

The Polynesian and other Pacific Islands vessels, like all other early types of vessels, were unable to hold a course in a gale. They left on their local voyages in fine weather with a reasonable prospect of continuance, and with a reasonably convenient wind. They were adept in judging weather for a day or two ahead. If they were caught by a storm, they not only lost their bearings by the stars and sun, but were liable to be swept away. Under such conditions an off-shore voyage of any distance was a gamble with the weather, the forfeit being their lives, or an involuntary trip to another island if they were lucky.

The reason, therefore, why the East Indian and Pacific peoples colonized distant islands was not because their vessels and navigation were good enough to take them to such islands, but because they were not good enough not to. Voyagers in island groups will tend to develop reasonably good craft, whether they be Polynesians, Caribbean Indians, Fijians or Caroline Islanders. But to keep a course in a gale without being swept away, one has to have a very good vessel indeed. The East Indian and Pacific peoples who developed craft which were efficient enough to take them off-shore but not efficient enough to ensure holding up against bad weather were ideal subjects for accidental voyages. When the gale blew itself out they might be hundreds of miles to sea in unknown waters with no way of fixing their position, or plotting their course, or knowing the position of their home island or their destination.

The evidence of a number of early observers makes plain the limitations of the Polynesian vessels in strong winds. The Polynesian sea-going double canoe of historical times was well adapted to staying afloat, but could not beat back into the wind satisfactorily. The late Tongan large double canoe with lateen sails, such as Cook saw, the Tahitian double canoe and the double canoe of the Tuamotuan islands near Tahiti were the best of the Polynesian sea-going vessels.[4] There is no evidence that their early craft were either better or worse than the craft of Cook's time. If anything one would expect that the later were at least as good as the earlier. When therefore we hear of the limitations of the double canoes from contemporary observers, it is a reasonable conclusion that they apply no less to the earlier craft in which the Polynesian ancestors came into their islands. But even if they had come into the Pacific in European-style sailing ships, the inescapable difficulties of navigation without instruments would still have applied.

John Williams, speaking of the trade winds from the east, referred to the 'impossibility of the native canoes working against them.'[5] Since he believed that the Polynesians came from the west, his testimony to their inability to work against the prevailing winds is all the more powerful. The trade winds are however overcome by westerlies at certain seasons of the year within the central belt of Polynesian islands and in the island chains which lead to it from the East Indies.[6] The meteorology is therefore consistent with the thought that the Polynesians might have come either from the east or west or both. What the evidence of Williams and many other observers shows is that the Polynesians could sail their vessels on a chosen course only when the wind was reasonably convenient.

Even the early Spaniards who ventured forth in their galleons across the Pacific could make little headway against the winds, and learned by costly experience to go with the huge eddies of which the tropical sides are the trade winds, and the northern arcs are the west winds of higher latitudes.[7]

Had voyagers before the days of large vessels and instruments been independent of local conditions of wind and current, they would still have had no way of finding and re-finding distant islands by their necessarily crude directional guides. In order to see the difficulties in proper perspective, it is desirable to see how the early voyagers navigated when out of sight of land. It is a remarkable demonstration of man's ingenuity in struggling with his environment.

The basic limitations on primitive navigation are simple and obvious. Concepts of following stars are somewhat beside the point on long journeys. For the stars do not shine during the day, the daytime is much longer than the night, and the sun is a very poor navigation guide. Furthermore, continuous sight either of the sun or the stars on long journeys in oceanic areas is a somewhat miraculous event. Many steamers have made passages of 3,000 miles by compass and dead reckoning by instruments without ever having a glimpse of the sun or a star. Now a sailing vessel which loses its bearings by the heavenly bodies changes its position in an unknown way with every change of current or wind that it encounters. This was what the Tongans told Cook happened to them. When courses were re-set by stars, or by directional angles with the east-west or north-south lines, or by a point on the horizon marked by stars which rose or set, or any combination of these, they were faulty courses. For the unknown lateral set with the currents, or drift with the wind, meant that the course was really being set from a series of new and unknown positions.

Very few theorists have attempted a detailed rationalization of how the Pacific Islanders navigated to distant islands. An astronomical expert who viewed with some favour the possibility of following stars to new islands stated that this involved keeping on a straight course in order that it could be re-traced, that the greatest hazard was that of sailing blindly in cloudy weather, and that Cook's accounts showed that his ships were driven to great distances off course by winds and currents.[8] An expert in air navigation has put forward the view that the Polynesians knew what stars would pass over the destinations at a given period of the year and a given time of night, aiming to judge the course by these aids. If no overhead star when needed were visible it was suggested that a steering star which was in line with the destination was used. It was also stated that the navigators were restricted to a knowledge of stars passing over islands with which they were familiar.[9]

The question that arises concerning all such theories, as of the more popular procedure of having no theory, is how, in the face of storms, variable winds, calms, and unknown currents, the locations of distant objectives could have been established in the first place or re-discovered when they had. No theory of the discovery and re-discovery of distant islands, particularly far south of the equator in areas of variable weather without predictable winds, can be made realistic in the teeth of such difficulties.

Any theory, whether of accidental or deliberate settlement, must meet all the facts. It is useless to work out hypothetical courses for 90 per cent of the supposed deliberate colonists and leave 10 per cent floating in the stormy expanses of the South Pacific without guidance or reliable winds. The testimony of the early observers shows that the Polynesian vessels could not work satisfactorily against the winds. As we shall see, their courses were either across the trade winds in both directions, or dependent on awaiting the seasonal changes in the winds.[10] How then could the presumed Maori voyagers who are reputed to have colonized the Chathams have come back in this area of variable and unreliable winds? How could the supposed Tahitian and Rarotongan colonists of New Zealand itself have kept a course through the vast area of variable winds that lies between the central belt of islands and New Zealand? And why did all the voyagers, including those in the central belt, stop making these voyages throughout the whole of the Pacific in later times?

There is abundant evidence of the navigation methods

used by the Pacific Islanders on the journeys they actually made.

The Tongans told Cook, Mariner, and Dillon that they went on voyages to Fiji, Samoa, and Rotuma. They said that they sailed by the sun and stars, and that when visibility was lost they depended on the direction of the winds and waves. De Bougainville, Andia, and Cook all testified to the same basic methods of navigation by the Tahitians, and Anderson established by his inquiries that by these methods they passed between Tahiti and the Tuamotus, but no farther.

Andia's evidence[11] bears out the fact that the direction of the winds and waves was considered no less important than the sun and stars. When the latter were obscured Cook found that the Tongans depended on the points from which the wind and waves came upon the vessel. Andia was told that similarly the Tahitians took note of the part of the vessel that the wind and the seas impinged on. The winds and seas acted as compass needles. Since however these were not stable in one general direction, the navigators had to keep checking their wind directions in relation to the heavenly bodies, which were the only certain guides when the voyagers were out of sight of land. If the heavenly bodies were obscured the navigator had no way of knowing if the wind had changed. As the Tongans told Cook, under such circumstances they were bewildered, frequently missed their intended port, and were never heard of more.

The Polynesians, like all early voyagers, preferred to sail at night, and for good reason.[12] There are more stars at night than the sun alone during the day. They therefore give a succession of clues from which the basic direction of the voyage and the wind direction at the time can be gauged. The Southern Cross points to the celestial pole, thereby giving a line on the south. In theory the altitudes of the stars above the horizon can be gauged as a rough check on variations in the north-south component of voyages, since they appear to rise higher in the sky when one moves towards the poles, but there is no evidence that the Polynesians used this clue, or indeed needed to on the actual voyages they made.

The evidence shows that the stars which rose or set progressively on the horizon beyond the destination were used as targets.

When the stars, including that nearest one, the sun, faded from sight, only the direction of the wind and seas remained.

The greatest authorities on Polynesian navigation were the Polynesians. The classic statements of their methods were those of the Tongans to Cook, and that of Puhoro, the Tahitian pilot, to Andia. Andia's account lay buried in the Spanish records until comparatively late times, like Cook's list from Tupia which shows that the very foundation of the speculations of Cook himself, Forster, de Quatrefages, A. Lesson, and others about Tahitians going to far islands was built on the sand. Puhoro told Andia how the Tahitians navigated on their trips of forty to fifty leagues or more, using the methods outlined in the preceding paragraphs.

Kotzebue, the Russian explorer, and Chamisso, his naturalist, who visited the Marshalls, Carolines and Marianas in 1817, and de Freycinet, the French explorer who visited the Marianas in 1819, secured details of the navigation methods in these North Pacific groups.[13] The navigators there gave the explorers much the same picture as the Polynesians did to Cook and Andia, with the addition, as reported by de Freycinet, that the Caroline pilots who visited the Marianas used the Pole Star.[14] This unique star, being near the celestial pole above the northern point of the earth's axis, gives a line on the north as well as a check on latitude, since it rises or sinks steadily in the sky as one moves north or south anywhere in the Northern Hemisphere.

Forster, having put on record that the Tahitians knew only the astronomy which applied in their local area, went on to make the truism that at a distance the appearance of the stars would be radically different.[15]

An ingenious way of recording directions of journeys when they had been fixed by experience was to register them, as it were, by lining up two landmarks on the home island which would thereafter give a permanent record of the direction. This had the added advantage that one could set one's course in the afternoon by the landmarks until they faded from sight, and then take up the course from the stars. John Williams gives an account of the use of this method by the people of Atiu in going to Rarotonga, 116 miles south.[16] Captain Beechey, who in 1824 visited Anaa, the Tuamotuan island 170 miles east of the Tahiti Group, was told by the people there of how they set their direction on trips to Tahiti by landmarks in the same way, and then watched out for Maitia, on the way to Tahiti.[17]

Obviously someone had to find out in the first place the appropriate courses. The voyagers had to establish them by initial trial and error. Between the extended coast-lines of the land-locked seas and gulfs of the Old World there was no great difficulty, because there was no life-or-death issue in hitting or missing one's objective, and the navigator, by striking the coast somewhere on his early journeys, could progressively improve on his steering lines by his heavenly guides by trial and error. In the case of islands, however, no such assurance applied, and the extent to which the voyager could go with safety in establishing his course was accordingly limited. Furthermore he had to get back for the knowledge to be transmitted. Every course to every island was a problem in itself, with specific circumstances of wind and current.

When the appropriate direction had been fixed on the early voyages, and its relation to winds and currents worked out, these data still had to be applied by judgement on each journey. There are no paths or signposts at sea, wherewith to preserve the accumulated knowledge of previous generations. Even if the direction had been fixed absolutely correctly in the first place, which would be rare, the application on each journey was subject to a high undetectable margin of error without instruments.

Let us take the simplest case, which is where the voyager is journeying by night due east or west on the equator by stars which progressively rise or set as they move due west across the heavens, passing directly over the point of departure and the destination, as well as over the vessel in between. On this course the directional angle of the journey and the altitudes of the stars on either hand are constant throughout. The overhead stars progressively become the horizon stars or vice versa, with no quarrels between their bearings as the journey continues.[18] All the voyager has to do is to follow the east-west line made by these stars. In doing this he is in effect trying to keep the lines from his eye to the star line in the same plane with the imaginary line which cuts the visible heavens in half and descends vertically to the plane of the sea and the horizon. Let us reduce the margin of error to a hypothetical half-degree, or one 180th part of the right angle between the star line and the horizon on the right or left hand, which is roughly the arc of sky covered by the moon. An error of a half-degree in judging star angles means an error on the surface of the sea of approximately thirty-four and a half miles.[19] This means that a vessel could swing or veer within thirty-four and a half miles on either side of the true course before the angle error with the stars would be detectable. In good visibility even a small island would come in sight. Islands on the equator are few and far between. As one moves south of the equator into the central belt of Pacific Islands, the bearings of the stars alter with the curvature of the earth and there is no longer a stable multiple star line over a long course. Nevertheless horizon stars which progressively rise or set at a point known to be beyond the destination give a fairly stable target over short journeys, albeit subject to an increased margin of error. South of the central belt are the great distances of sea which extend to New Zealand and the Chathams. Concerning the navigation methods which early voyagers might have used in these areas there is no evidence, nor evidence of any voyages.

The prime navigating star was the Pole Star. All of Polynesia with the exception of Hawaii lies in the Southern Hemisphere, which lacks a visible Pole Star.[20] It was in the Northern Hemisphere that Columbus and those who followed him learned to come on a rough diagonal course to where the Pole Star was the right height above the horizon, and then keep it at that height as they moved east or west across the oceans to their destinations.

Here we see the dilemma of the reconstructionists who have attempted a general theory of Polynesian long-distance navigation. If all the Polynesian islands were strung out near the equator there would be no difficulty. If all of them were in the Northern Hemisphere a Pole Star theory would no doubt have been adopted. But a general theory must embrace all the islands and not just some of them. New Zealand and the Chathams were inhabited by Polynesians, and traces of Polynesian occupation were found on Norfolk, the Kermadecs, and Pitcairn. All these islands are well south of the equator, at great distances from the central Polynesian islands, in areas without benefit of a Pole Star, and subject to variable currents and winds. No feasible sailing directions are recorded in Maori traditions.[21] Any suppositious ones are subject to a much greater margin of error than east-west courses on the equator or by the Pole Star, and yet these southern areas are most subject to set and drift.

The truth is that astral guides were only a small element of the problem of primitive navigation. The Western Caroline Islanders knew the Pole Star, yet the distances they traversed were no farther than those of the Polynesian voyages. The facts were the same everywhere, as Madeira, uninhabited for 2,000 years only a few hundred miles from ancient maritime centres, and all the other uninhabited oceanic islands throughout the world, plainly show. If anyone thinks that New Zealand, being a large land area, might have been an exception, let him explain how the steering line was established, how the certainty of bad visibility and storms in the area was overcome, how drift and set were known, how distance was judged, how the voyagers made progress against adverse winds, how they got back again to their small islands, and how the western Europeans with their extended coast-line did not get even to the nearer islands until the days of large sailing ships and instruments. Nor is there any point in guessing at such things, when the testimony of the men who did the voyaging at the time of

European contact shows so plainly what could and what could not be accomplished.

It may be tempting to think that distant islands could have been found by search[22] if they were not picked up at first. This was certainly the case on short journeys when there was a margin of time and the error in calculating distance traversed was not great. On long journeys, however, the primitive voyager had no precise means of determining the distance he had come. All that he could do was to estimate distance by average sailing in a given time, corrected for changes in winds and currents if he knew them. This was the time-honoured method of dead reckoning. The farther one went, the bigger the possibility of error. With a high margin of error in direction and distance, how does one know when or where to begin to search? One cannot know whether one has overshot one's mark until all hope of striking it has gone. One then has no clue as to whether it is over one's left shoulder or one's right. Supposing one chooses the left, at what angle of the quarter-circle will one go? How far will one go before taking another? So one has to search all that quarter-circle and then go over and do the same thing in the other. But one piece of ocean looks very much like another, and in such a search one cannot judge when one has come into the other quarter-circle. One may therefore be searching the same piece of ocean as before without knowing it.

Very few islands in the world have been found by deliberate search when their locations as determined by instruments were not known. There are however one or two cases which give evidence on the difficulties.

When John Williams made his first attempt from Aitutaki to reach Rarotonga 146 miles south, he knew its approximate direction and distance from some Rarotongans who had been brought to Aitutaki by a European whaler, and who accompanied Williams on his search. Williams had a ship with a mast and a telescope. Rarotonga is an island with high points. They looked for Rarotonga for a week without success, and then gave up.[23]

The Tahiti Mission ship, which knew of Manihiki, 600 miles north of Aitutaki, from accidental voyagers who had been blown away from it by storms, looked repeatedly for the island over a period of years before it was found in 1849.[24]

When the Spaniards on Guam, 300 miles north of the Western Caroline Islands, learnt of the direction and distance of these islands from accidental voyagers, and from a Spanish ship which had seen them by accident, they sent a ship to search for them. It looked for them for nearly a month without seeing any of them, and the search was given up for another decade.[25]

Nor can the difficulties be overcome by imagining fleets of canoes fanning out to increase the range of visibility on long journeys, although they certainly did so on short ones. Long journeys mean travel night after night with no assurance of fine weather. The ocean is too deep for anchors. How then could the vessels keep in touch at night in squalls, or when the sky was overcast? A practical test of this difficulty is to go out in similar circumstances on the sea in a small boat, or even to look out of the back door. The European sailing ships had the utmost difficulty in keeping together, even with high look-outs and telescopes and high masts to look for, and always used to appoint rendezvous at determined positions, so that when blown out of sight of one another they could come together again. The Spanish ships kept to an agreed line of latitude to facilitate their keeping together, having the advantage of quadrants to determine it, and yet were continually losing touch. Cook was separated from his second vessel on the second voyage, and did not see it again until both got back to England.[26] The difficulty is doubly enhanced by the fact that voyagers without ways of determining distance accurately have no way of knowing how far they are from their destination, and on a long journey must therefore be presumed to have fanned out long before the possibility of reaching it arose. But since they would have to keep in sight or sound of one another, ten canoes which might be imagined as having stuck together in the face of all the difficulties would increase the range of vision by only forty or fifty miles. Again there is evidence of what was actually done on the short journeys, in de Freycinet's account of how the Caroline Islanders used conch horns to keep in touch when visibility was bad.[27] But over long gaps things were different. No fleets of galleasses colonized Madeira or the Azores, nor fleets of dhows the Seychelles or Mauritius.

The basic limitation on all navigation before the days when courses could be plotted was unknown set and drift. The local conditions at all times of the year, and on all courses studied separately, had to be learnt by experience. The early Spaniards in crossing the Pacific made fantastic errors as the result of unknown set and drift before they realized how they were acting. Gaetan, a pilot on Villalobos's expedition in the sixteenth century, after crossing from Mexico to the Philippines, thought that the distance was 3,000 miles less than what it really was. Saavedra, when coming slantwise from New Guinea towards Mexico, discovered some islands which were thought to be half-way to his destination, which would have put them in an area where there are no islands. Despite two tries he did not get anywhere near Mexico, and his ship each time returned to its starting point.[28]

All that has been said about the difficulties of navigation by the sun and stars without instruments has to be qualified by the fundamental limitation that when the skies are obscured these are no use at all.

When Will Mariner was living among the Tongans from 1806 to 1810 after the wreck of his ship, he once made a voyage with Finau, a chief of Tonga.[29] They were overtaken by fog, and, precisely as Cook had recorded a generation earlier, the navigators took their line from the direction of the wind as it had been at the time when sky visibility was lost. Mariner had a small compass which he had salvaged from the wrecked ship. From it he saw that the wind had changed direction and that the canoe, by taking its course on the wind, was going to miss its destination by a big margin.

He prevailed on Finau, on pledge of his life, to let him give the steering directions, reckoning that he was lost anyway otherwise. Mariner changed course and they went on all night. One may imagine the tenseness. In the dawn light their destination showed up ahead. Finau was so pleased with the white man's magic that he used the compass on every occasion, whether necessary or not. Since Mariner could not explain satisfactorily why the needle pointed north, Finau's firm opinion was that it was kept there by a special god.

This does not sound like the sort of navigation that could ensure landfalls on distant islands, at any rate by deliberate intent. Limitations on visibility are fundamental difficulties in navigation by the heavenly bodies. No amount of skill on the part of Polynesian navigators could overcome them; or for that matter on the part of European ones, before compasses and precise measurement of distance were applied to the problem.

The Tahitians, like the Tongans, lived in areas without a Pole Star which, like the visible Pole Star in the Northern Hemisphere, could give a fairly accurate check on the north-south component of voyages. The Tahitians are reputed to have colonized New Zealand in their sea-going double canoes, maintaining two-way contact in the colonizing period over the 2,500 miles which lie between. None of those who have said so went in a Tahitian double canoe, and those who have said so did not include the Tahitians at the time of European contact. The reconstructionists do not explain the winds which were used by the Tahitians in their supposed traverses. William Ellis says that he made several voyages in Tahitian double canoes, that in fine weather and with a fair wind they were tolerably safe and comfortable, that when the weather was rough and the winds contrary they were 'tossed about completely at the mercy of the winds', and that on occasion they were blown out of the Tahiti Group.[30]

A navigator who apparently had an appreciation of the difficulties of oceanic navigation noticed that a sacred calabash in Hawaii had certain holes in it, through one of which the Pole Star could be seen if viewed at a certain angle. He connected this with the prevailing theory that the Hawaiians visited Tahiti in early days, and pictured the voyagers returning north from Tahiti until the Pole Star came into view through the hole at the right latitude, and then turning west.[31] It is however arbitrary to choose Tahiti as the destination, since no similar calabash has been found in Tahiti or anywhere else. Nor was it explained how destinations were known in the first place. The idea might more appropriately have been applied to imagining local trips in the Hawaii area, since that was the only place where the calabash was. An ethnologist who examined the matter stated that while he knew of the use of a calabash as a royal travelling receptacle in Hawaii, he knew nothing of calabash sextants, and invited the production of the calabash in question.[32]

Other navigators have been sceptical of the view that the Polynesians navigated to Hawaii and New Zealand and back. Of the great number of seafarers who have not expressed that view, early explorers in the days of sail figure prominently. Many of them found the notion of deliberate voyages so unrealistic that they thought there must have been chains of islands or a lost continent connecting the father islands in former times. Moerenhout and Dumont d'Urville thought this. Dumont d'Urville suggested that the animals which should also have been in the islands on this view might have been hunted to extinction, but no fossils have been found.[33]

The difficulties associated with two-way contact with islands after they had been found, great as they are, are as nothing when compared with the difficulties involved in the thought of deliberate discovery in the first place. A hypothetical explorer could not count on finding land, and must therefore be thought of as being prepared to go twice as far as the supposed islands he discovered, as well as spend time in searching. On the many times when land was not found, the supposed discoverers would have had to come back without being able to wait for a favourable wind. Double or treble the time means ten times the risk of storms, since fine weather can be predicted for only a limited time ahead.

Late European suggestions – not, be it noted, old-time Polynesian ones – have been made to the effect that the supposed colonists derived guidance from the flights of migratory birds.[34] As against the thought that the flight of migratory birds could be followed, one might think that the fact that their seasonal movements are swift and short, their height in the sky unpredictable, and the width of their zone of flight unknown would create difficulties for the navigators. However that may be, one disability about the birds would appear certain. They must be visible to be of use, and visibility on long journeys is not constant. As against the thought that flights of migratory birds might have revealed the presence of distant land which would not otherwise have been known, there is evidence that mere knowledge that distant islands existed solved nothing in itself. The trouble was to find them in the face of unknown set and drift and all the other difficulties. The Raiateans knew the broad location of the Samoan islands in Cook's time, as Tupia's data show, and yet there was no exchange of visits. The searches for Manihiki and Rarotonga and the Carolines, despite their comparative nearness, and the fact that their direction and approximate distance were known, show how far short such knowledge fell of the conditions for deliberate discovery of distant land. Above all when such far islands had been found there was no way of fixing their position, and no certainty of ever finding them again. Navigation does not rely on repeated double miracles.

How then were contacts established at the extreme range of authenticated deliberate voyaging? If deliberate probes were imagined to have taken place, this would have involved the chance of a double trip coming back into the wind. Again, Anderson's inquiries give the clue, when he heard from the Tahitians of the return of the canoe which had been blown to Mopihaa, and of the way in which knowledge of other islands was brought by accidental voyagers. Sooner or later the courses and approximate distances would

be established by such occurrences. Within the range of
effective contact, the distinction between accidental and
deliberate voyaging would be in due course effaced. So the
contact areas as determined by the natural groupings and
the local circumstances of wind and current would be
established progressively and without design.

Now and again accidental voyagers no doubt got back
again to their own contact areas at a distance. Chamisso
relates an incident where some Caroline Islanders who had
been carried to the Marshalls pushed off in the direction in
which they thought their homes might be, and by good luck
came on Nukuoro, on the southern edge of the Carolines.[35]
This was obviously little more than an accidental voyage in
the reverse direction and in no sense deliberate navigation.
Furthermore, for such return trips to be successful, there
would have to be sufficient knowledge of the home contact
area for the final stage to be completed. It might be suggested on first thoughts that such incidents might have led
to deliberate voyages and colonization between the contact
areas, but that is really tantamount to saying that a common
contact area would have developed, since the vague notions
of relative positions would have been progressively replaced
by more exact ones if the areas had been within effective
range. The contact areas in historical times, involving as
they did detailed knowledge of the local meteorology, landmarks, currents and star courses, were obviously the outcome of a long process of internal development and were
fundamental unless and until some advance in navigation
was made. Much the same pattern applied independently
in oceanic areas all over the world until the days of instrumental navigation and large sailing ships, which incidentally were inter-dependent, in the sense that neither was
much use without the other.

While the myth of deliberate long off-shore voyages in the
days before navigation instruments is not supported by any
evidence, the Polynesians and other inhabitants of the
farther Pacific Islands deserve their reputation as outstanding voyagers. The Caroline Islanders in the North Pacific

made journeys comparable with those of the Polynesians. The farther voyages of the Tongans, Tahitians, Tuamotuans, Fijians, Caroline and Marshall Islanders, with no extended coast-lines before or behind them, in craft which were liable to be swept away, and without instruments, remain as among the most daring voyages of which there is reliable record. This was the effect of the unique environment of the Pacific Islanders. The reason why the Polynesians appeared to have gone a great deal farther than anyone else was because the islands which were accidentally settled by them were much farther apart than those which were inhabited elsewhere.

The nature of the Polynesian voyaging is shown by the accounts of the Tongan journeys in the farther parts of their large contact area, which extended from Samoa to Fiji. Will Mariner's evidence[36] confirms Cook's and gives a good idea of the type of cruising in old-time Polynesia.

Occasionally a daring Tongan chief went off to join in the Fijian wars. The attention of the Tongans, according to Mariner's reports of what they told him, was drawn to the Fijians and their wars as the result of accidental contacts from east to west, no doubt arising from the prevailing winds. Apparently the infrequent visits which were made by the Tongans to Fiji were hit-and-miss affairs, extending over years. After fishing in troubled waters among the Fijians, they would come back to Tonga with a convenient wind from the west, or try to. One chief, Tui Hala Fatai, after being two years in Fiji, came back to Tonga, but lost a canoe with some of his best men in a gale while doing so.

Another Tongan chief, whose name Mariner renders as Cow Mooaly (Kau Moala), told Mariner that after adventuring in Fiji for a couple of years, he decided to come home. In due course Vavau, the northernmost Tongan group, came into sight. He could not make the land because of the wind, and decided therefore to run for Samoa, a long way to the north-east. He could not make this either, and was blown onto Futuna, some distance to the north-west of Tonga. The people of Futuna knew no country other than their own, and had no large canoes – a sufficient commentary in itself on their range of contact. After a year the Tongan chief decided to push off for Fiji. He came west to Rotuma, which was a perilous trip indeed. Here the people treated him as a god, having never seen such a large canoe, which was a sign to Mariner, as well as to us, that Rotuma was not on any very frequent sailing schedule from the main western archipelago. Dillon's evidence a decade or so later shows indeed that Rotuma was at the extreme range of effective contact, for he found accidental voyagers from Rotuma scattered from Samoa to Tikopia, and heard of a Tongan expedition which had set out for Rotuma and never been heard of since.[37]

Cow Mooaly again set off for Fiji, taking with him some Rotumans. Yet again he was taken off course with the winds, but managed to make Fiji. Here he joined again in the local wars as the ally of one of the Fijian factions. Finally he got back to Tonga safely, after having been away for many years.

All this happened in the Western Polynesia-Fiji area. The picture given by such an account is hard to reconcile with the suggestion that the Polynesian ancestors deliberately explored for and maintained contact with islands 500 to 1,500 to 2,500 miles away in some hypothetical early colonization period. The procedure of ante-dating the voyaging to such a period, and suggesting that it stopped short in later times in every part of the Pacific, raises the question of what differing navigating techniques the earlier people might have had as compared with the later, and how it could have come about that such techniques could have disappeared everywhere without trace or memory.

The sort of voyaging of which Cook, Mariner, and Dillon tell shows the daring, the romance, and the difficulties of offshore cruising in the early Pacific. The Europeans who observed these journeys, knowing something of navigation difficulties in the days of sail, even with quadrants and compasses, were continually amazed at these feats. They repeatedly say that no European would have dreamed of attempting them without instruments. But later Europeans were apparently not impressed or satisfied with anything less than imagined voyages of a thousand miles or more. It is the sophisticated Europeans, with their Mercator's projection, their navigation aids, and the accumulated knowledge of four centuries of Pacific exploration, who have forgotten the elementary difficulties of primitive navigation.

Here then are facts, as opposed to the 'thousand conjectures of speculative reasoners' of which Cook spoke. There is de Bougainville's, Cook's, Andia's, Anderson's, Morrison's, Mariner's, Dillon's, Ellis's, and Turner's evidence on the short range of voyaging in Polynesia. We shall see later that the same applied to the Micronesian groups in the North Pacific and the Melanesian in the west. There is the evidence of Madeira and all the other uninhabited islands throughout the world. There is the inadequacy of all craft before the days of large sailing ships. There is the great margin of error in navigation without modern aids. There is the fact that when the sky is overcast the navigator is robbed of his heavenly guides. Finally there is the storm, with power to turn short navigated journeys into long un-navigated ones.

# CHAPTER THREE

# The Polynesian Dispersal

\*

THE Polynesian population in 1800 was somewhere round 800,000.[1] Let us assume that there had been a slow population increase, such that at the end of each generation of twenty-five years there were eleven people for each ten people there had been at the beginning of the generation. This represents an increase of 10 per cent per generation on the average. The rate of increase in Samoa today is 100 per cent per generation. On a figure of 10 per cent the number of Polynesian ancestors in 800 B.C., wherever they were, would be fifty. The figures are entirely arbitrary, but prove the point. A handful of people coming into Polynesia 2,000 or 3,000 years ago, and increasing at a moderate average rate, could easily have propagated the Polynesian population of historical times. In the light of this the necessity of imagining shuttle services of Polynesian colonists in order to account for the population disappears, in the same way that it is unnecessary to imagine that the British settlers brought shiploads of rabbits to New Zealand in order to account for the countless millions that arose there.

The same demonstration applies in the case of each of the natural groupings. One canoe-load of people, borne onto one of the islands in the early centuries of the Christian era with a rate of increase of 5 per cent to 10 per cent per generation, could account for the total population of the entire grouping in historical times.

The first European after Cook who moved fairly systematically round the islands of the central belt of Polynesia and left a full account was John Williams, the head of the London Missionary Society's post in Raiatea from 1817 to 1839. Trained as a craftsman, he was a man of practical bent and possessed of great drive and energy. At first he depended on casual passages in tramp sailing ships, but while stranded at Rarotonga for a year, he built a small schooner mainly out of local materials, which he called the *Messenger of Peace*. Chief Makea of Rarotonga put his people to work on it for Williams, and Makea himself sat on a stool on board, working the bilge pumps with fascinated curiosity. When the vessel was ready, Williams and Makea and a crew of enthusiastic Rarotongans sailed to Aitutaki, 146 miles to the north. This was the first time Makea had ever been to sea. Williams had a quadrant and a compass, and he knew the position of Aitutaki, so this time he landed on his target, which was very different from what had happened previously when he tried to find Rarotonga from Aitutaki.[2] After two trips from Tahiti to Tonga and Samoa, Williams met his death at the hands of the natives of Erromanga in the New Hebrides, as he came in to the beach in a ship's boat.[3]

The fact that Williams, from 1817 to 1839, was intimately associated with the establishment of the first continuous European contacts between Tahiti and the southern Cooks and Samoa, which form the Polynesian heartland, will be a sufficient explanation of why his name is quoted here only less frequently than that of Cook himself.

The notes which Williams has left of various accidental voyages which came to his notice give an invaluable picture of their potency for involuntary colonization. Taken with a few other notes left by other early nineteenth-century observers, these accounts give a revealing and at the same time final glance into the Polynesian dispersal. If anyone fears that the picture of settlement by accidental voyages is any less dramatic than the fiction of deliberate settlement, let him take note of the following stories.

John Williams never saw Manihiki-Rakahanga, the twin atolls situated some 600 miles to the north-west of Aitutaki. Contact was not made with them until ten years after he was dead. Yet he wrote some notes on their ethnology. He said that the people were more like the Tuamotuans than the Tahitians.[4]

When Williams set up a mission station on Aitutaki, he

learned about Manihiki because some accidental voyagers had arrived from it on Aitutaki about sixty years previously.

That was not however the only information Williams heard about Manihiki-Rakahanga from accidental contacts. One of the native missionaries who was working on Rurutu, some 1,000 miles to the south-east of Manihiki, had a small European-style sail-boat. Some Americans had come to Rurutu – Williams does not say how or why. The missionary, accompanied by the Americans, his wife, and some Rurutuans, set out for Tahiti, some 350 miles north. Presumably they had a compass, since these were supplied to the native missionaries in the outlying islands. The boat was caught in a storm and the destination was missed. A compass is no good for finding small objectives if the extent of veering off course is not known. Six weeks later a low island came in sight. They hove to and some canoes came out. They said the island was Manihiki. It was from this contact that Williams indirectly got some of his information about the Manihikians. The Americans and one or two of the Rurutuans decided to go and make contact with the local chief to see if they could get supplies.

While the vessel was waiting for the envoys to reappear, a gale came up and swept the boat off-shore again to the north. Here another island came in sight, which was the twin atoll of Rakahanga, about twenty-five miles away. The Manihiki-Rakahangan custom was to live on one island at a time, letting the fish and vegetation recover on the other. At that time the islanders were on Manihiki, so Rakahanga was deserted. The missionary and the remaining Rurutuans, now minus the Americans, landed on Rakahanga and found the native huts left just as if the people were all out visiting. There were even some human heads with flowing black hair. The voyagers stocked up on food from the island and decided to push off again, as any of us would no doubt have done in the same circumstances. The wanderers by this time had no notion where they were going. The prevailing winds and currents decided that they would go to Western Polynesia, for after a few more weeks had gone by, another island hove in sight. This was Niuatobutabu, between Tonga and Samoa, 1,000 miles west of Manihiki. Here they were received with kindness after their wanderings of over 2,000 miles at the whim of the elements.

That is not the end of the story, for if it had not been for a lucky chance, the survivors would have remained where they were and all that Williams would have known of them would have been a second-hand report that they had disappeared after setting out for Tahiti. Some time after, Williams made one of his trips to the west, and called at Tonga. There he heard that a native missionary was working at Niuatobutabu. He went there and found the widow of the missionary from Rurutu, the husband having died a short time before.

There is a loose string in this story, which is stranger than many better-known ones in the long annals of the sea. What happened to the Americans who were left stranded on Manihiki when the boat left? Williams, when he heard about them from the survivors, hoped that they would sow the seed of the Gospel in Manihiki. But when the island was found by the missionaries ten years after Williams himself was dead, no sign of them apparently remained.

By way of finishing off the evidence of accidental voyages from Manihiki, that the island still existed was again revealed to the missionaries in 1849, when a ship found a lost canoe containing another pathetic little company who had been blown away from Manihiki. So with this further clue, the Mission ship, which had searched repeatedly for the island over a period of years, finally found it, nearly thirty years after its existence first became known to Williams. This is a commentary in itself not merely on the difficulties of navigation without instruments, but on the final triumph of being able to fix positions so that contact could be maintained.

In the years that followed, canoes were always being blown away while passing between Manihiki and Rakahanga. Eventually the missionaries persuaded the people to give up their migrations between the two islands and settle each separately, in order to prevent this continual drain of life.[5] Yet they were only twenty miles or so apart. This does not square very well with the idea of long voyages of hundreds and indeed thousands of miles. It does accord however with Cook's view that in these accidents, continually repeated through thousands of years, might lie the secret of the peopling of Polynesia. Accidental trips from Manihiki-Rakahanga alone could have populated quite an extensive area in Polynesia, had they happened to be among the first islands to be peopled. Yet these islands were only as two pin-pricks among the Polynesian islands.

From Raivivae, on the southern fringe of Polynesia, an epic voyage occurred during Williams's time in Polynesia.[6] A vessel with a number of people was lost and left without bearings, so that it was carried to the west. After a time some of the people began to die. As the weeks went by, the toll of the dead mounted, until it was twenty. No doubt the weaker went first. So three long months went by. Then one day some land popped up ahead. This was Manua in the Samoa Group, some 1,500 miles from Raivivae. A number of islands lie between the two, but the voyagers who died because they were not sighted were less lucky than those who lived long enough to see Manua.

Again the question arises how Williams knew about this, and again the answer is that he happened to come across the survivors on one of his two visits to Samoa-Tonga.

On one of these trips, both of which were flying visits, not periods of residence, Williams found still another lot of accidental visitors to far distant islands. This time it was some Aitutakians who had been carried for 1,000 miles to Niuafoo, north of Tonga. Again Williams came as the Good Samaritan who took them home.[7] Thus the voyage finished up as a two-way one through the intervention of a European ship, which was a departure from the outcome of the many previous incidents that peopled Polynesia.

What determined the chances of survival on the longer accidental journeys?[8] It might be thought that the islands of

Polynesia must have been deliberately colonized because planned provisioning for the longer voyages to Hawaii and New Zealand and Easter Island was essential to survival. An ounce of demonstration is worth a ton of speculation, and these accounts by Williams give the demonstration. These long voyages which he tells of were quite unexpected. Men can live a long time without food, and an occasional fish or sea-bird would help them to survive. Water would be a more serious matter if they went too long without rain, or did not catch enough fish to squeeze the juices from. Yet some survived these authenticated journeys which were comparable in length to the long voyages to New Zealand, Hawaii, and Easter Island.

After such long involuntary traverses, one of a mere 500 miles from Rurutu to the Tahitian islands may not sound spectacular. A chief of Rurutu with a number of his people was taken to Raiatea in Williams's time.[9] The incident is mentioned particularly because Rurutu or Oheteroa was the island Tupia knew of. Anderson considered that the Tahitian knowledge of such farther islands was derived from accidental migrants. Here then is confirmation that such voyages occurred from Rurutu to Tupia's own home. Since Raivivae and Rimatara, two more islands in Cook's and Forster's Tahitian data, are near Rurutu, the same applies to them. One would expect also that Tubuai would have been heard of in Tahiti from accidental voyagers, and it may well be the 'Toobooai' which Forster identified with one of the Marquesas Islands, as his chart shows.

Williams was only twenty-five years in the Pacific, as compared with the untold centuries that the Polynesians had been there before him. His glimpses of the islands beyond the Cooks were fragmentary. Yet the few accidental voyages which came to his notice ranged from Raivivae in the south to Manihiki 1,000 miles to the north, from Manihiki to Aitutaki 600 miles south, and from Raivivae and Tahiti to Tonga and Samoa. How many more during these twenty-five years went into the void where there was no land, or came on islands where their different dialects and customs spelt their doom, or were carried to islands which Williams did not visit, we can only guess.

One thing will not have failed to attract the notice of those who remember the prevailing easterly winds, and the currents that accompany them, and that is that while some of the voyagers in Williams's stories went south, others north, and most west, none of them went from west to east. Nevertheless Williams believed that the Polynesians came from the west in the first place, because he knew that the winds were not invariably easterly. He said that he was well aware of the impossibility of the native canoes proceeding against the prevailing wind, but that they could have come from the west when westerlies blew.[10] He did not deduce a firm concept either of accidental voyages or deliberate settlement so far as the arrival of the Polynesians in their islands was concerned. He believed that some contact had occurred between the Cooks and Tahiti because there appeared to be traditions in both groups of such contacts.

Peter Dillon, the sailing captain who visited Tonga in the early nineteenth century, was told by a chief there that a canoe from Aitutaki had finished up on one of the Tongan islands with five survivors out of ten after being lost at sea for five months.[11]

William Ellis tells of the surprise that awaited the first missionary to visit the lonely little island of Rapa, which is situated far to the south of the main Polynesian islands. Here they found a man named 'Mapuagua' who had come in a storm twelve years before from Mangareva, with six other people including women.[12] They had come over 600 miles on a raft with the winds and currents. Mapuagua was probably one of the luckiest accidental voyagers that ever was projected into the Pacific wastes, because Rapa is only five miles wide, with no islands to speak of on either side of it or beyond it for a tremendous distance. One may conjecture how many vessels blown away from Mangareva and the islands near it over many centuries, had been less lucky.

Since all the voyages that Ellis knew of, whether accidental or deliberate, were from east to west, he thought that some of the Polynesians might have come from America. He based this view on the fact that the prevailing winds and currents came from that direction, and knew from experience the limitations of the native craft in going against the wind.[13] A succession of other missionaries, commencing with Williams,[14] opposed this view, because as time went on the capabilities of winds from the west to convey ships became known. Some of the missionaries soon realized that winds blowing from the west could have caused accidental settlement.

Sheldon Dibble, the head of the mission in Hawaii from 1830, suggested that the Polynesians had been distributed round the Pacific by accidental voyages.[15]

George Turner was one of the first white missionaries to reside permanently in Samoa. At Rotuma, which he visited in 1845, he saw twenty people, both men and women, who had been picked up by a whaling vessel after being blown away. Turner quoted this as an example of the way islands were settled, saying that these people, if they had come on an uninhabited island, would have called it after their own island and peopled it.[16]

On the same trip, on one of the islands of the New Hebrides 500 miles west of the Fiji-Tonga-Samoa area, Turner found some Tongans and Samoans. They had been blown away while passing from Savaii in Samoa to Tonga. Again women were numbered among them, again it had been a one-way trip, and again they had resumed their lives where fate had taken them. One of them, Sualo, a Samoan of Savaii, had indeed become a famous man in this new community, having devised a way of repelling marauders. This simply consisted of rushing into the middle of them with a two-handed weapon and laying about him, instead of waiting to be picked off. This practical demonstration of the ancient maxim that the best form of defence is attack had earned him much prestige.[17]

Another remarkable epic of the storm, incidentally proving that accidental voyagers were borne over long distances from west to east, was recounted by Captain Beechey, an

English naval commander who visited the eastern islands of Polynesia in 1824.[18] On one of the Tuamotus he found a number of people who had set off from Anaa for Tahiti three years previously. So far from getting to Tahiti, they finished up on an uninhabited island 420 miles behind their starting point.

Three of the fine canoes for which Anaa was famous set off for Tahiti with 150 people of both sexes and all ages. The vessels were lined up on landmarks on Anaa which were known to point in the direction of Maitia, the nearest of the Tahitian islands. The distance to Maitia was about 170 miles. The use of Maitia as a navigation aid shows the importance of intervening islands. They set off with a convenient wind in fine weather and made such good progress that they began looking for Maitia. If they went at seven knots with a very strong wind, as Cook found the Tongan canoes did, we may judge that they had gone somewhere round 120 miles in seventeen or eighteen hours at this point. Had the wind held for only a few more hours, they would have made land. Instead, however, a westerly gale came up and blew them around for days, during which time they were much battered by waves sweeping over the vessel. They lost contact with the other two canoes, containing over 100 people, and never heard of them again. In their own canoe were twenty-three men, fifteen women and ten children.

Eventually the storm blew itself out and they set sail again for the west towards where they hoped Tahiti might be. After two days, however, during which no land came in sight, they were becalmed for many days. They grew exhausted from paddling, and their food and water ran out. Since they had taken enough for three weeks, they must by this time have been lost for a long time. Some of them drank sea-water. Then they began to die. The others in extremity for a time ate their companions' flesh, although ordinarily they were not cannibals. Then Tuwarri, who told Beechey the story, managed to gaff a shark which kept the survivors going after half the original forty-eight had died. Finally another storm came up, again from the west, and was actually welcomed because it meant life-giving water. For several days they were blown before the wind, and so eventually onto an island 420 miles south-east of Anaa, and 540 miles from the point near Maitia where the first westerly gale had hit them. That had happened three years previously, during which time they had subsisted on some deserted Tuamotu atolls without knowing where they were.

No better example of the loss of bearings that occurred in such incidents, or of the capacity of winds from the west to transport accidental settlers on occasion, or of the fully-fledged little communities, complete with men, woman, and children that could arise, could be imagined.

Dr Lang, a churchman of Sydney in Australia, plied back and forth across the South Pacific on a number of occasions in the early nineteenth century. He interested himself in the problem of the Pacific migrations, and noted the frequent occurrence of westerly winds even in the tropic areas where the prevailing winds are easterly. He collected evidence of the type of voyages that were made in the South Pacific, and came to the conclusion that the long ones were solely accidental, and by no means exclusively from east to west.[19]

William Wyatt Gill is a somewhat later missionary who lived in the Cook Islands for twenty-two years, and who had experience in the newly discovered atolls to the north of the central belt, and in New Guinea.[20]

Gill says that in 1862 he saw on Manua in the Samoa Group people who had been blown there accidentally from Moorea in the Tahiti Group, a distance of 1,250 miles, with no lives lost.[21]

Another of Gill's accounts tells of an accidental voyage from Manihiki to the Ellice Group north of Samoa, a distance of over 1,000 miles, during which half the party perished from want of food and water.

The most significant of Gill's reports is the following, because it was from west to east and bridged the gap from the western islands to the Cooks. Fakaofo is an island about 300 miles north of Samoa. In January 1858, says Gill, a numerous family was conveyed from Fakaofo in a westerly gale, coming eventually to Mangaia in the southern Cooks via the desert atolls of Nassau and Palmerston. This was a distance of 1,250 miles in which the east component was about 700 miles. This confirms the occasional persistence of westerly influences and their potency for accidental settlement from west to east, as Gill himself points out. The fact that these people continued on from two desert atolls shows how such lost wanderers could pick and choose between alternatives, and were not necessarily driven by gales although their courses were determined by the direction of the winds at the time.

William Pritchard, who was born in Tahiti and lived for many years in the mid-century in Western Polynesia-Fiji, where he was British Consul,[22] after reviewing the legends of Fiji-Tonga-Samoa, says: 'Apart from these legendary accounts, it cannot be doubted that the early migrations of the ancestors of these islanders were involuntary rather than the result of roving dispositions, or the pressure of limited and over-populated homes; that, in fact, they were blown away from their earlier homes in their frail canoes.' Pritchard then remarks that no such voyages from west to east were known.[23]

The controversy among the earlier European observers who saw things for themselves, apart from those who thought the facts could be best explained by former land connexions, was rather over where the people came from than how they got there. The truth of the matter is that the prevailing trade winds are occasionally overcome by winds from the west in the Pacific Island belts, and in the South Pacific cyclonic storms generated south of the equator move onto the central islands.[24] The meteorology within the Pacific Islands themselves is therefore not inconsistent with the view that settlement occurred either from the east or west or both.

The accounts of accidental voyages which have been given are of those which actually finished on a distant Polynesian island with men and women survivors, because such survivors were the living proof of the potentialities of such voyages for the colonization of Polynesia in early times.

Occasionally European vessels met such waifs of the storm in mid-ocean. An interesting incident of this nature was told to Dr Lang of Sydney by a whaling captain.[25] His vessel came upon a large canoe with a number of people in it several hundreds of miles from the nearest land. They had been blown off one of the Tahitian islands. The whaling captain took pity on them and gave them a compass, telling them to follow the mark on the card which he pointed out to them. One may imagine the mingled hope and scepticism with which the Tahitians followed the direction of the compass line. Eventually the Tahitian islands showed up ahead, as the whaling captain found later. The travellers then concluded that the compass, like an eye, had seen the land all the time. This again shows the inability of primitive navigation to re-establish a course when bearings had been lost.

After 1860 no more big canoes were being built in Polynesia. Yet accidental voyages still went on in the South Pacific, although for the most part confined to small canoes. Some tales from the Gilberts[26] in later times throw light on the capacity of men to survive such ordeals. A missionary in the twentieth century left a report of a couple of Gilbertese who awoke one morning to find themselves out to sea. Their small boat had drifted off shore during the night. They caught a sea-bird after some days, and a few days later caught another. Then for a long time they had no food at all. They then caught a shark, but were unable to eat it after being starved for so long. When they were at their last gasp, an island showed up. It was not far from Truk in the Carolines, some 1,400 miles from their home island. The Truk officials arranged for the wanderers to be returned, otherwise the incident would probably not have been heard of.

The classic of all such records for endurance is the story of the Gilbertese youth in World War II who took to a canoe to escape the Japanese. He drifted 1,500 miles to the Admiralty Group to the north of the New Guinea area. For no less than seven months he kept alive on fish. In the light of this, given a stout heart, an iron constitution, and some fishing tackle, nothing is apparently too much to believe as far as survival on long accidental voyages is concerned.

Such incidents were evidently not rare in the Gilberts, for the Gilbertese had a customary law that when some of their people disappeared in storms, after a certain time their property was divided.[27]

Throughout the century from Cook to 1860, when the old order in Polynesia had gone for ever, the tale is thus the same – a steady succession of accidental migrants, starting their journey in any direction with the storms, and then, when the gale had blown itself out, going with whatever seasonal wind was blowing at the time. For the most part the dominant winds were from the east, but not invariably. One century is not long, and the voyages which were recorded were no doubt only a fraction of those which occurred even within that century. Yet those few which attracted notice could have colonized the central islands of Polynesia, either from the west or the east. Extend the time back for twenty or thirty centuries, and the thought that any other explanation is necessary to explain the peopling of the Pacific becomes superfluous. For each little party of men and women who were borne to a new island in this way bore within them the seed which would in course of time, with only a small rate of increase, populate not only that island, but all the others which were accessible from it. For a thousand years at least before Cook, it would be seldom when some canoe was not sailing aimlessly somewhere in the Pacific. In early times accidental voyages were no doubt fewer, since the population would be smaller, but on the other hand those who came on land were more significant, since there would be more islands and parts of islands awaiting their first settlers. Accidental voyagers had a hundred generations, with scores of such involuntary incidents in each generation, in which to hit or miss each of the natural groupings.

Most accidental voyagers were no doubt overwhelmed by storms or exposure, or were carried onto islands which

were already populated. Of those who came on an uninhabited island, most would be men who had been carried
away while fishing or while going on forays against neighbouring islands. The great events of the prehistory of the
Pacific were when an isolated canoe with women aboard
happened for the first time on a new island group. In the
early days it would be a very infrequent event, since the
population would be fragmentary. Possibly it happened only
once in 500 years, but several thousand years is a long time.
When it did happen, the seed of human continuity and
increase throughout that island group was sown. No doubt
in the case of the bigger island groups several such canoes
started separate involuntary colonies on different islands in
the group, which in due course expanded and inter-married.
As the population grew, other involuntary voyagers were
launched into the Pacific wastes, most to die, a very occasional handful to carry their seed to a new island.

Always must it be kept in mind what magic is effected
by slow population increase over a long time when the food
supply is adequate and natural enemies few. While there is
room to expand, and a sufficiency of food, the increase is like
compound interest – slow at first, but cumulative as more
population arises to beget more population. The high fertile
islands of Samoa, Tonga, Tahiti, the Marquesas, the Cooks,
Hawaii and New Zealand were suited to such steady and
progressive increase from small beginnings. A few little
knots of people coming onto each of them in early times can
easily account for the populations in historical times. Take
any rate of increase, however small, and it will be found that
this applies. Nor is it necessary to imagine that the early
canoes with women aboard which started the settlement of a
new island group brought the animals of historical times
with them. The food plants, where imported, could also
have come in later canoes.[28]

All the stories of accidental voyages which have been
repeated are authentic beyond all doubt, because the early
missionaries and others who recounted them actually found
the survivors on the islands to which they had gone so un-

willingly. All of them were blown away in storms. These were not however the only types of one-way voyage which there is reason to believe occurred in old-time Polynesia.

When the English missionaries in Tahiti fell foul of the local people on one occasion, they were threatened with being sent out to sea, which may indicate that this was sometimes done by the Polynesians to their enemies.[29] Captain Porter, an American naval commander who visited the Marquesas in 1814, was told that a chief, when his people were hard-pressed by enemies, had prepared to put out to sea with them on a desperation voyage of self-exile in order to escape annihilation, although he had not actually done so. Porter was also told that deliberate exiles sometimes set off for traditional islands and were never heard of again.[30] In the early nineteenth century a statement was made by a Rotuman that larger canoes had been retained on Rotuma so that when population pressure arose, expeditions of voluntary exiles might go off in them.[31] George Turner records a case of some Manihikians who, having learned that there were islands to the west from European sources, pushed off with a daring born of ignorance to visit them, and came eventually on one of the Tokelaus.[32] Later again the missionaries on Uvea reported that similar incidents occurred,[33] while other instances, in which young males went off on trips of self-exile from Tikopia, are on record.[34]

While no authenticated instance of forced exile or voluntary self-exile of a party containing women is on record in historical times, this means no more than that it would probably be a rare event.

Such voyages of exiles, whether arising from desperation or misplaced optimism, or from the whim of conquerors, were merely variations on the accidental voyage-theme. Not being blown off by storms, such exiles would tend to go with the prevailing winds and so be borne into areas which were already populated. Such parties might have made preparations for the journey, but would not differ in this from canoes

71

blown off-shore while passing between islands. Such exiles, if they did not meet land soon, would certainly be parted from any other canoes by strong winds at night. If they kept together for more than a night or two it would be rare, let alone for the weeks and months which were involved in the longer distances. For these reasons it is doubtful whether exiles had any great significance in the Polynesian dispersal except possibly in secondary east-west voyages after the population had built up in the central and eastern groups. But the distinction between voyages of exiles and voyages arising from storms is academic, for all alike, if they survived to carry the seed of human life to a new island or group, did so as accidental settlers in isolated canoes. They were all accidental settlers, arriving as handfuls of people by one-way journeys.

It is not appropriate to describe voyages arising either from storms or exile as drift voyages. The accidental voyages of the Pacific Islanders, as the accounts of them show, arose from their inability to re-set their courses when blown away and lost at sea, or when committed to unfamiliar waters. The essential things about these incidents were that those who figured in them were lost, and were unable to come back into the wind which was blowing at the time. They could however exercise a choice as to whether they would sail across the wind or run before it. Furthermore, they had their sails and steering paddles, and could control their vessels. Gill's story of the numerous family who came to Mangaia via Nassau and Palmerston is evidence that accidental voyagers could and did exercise some option over their fate within the margin allowed to them by the winds and currents at the time. Even less appropriate a term than drift voyagers would be that of castaways.

On the issue of whether the Polynesians were distributed from Western Polynesia or Eastern Polynesia, in the first place, the records of accidental voyages can throw no light, since some occurred in both directions. The answer is established beyond reasonable doubt by the linguistic research of Dr S. H. Elbert, who has shown that Western Polynesia was the ancestral speech area of the Eastern Polynesian tongues, and that Hawaiian and Maori are derived from one or other of the latter. He conjectures, without reaching a final con- clusion, that the original hiving-off of the Eastern Polyne- sian speech had occurred by the third century A.D., and that Hawaiian and Maori were established somewhere round A.D. 1000.[35]

Reconstructions of the probable course of accidental migration to the peripheral groups of the eastern area of Polynesia, using the evidence of actual accidental voyages where available, and the meteorology, are in marked accord with the cultural affinities. They cannot establish precise origins, but can throw light on the broad pattern of distribution.

A word of explanation is due here on the use of cultural evidence in this book. Some cultural items are more resistant to change than others. The words for basic things such as 'water', 'air', 'walk', and the like are comparatively endur- ing. General cultural items, such as arts and crafts, habits of dress, and social customs, may be less so, being more subject to local circumstances. For these reasons the primary cultural evidence which is used in references to cultural similarities is that of basic vocabularies, other cultural ana- logies being used merely as probable corollaries or illustra- tions of such affinities as are indicated by more fundamental evidence, most of which is not cultural.

Coming to the Cooks, we have seen evidence that a number of accidental voyages from Tahiti occurred, as well as one from Fakaofo north of Samoa. Williams found that the Rarotongans knew of a traditional island, Manua, to the west,[36] which was no doubt the Samoan island  But since the set of the prevailing winds is from the Tahiti-Tuamotu area, it is not surprising to find that culturally the Cook Islanders resembled the peoples of these eastern groups rather than the Western Polynesians.

In the case of New Zealand, the same prevailing winds and currents come as a broad band through Eastern Poly- nesia to within 800 miles of New Zealand, whence a region of variable winds, where anything might happen to a canoe according to the caprice of the weather, stretches down to New Zealand. Again one finds that there were close affinities between the Eastern Polynesian cultures and those of New Zealand. This does not necessarily mean that a canoe could not have come from the Samoa-Tonga-Fiji area by a north-west storm into the region of variable winds and so to New Zealand, but if so it left no noticeable impact on the cultures.

In the case of New Zealand there is little objective evidence of accidental voyages to guide us in determining origins. The Maoris in the middle of New Zealand told Cook that their grandfathers said that four men in a canoe from islands to the north had come ashore and been subsequently killed.[37] No late accidental arrivals have been recorded. They may well have taken place even in historical times, since such incidents would not necessarily attract attention. Evidence is not however entirely lacking that canoes could be borne to New Zealand with the winds and currents, for in 1953 an empty canoe from some Pacific island came ashore on the east coast of the North Island.[38] The record in the case of New Zealand is therefore almost as negative of accidental voyages as of deliberate, in respect of migrants from the islands outside New Zealand itself.

The Chatham Islands are located 500 miles to the east of New Zealand, and frequent westerly winds sweep from New Zealand in their direction. Horatio Hale, the American ethnologist who visited New Zealand in 1840, was told by an English sailor who had lived in the Chathams that the people there said they were descendants of Maoris who had been driven from the East Cape of the North Island of New Zealand in a storm about ninety years previously.[39] Many of the relics which had been found by the fossickers in the Chathams and New Zealand resemble one another closely. The only record of a deliberate voyage by Maoris prior to 1840 is that of a party who in 1835 performed the remarkable feat of capturing a whaling ship and forcing the captain to take them to the Chathams, which they conquered and occupied.[40] Many accidental migrants had in all probability preceded them.

The compact Marquesas Group lies 350 miles to the north of the easternmost Tuamotu islands. We have seen that accidental voyages occurred to north and south in the central belt. There is therefore no difficulty in picturing accidental voyages between them and the Tuamotus. Indeed, when we consider how Beechey's friend Tuwarri and his companions were blown 540 miles to the east, there is no difficulty in thinking that accidental voyages could have occurred from any of the Tuamotus, including the larger ones to the north-east of Tahiti. Again the cultural evidence shows affinities between the Marquesas and the other Eastern Polynesian areas. Again there are no records of deliberate voyages to and from the Marquesas from any other islands by native craft without navigation aids, so far as a diligent search of the published literature can establish.

Finally we come to Hawaii. This group is about 1,800 miles from the Marquesas lying to the south-east, and somewhat more from the Marshalls to the west. The winds blow fairly consistently from Hawaii to the Marshalls. Being unable to beat back satisfactorily against them, the early Spaniards who came from Mexico to the Philippines learned to go north on the return journey and pick up the Japan Current to California. Trying to get the Hawaiians from the Marshalls against the prevailing winds is a difficult thought, whether by accidental or deliberate journeys. Not even a cyclone[41] can be invoked with any realism, for cyclones are twisters which could start an accidental journey, but could not be expected to bear either accidental or deliberate voyagers for 2,000 miles. Nor are the winds and currents propitious for voyages from Hawaii to the South Pacific. On the other hand Hawaii is favourably placed for accidental voyages from Eastern Polynesia. The trade winds south of the equator bear towards the north-west in the general direction of Hawaii, and at certain times of the year extend over the equator as far as seven degrees north. Here there is a zone of calms and light breezes, beyond which are the prevailing easterlies. South-west gales blow from time to time in the Hawaii area. In the Eastern Polynesian area itself, westerlies and south-westerlies blow strongly on occasion. Canoes could thus come from any part of Eastern Polynesia in a storm, and then come under the influences bearing towards Hawaii.

Again the cultural affinities are compatible with the view that the people who were decisive in establishing the Hawaiian cultures came from Eastern Polynesia, for they are of much the same character in both areas.

The usual view that the Hawaiians were derived almost exclusively from Tahiti cannot be proved or disproved. Some canoes may have come from anywhere in Eastern Polynesia. The cultures of the Eastern Polynesian area have a broad affinity, which may have been closer in earlier times. So far as the direction of the winds and currents throws light on this, a no less probable source of accidental migrants would be the Marquesas. Since it is reasonable to think that the early canoes with women were few and far between, a great deal depends on which area of Eastern Polynesia supplied the main components in this early settlement period. Since there might have been several knots of settlement on different Hawaiian islands from different parts of Eastern Polynesia, and since the precise course of initial settlement in Eastern Polynesia itself cannot be traced, the only thing that can be said with any certainty is that the decisive Hawaiian ancestors were Eastern Polynesians.

David Malo, a Hawaiian who was born somewhere round 1793, and who wrote notes on early Hawaii, said that the ancient lore of the Hawaiians contained the name Polapola,[42] which looks like the name of the Tahitian island of Borabora. Since this traditional name was uncommon in other parts of Polynesia, its occurrence in Hawaii may possibly be regarded as a slim clue to an accidental voyage from the Tahiti-Tuamotu area.

In 1814 Captain Porter, the commander of the American naval unit which visited the Nukuhiva area of the Marquesas, was told of deliberate exiles who were described as having set off for traditional islands to the west.[43] If true, these happenings might have been of some importance as far as accidental voyages to Hawaii were concerned. In the light of accidental settlement, the thought that all the Hawaiian ancestors came from one group in Eastern Polynesia is unrealistic. The stories Porter tells, however, may possibly throw light on the importing of livestock and food plants into Hawaii. Hawaii had the pig, dog, fowl, seedless breadfruit, and seedless banana, *taro* and *kumara* at the time of European contact. The distribution of the food plants in Polynesia is a subject which is full of uncertainty, as a later chapter will show, but the livestock and seedless plants certainly came to Hawaii in human vessels. It is reasonable to believe that some at least of them were taken by deliberate exiles, although this is not a completely necessary belief, as they might all have arrived capriciously on other types of accidental voyage. The conveyance of deliberate exiles to Hawaii would be more likely from the Marquesas than from other parts of Polynesia, since such exiles would not leave in storms, and would differ from accidental voyagers driven to the north-east in the first place. Porter was told that the grandfather of one of the chiefs of Nukuhiva had gone off with four large canoes furnished with livestock and food plants, and had not been heard of again. Such expeditions of exiles were reputed to be frequent, some hundreds of people having gone off in this way in living memory, specially large canoes being used. The priests encouraged these ventures, professing to know by second sight that the exiles had arrived in traditional islands which abounded in breadfruit and other delicacies. Their fate remained unknown, which does not accord with the thought that their navigation was equal to retracing their courses.

In this chapter a review has been made of the records of accidental voyages across the larger gaps between the Polynesian groups in the hundred years between Cook and the passing of the old sea-going canoes. The accounts of voyages across these gaps are confined to accidental ones because no accounts of deliberate two-way contact have been found. Ellis mentions[44] a voyage in a large canoe from Rurutu to Tahiti, which he suggests had taken somewhat longer than a direct course. A voyage from Tahiti to Rurutu, a smaller target, would have been necessary to establish evidence of two-way intercourse. Ellis also mentions a voyage from the Tuamotuan island of Hao to Tahiti, bringing the Tahitians knowledge of this island which they had not had before, and of a voyage from Tahiti to the islands near Mangaia. That these two latter voyages were not evidence of two-way contact is demonstrated by Ellis himself, for he goes on to say that comparable voyages in the reverse or eastern direction were unknown.

In later times, when missions had been established in the Australs, which are the nearest islands outside the Tahiti-Tuamotu area itself, Ellis tells of how Tahitian missionaries and chiefs occasionally went between these islands and Tahiti or Raiatea in European-style vessels, but by that time the courses had been established by the Europeans and compasses had been introduced. Pomare of Tahiti had a cutter with a European navigator and extended his dominion over the neighbouring islands. The unique maritime cultures of the Pacific Islands were passing for ever.

The early Europeans who debated whether accidental settlement occurred from west or east were brought to grips with a problem that was not easily solvable within Polynesia itself. What the facts of Polynesia show is that accidental settlement is the only theory that can explain how people came to be on the farther islands of the world. The Europeans who lived longest in Polynesia in the early days and saw things for themselves put forward the same view that Cook had, and for the same reasons.

# CHAPTER FOUR

# Where did the Pacific Islanders come from?

*

FIVE possible gateways or routes to the Pacific Islands have been suggested from time to time by various writers. All of them are in accord with the potentialities of the winds and currents to convey vessels with human freight. One is the route formed by the Caroline Islands chain and its extensions the Marshalls and Gilberts. A second is by the Japan Current to Hawaii. A third is from the Americas to the eastern Pacific Islands. A fourth is from Australia to New Zealand. The fifth is from the chain of islands formed by New Guinea, the Solomons, and the New Hebrides.

The Caroline Islands lie between the East Indies and the farther islands of the Pacific. The nearest of them are about 400 miles east of the Philippines, and a slightly less distance north of the Moluccas and western New Guinea.

For nearly 200 years the early Spanish voyagers came across the Pacific passing north of the Carolines, yet these islands did not attract any deliberate attention from them till 1696. As early as 1565 the Spaniards had come from Spanish America and established a trading post at Manila in the Philippines, and later another Spanish post was set up at Guam in the Marianas, north of the Carolines.[1]

How then were the Spanish first induced to make deliberate voyages to the Carolines? Did Spanish vessels from Manila, with their quadrants and compasses, and with the extended coast-line of the Philippines behind them, push off into the uncharted seas to the east on deliberate probes for new islands? Did the Caroline Islanders themselves come on deliberate quests in their fine praus? The answer by this time is becoming commonplace. The Carolines first attracted the deliberate attention of the Spaniards through accidental voyagers.

In 1696 a party of Caroline Islanders was blown to Samar in the Philippines. The Spanish missionaries there were induced by this incident to make contact with the Western Carolines, but tragedy overtook the first envoys and the attempt was discontinued. Then in 1721 some more Caroline Islanders were blown to the other Spanish post of Guam. The Spanish missionaries there were induced by this to set up a mission in the Western Carolines, but again tragedy supervened, the missionaries being wiped out by the islanders. So the Carolines, Marshalls, and Gilberts were left more or less to themselves for another century or more.

For the accounts of these first contacts with the Carolines, we are dependent on the reports of the Spanish missionaries. The report of the missionaries on Samar is comparatively short, but the main facts are clear.[2] The report of the missionary on Guam, Juan Cantova, is a thorough and valuable document.[3] Such first contacts, before derived knowledge through European sources could arise, are all-important as evidence of the range of deliberate voyaging in pre-European times. All those which throw light on that range in the Pacific Islands have been searched for, and all those which have been found, other than such as are purely repetitive of earlier evidence, are reviewed in this book.

On the day in 1696 when they started their long involuntary voyage of 1,000 miles to Samar in the Philippines, thirty-five Caroline Islanders including a number of women and children were passing between two of their islands. Some of them were important personages in those parts, including relatives of the local overlord. No doubt they had one of those praus which so excited the admiration of all the early Europeans who saw them. They were large single canoes with a substantial outrigger, not double canoes like the Polynesian sea-going vessels, although the balancing principle is obviously the same in both. A gale came up and blew them away. For days and weeks and months the wanderers were at the mercy of the winds blowing from the east. During this time they caught fish by trailing funnel-shaped traps in the water. Five of them died. Eventually they despaired of fighting the winds in their attempt to regain their islands, and ran with the wind. Some seventy days after their journey started, they came on Samar, the easternmost of the Philippine Islands. A man of Samar, seeing a strange type of craft, waved to them to come in through the reef. They were terrified, so he swam out and piloted them in.

The Spanish missionaries on Samar interviewed the involuntary visitors from the unknown world to the east, being helped by two previous accidental migrants from the Carolines who were already on Samar. Here we find more evidence of the perennial process of accidental migration in the Pacific Islands. The voyagers told the missionaries that the Caroline Islanders believed they were the only people in the world – a commentary on their range of deliberate contact. One of the Caroline Islanders had been blown before to an island without seeing any people there, and had got back again to the Carolines. The missionaries supposed the island to have been one of the Philippines. But Zuniga, a later missionary in the Philippines, evolved his theory of the American origin of the peoples of the Pacific Islands and the Philippines because the missionaries knew of no cases of easterly voyages from the Philippines by local voyagers.[4]

In 1721 a second lot of Caroline Islanders were blown to an island near Guam in twenty days, and a week later another party of six who had been separated from them in the storm came there too. They were the remnants of a flotilla of six canoes in all, which had been passing from their home island of Faraulep to another island. This time the gale had come from the west.

Juan Cantova, a Spanish missionary on Guam, questioned the islanders over a number of months, learning their language. *He found that the Caroline Islanders at the time of the inquiry did not visit Guam. Faraulep is about 300 miles from Guam, these being the nearest inhabited parts of the Carolines and Marianas respectively. All the Western Caroline Islands, on the other hand, from Yap and the other westernmost islands to Truk in the east, were in contact with one another. All these islands can be reached without crossing gaps of more than 170 miles. These informants of Cantova, numbering people familiar with all parts of the Western Carolines, also knew of islands to the east of Truk, including the largest island in the Eastern Carolines, Ponape, but the information came from inhabitants of these islands who had been driven thence to the western Carolines by storms. Ponape is 400 miles east of Truk, with a small uninhabited atoll, Oroluk, about 220 miles from each.*

Cantova wrote his report, together with a chart of the islands, purely on the information he got from the accidental voyagers. He wanted detailed information in order to show his superiors that an extensive region still awaited missionary enterprise. Again the witness was soon dead, for Cantova achieved his ambition of being sent to the Carolines, where he was killed.

Kotzebue, the Russian explorer, and his naturalist Chamisso, were the first Europeans to make contact with the Marshall Islanders and question them about their range of contacts.[5] The Marshall Islands lie several hundred miles east of Ponape, and a similar distance north of the Gilberts. *When Kotzebue and Chamisso interviewed the islanders about their range of contacts in 1817, the voyagers were visiting both for friendly and warlike reasons all the islands in their own group with the apparent exception of the outlying atolls of Ujelang, Eniwetok, and Taongi. From the information he received, Kotzebue made up a chart which shows the Marshall Islands apart from the outliers. The Marshall Islanders, said Chamisso, knew nothing of the Gilbert Islanders, several hundred miles south, unless their references to 'Repith-Urur' might refer to them, which they very probably did in the light of later knowledge gleaned by an ethnologist in the Marshalls concerning the probable meaning of the words.[6] But in any case Repith-Urur, wherever it might be, was known only from accidental voyagers.*

When Captain Hudson and Horatio Hale, of the United States Exploring Expedition of 1838–42, visited the Gilberts and the Ellice Islands in 1841, these islands were still little known. *The Americans found by systematic inquiries that the Gilbertese visited only their own central string of islands, and that contact even within them was limited and discontinuous. The southern*

*Ellice Islanders showed no sign of knowing the Gilberts or other islands to the north.*[7]

The Gilbert Islands and the Ellice Islands each form a thin chain across the prevailing winds and currents, which make voyaging hazardous. Despite their nearness, the Gilbertese and the Ellice Islanders differed noticeably among themselves according to the testimony of all the early explorers. Thus Hudson and Hale found that some of the islanders were predominantly like those of the Carolines in their appearance and culture,[8] while others, including the southern Ellice Islanders, were like the Samoans.[9]

Accidental voyages are recorded over the whole area of the Marianas, Carolines, Marshalls, and Gilberts. Kotzebue found on one of the Marshalls two men who had come by an accidental voyage from the Western Carolines. They had been blown west of home, eventually finishing up 1,200 miles east of it, still thinking they were west of it.[10] Here is another example of the loss of bearings which beset primitive navigation. De Freycinet collected stories of involuntary migrants from the Carolines who came on the Marianas during the Spanish occupation up to the early years of the nineteenth century.[11] They arrived about once in each generation. Chamisso was told by a Caroline Islander that Ponape was known to his people from accidental voyagers,[12] as it had been in Cantova's time a century before. Chamisso says that Caroline Islanders were frequently driven in the opposite direction to the Marshalls.[13] Many lesser accidental voyages within the groups themselves were recorded by these explorers.

Cantova had found that the Caroline Islanders had no knowledge of the Marianas. In Kotzebue's day, with Spanish encouragement, they were sending up annual trading fleets to Guam. The vessels with which they crossed gaps of 300 miles and more in the Caroline-Marianas area were developed in the Western Carolines themselves, according to the ethnologist who studied the derivation and improvement of the Micronesian prau.[14]

Whence came the Micronesians, as the explorer Dumont

d'Urville called the peoples of the Marianas, Carolines, Marshalls, and Gilberts?[15] Suffice it to say here that, applying the indications of the meteorology, the most obvious source areas of accidental settlers of Micronesia are the southern Celebes, the Moluccas, the New Guinea area, and the islands lying off New Guinea to the east. In the west of this region the south-west monsoon blows violently at certain times towards the Carolines, while from eastern New Guinea come winds and currents which eventually swing round into Micronesia. The Bonin Islands, which lie nearer the Asiatic mainland than Micronesia, were uninhabited when the Japanese occupied them in comparatively late times, whereas human occupation in western Micronesia has been taken back by radioactive carbon dating to somewhere between 1327 B.C. and 1727 B.C.[16] This does not favour the thought that any appreciable amount of accidental settlement of Micronesia occurred direct from the Asiatic mainland.

The fundamental facts of the voyaging into and within the Micronesian areas are shown by the evidence to be much the same as in Polynesia. Accidental voyages, not deliberate ones, bridged the larger gaps. The limit on off-shore voyaging was the range within which the local conditions of wind, current, and weather could be known and judged. This knowledge was of necessity built up within the natural groupings themselves. The existence of and course to every island had to be worked out. The limiting factors were unknown drift and set outside the area which could be effectively tested; the weather, which could be judged with accuracy for a day or two ahead, but not in the nature of things for longer; the cumulative error in estimating distance from dead reckoning; and the high margin of error in non-instrumental navigation by the heavenly bodies, which faded from sight in cloud, haze, or storm. The off-shore voyages of several days in the archipelagoes were a wonderful achievement in adaptation to a peculiar and unique environment.

The question of whether the Polynesians came from some

point or points in Micronesia will be discussed later in the chapter in the light of the Pacific-wide evidence.

Far to the north the Japan Current sweeps from Formosa to California. In the early nineteenth century a Japanese junk came on Hawaii with living seamen on board after an accidental voyage.[17] But this current cannot account for the presence of the Polynesians in other parts of the Pacific, or for the Hawaiians themselves. For many indications, including the close similarity of the languages, show that the Hawaiian culture and the cultures of Eastern Polynesia were derived one from another at a time or times later than when any or all of them were derived from Western Polynesia, and the meteorology is favourable to accidental voyages from Eastern Polynesia to Hawaii, but not in the reverse direction.

What then of the Americas as the source of the Polynesian or other Pacific peoples? If there are American Indian elements in the Polynesians, either in part or wholly, they could have come to Hawaii in the same way that the pine logs which made the best Hawaiian canoes were borne there, or to Eastern Polynesia with the prevailing winds and currents. The experimental voyage of six Europeans in the Kon-Tiki raft[18] is evidence that the latter could have happened, provided one replaces the Peruvian vessel which towed them out to sea by some primeval form of energy. A derelict ship once drifted from off the South American coast to Eastern Polynesia.[19] Nor is there any need to think that migrants from America who had been carried away or had decided to chance their fate must necessarily have come from North America to get to Hawaii, or from South America to get to Eastern Polynesia, for they might have been borne at the whim of the winds and currents from any of the middle parts of the western American coast to any of the eastern islands or beyond them. On the other hand there are good reasons for believing that such incidents would be few and far between. The American coast-line had few islands near it to encourage the development of voyaging and so of accidental migration. The Inca coastal journeys were in a settled weather area, and there is no evidence that they had been going on in very early times. Accidental voyages from continental coast-lines are different from those from islands, because the voyager knows whether he is west or east of home, and in making back can depend on reaching the coast somewhere if he survives at all. At night sea breezes blow shoreward. Off the South American coast the prevailing winds and currents towards the west do not commence until one is well out to sea. There were scores of oceanic islands nearer to continents than Polynesia to the Americas, and yet were uninhabited, including some off the American coast itself.

None of this means that migrants did not come occasionally by accident on some of the Pacific islands after having been conveyed from America either as the result of storms or deliberate exile. Women were, however, necessary to the establishment of continuing settlements. There is no necessity to believe that women came from America to the Pacific islands over distances of 4,000 miles before women arrived from the west by a series of far shorter migrations.

On the other hand all the evidence is against the thought that American voyagers ever deliberately set out to see if there were lands to the west, and, having found them, returned over thousands of miles and brought deliberate colonists back again. This implies that they were prepared to go on the outward leg for thousands of miles with no assurance that there was anything there, and knowing they must come back a comparable distance against the predominant winds and currents. Furthermore, any theory that suggests that voyagers were going back and forth in earlier times must explain why they were not in later.

The American and Polynesian cultures[20] were neither more nor less like one another than those of many peoples who are known to have been segregated from one another for a very long time. The American theory originated with Zuniga in 1803, and William Ellis favoured it later.[21] Dr Lang had the opposite view, arguing that all the American Indians were Polynesians.[22] Since then the debate, conducted mainly on cultural grounds, has continued without decisive result. Compilation of a number of analogies or differences between stone statues or folklore or arts and crafts or customs or fragmentary word resemblances cannot of itself establish whether either of two peoples came from the other directly, or both from a third area, or whether these features were not developed independently because of similar environments.

The only firm evidence of direct contact between America and Polynesia which exists to date is botanical.[23] It does not reveal conclusively whether Polynesian accidental voyagers went to America and returned, or whether migrants came on one-way voyages from America, although the latter would be the simpler view. The sweet potato, and also cotton, came to Polynesia by human agency from America. The Polynesian name was 'kumara' in varied forms. A botanist in the nineteenth century recorded the Quichua Indian form of the word in Ecuador as being 'cumar'.[24] This is presumptive evidence that the name, as well as the plant, came from America, although Captain Porter thought that the Marquesan word for pig (puaka) came from the Spanish 'porca'.[25] Many varieties of kumara occurred in Hawaii, which shows that it must have been there for a long time.[26] The facts of the cotton have been described as paradoxical by Professor Heine-Geldern, as indeed they are on any view of deliberate long navigation. A variety of American cotton which was fairly certainly introduced into Hawaii prior to the fifth century A.D. was found growing in a wild state there by the early explorers. Its American habitat was apparently South America. A different variety of American cultivated cotton was found in Eastern Polynesia. It must have come from Central rather than South America. Why then was each cotton variety localized, why was cotton taken to Hawaii and then allowed to go wild and stay that way, why was the Hawaiian cotton a very early variety, and how did the Eastern Polynesian variety come from Central rather than South America?

The simplest explanation would be that the Hawaiian

cotton, and perhaps the Hawaiian *kumara*, were brought in very early times by one-way migrants from America who did not leave descendants, whereupon the cotton went wild; and that other migrants from America brought the cotton and *kumara* to Eastern Polynesia, not necessarily before the Polynesians had become established from the west. Since the Hawaiian *kumara*, as well as the cotton, was seeded, and had developed many varieties, both plants may have been established from seeds brought at a very early date by two or three people borne from South America in a small canoe, the later Polynesian arrivals recognizing the *kumara*, but not understanding or cultivating the cotton which had gone wild. The *kumara* could however have been brought in early times by Polynesian accidental migrants who did not leave descendants.

A less feasible explanation might be that the two cotton species and the *kumara* were brought back severally by Polynesian accidental voyagers who had been borne to America in the belts of westerlies to the north or south of the central zones, and had pushed off again and hit on the eastern islands of Polynesia.

The pigs of Polynesia did not come from America. The pig was a native of the East Indies and yet got as far as the Marquesas and Hawaii. He could not have swum across the larger gaps, but must have crossed them in human vessels. This shows in itself that the argument that the human vessels could not have got to those islands from the west is invalid.

Those who, like Cook, prefer concrete evidence that things could and did happen to the 'thousand conjectures of speculative reasoners' will find that evidence in the central belt of Polynesian islands. The recorded facts give direct proof that all the vital links in that chain could be and were crossed. Dillon found accidental voyagers from Rotuma in Samoa, and commented on the fact that sustained westerly and north-westerly winds blew in that area, giving a specific instance where a ship was blown from near the equator in the western Pacific to Samoa. Gill recorded that a 'numerous family' had come to Eastern Polynesia by an accidental voyage in the season when westerlies blew. Beechey found twenty men, women, and children who were established on unknown Tuamotuan islands after being driven over 500 miles to the east by two successive westerlies.[27] As against this there is no evidence of accidental voyages from America compared to the authenticated voyages of involuntary west-east migration. The argument that such voyagers from America could have come into Polynesia is irrefutable. The argument that such incidents were more likely than those in the contrary direction into Polynesia is disproved by the weight of the evidence of what actually was seen to happen.

The linguistic evidence is impossible to reconcile with the view that the decisive Polynesian ancestors came from America. There is no significant linguistic affinity between the American and Polynesian speeches, whereas there is between the Polynesian, Melanesian, Micronesian, and Indonesian, showing that the four latter arose from a common speech area at some time.[28] It does not follow that the latter tongues could not have been derived from America, so long ago that all affinity has been lost, for languages, including even their basic words, change slowly over a long time. But Dr Elbert's demonstration that the Tonga-Samoa area was ancestral to the speeches of Eastern Polynesia, and that the speeches of the Marquesas and Hawaii were derived from Eastern Polynesia,[29] shows that the flow of decisive Polynesian migration was from west to east, not the other way. This in itself does not dispose of the possibility that Americans might have by-passed the intervening islands and so arrived in Samoa first, coming back into the eastern islands. That view could however only be held at the sacrifice of the notion that the Polynesians must have come from the east because the prevailing winds and currents are in that direction. Furthermore, the affinity of the Polynesian, Melanesian, Micronesian, and Indonesian speeches would have to be explained by the suggestion that they all came from Samoa or some other unknown point in the Western Pacific or the East Indies to which Americans had been borne, since it could not be argued that they had come independently from America so long ago that all affinity had been lost with the parent American speeches, and yet not so long ago that they have not retained a Pacific-wide affinity among themselves.

The conclusion that the American theory of the origin of the decisive ancestors of the Polynesians or other Pacific Islanders will not hold water is without prejudice to the probability that occasional accidental migrants from America arrived before the Polynesians but did not leave descendants – a view which would explain the Hawaiian cotton and possibly the Hawaiian *kumara* – and that occasional migrants arrived from America in Eastern Polynesia, not necessarily before the Polynesians, bringing the Eastern Polynesian cotton and *kumara*, but making no noticeable impact otherwise.

What of Australia? Westerly winds sweep over the thousand miles or more which separate that continent from New Zealand. The fact that the Australian blacks were not in later times a maritime people[30] is not conclusive, as they may have done some voyaging in earlier days, particularly in the Tasmanian area and on the southern coasts. But the people of New Zealand show no characteristics of language or general culture reminiscent of such an origin, and no relics of aboriginal type have been found.

Finally we come to the New Guinea-Solomons-New Hebrides area. No one doubts that the ancestors of the negroid peoples of Fiji came for the most part from some of these islands to the west. The question is whether the Polynesians could have come from some point or points in the New Guinea-Solomons-New Hebrides area.

Many theorists have thought that the Polynesians must have skirted the New Guinea-Solomons-New Hebrides on their migrations into their islands, because it was considered that dark peoples – Papuans and Melanesians – had filled up that area before them. Since, however, the Caroline chain of islands, leading through the Gilberts to the threshold of Polynesia, appeared to offer a solution of the impasse, the

Micronesian route for the Polynesians has become the conventional one. It has been considered to be supported by the fact that the Micronesians and Polynesians had some cultural elements in common, including language affinities. The theorists who have held these views have been influenced by the assumption that fairly massive purposive migration took place.[31]

When the Spaniards Mendana and Quiros discovered Santa Cruz, lying between the Solomons and the New Hebrides, in 1595, they found tawny people there as well as black. Quiros said that the people of Santa Cruz were like those whom Mendana and his companions had seen in the Solomons in 1568. Quiros thought that both the dark and tawny people in the Solomons and New Hebrides might have come from similar dark and tawny people whom he saw at about the same time in the Philippines.[32]

Quiros's evidence throws no light on whether the tawny people who then existed in the Solomons and New Hebrides did or did not come from the Philippines or anywhere else in the Pacific area, including Polynesia itself. When Englishmen from Penang and Singapore visited the hinterland of Sumatra in the early nineteenth century, they found very dark people check by jowl with others as tawny as Chinese.[33] Much the same applied in many other parts of the Pacific. What Quiros's evidence does show is that there were tawny people in the western islands as well as dark, and that those islands were not occupied by a solid phalanx of dark people at that time.

In New Guinea the idea that a uniform negroid appearance was presented by people speaking languages less like Polynesian than were the Micronesian is also not sustained by the evidence of early observers. New Guinea was the home of brown Polynesian-like people no less than of negroid ones. This applied as late as the time of William Wyatt Gill, who visited New Guinea in 1872, when it was still little known. He found the south-eastern parts solidly occupied by people whom he said were of nearly the same appearance as the Samoans and Rarotongans and who had a number of basic words in common with the Rarotongan speech. Who could judge better, since Gill had lived among the Polynesians for twenty years, and was associated with native Rarotongan missionaries working in New Guinea, who themselves commented on the physical and linguistic affinity noted by Gill? Gill was told that in the interior there were numerous brown people resembling those in the southeast. On the other hand, to the west of the Polynesian-like people, towards the Torres Strait area, there are people of markedly different appearance, with black skins and fuzzy hair. So sharp was the cleavage that a black man coming among the Polynesian-like people looked bizarre.[34]

Gill's view was that the Polynesians came from the Polynesian-like people in the New Guinea area. He drew a distinction between the Polynesians and the Gilbertese, considering the latter spoke a markedly different language from the former.

Again Gill's view does not necessarily follow from the facts, since the Polynesians and the Polynesian-like people in New Guinea may have been derived independently from a third area, or the latter from the former. Again, however, his evidence is destructive of the thought that the New Guinea area was an ancient and exclusive preserve of strains alien to the Micronesians and Polynesians.

The evidence from cultural features such as dress, arts and crafts, beliefs, and customs is also inconclusive in itself. They are too mutable to be relied on. The proof is that this type of evidence has been used to support divergent views. General cultural evidence has been produced to prove that the Polynesians were Americans, others have opposed this on cultural grounds, and others again have argued that the Americans were Polynesians. The same difficulty, and the same inconclusive result, has applied to the use of cultural evidence of a general character in Micronesia and Melanesia.

The later theorists who thought the Polynesian ancestors came through the Micronesian chain have quoted cultural evidence. It has been stated that the Gilbertese wore helmets of Cook Islands type.[35] This could be explained as an exotic feature which came by accidental voyages, like those which Gill recorded to the Ellice Islands. R. P. Lesson, the naturalist of Duperrey's voyage in 1822–5, who thought the people of the Micronesian area were partly Mongols, said that some of the Gilbertese and southern Marshall Islanders wore headgear of Chinese type.[36] It has also been suggested as evidence of the Micronesian origin of the Polynesians that both they and the Micronesians used slings in their wars, whereas the people of the New Guinea-Fiji chain used bows and arrows.[37] But Cook was told that the Fijians, some of whom he met in Tonga, used slings as well as bows and arrows,[38] while George Brown, an early resident of the islands near New Guinea, said that in large areas the bow was unknown.[39] On the other hand the Polynesians were well acquainted with the bow and arrow, using it for sport.[40] Some of these things may be explained by borrowing,[41] but if so cultural items of this character are no test either of barriers or affinities.

Pottery was known in many parts of the New Guinea-Fiji chain, but not in Polynesia, apart from a few occurrences in Tonga. Professor Macmillan Brown thought that this was evidence that the Polynesians must have preceded the pottery-making peoples who surrounded them in the Pacific area.[42] But George Brown said that there were whole areas in the islands to the south-east of New Guinea where pottery was unknown. Furthermore, the volcanic islands of Polynesia had no suitable material. New Zealand had clay, but the people there did not invent or re-invent the art.[43]

All these things show how complex and variable were the circumstances of environment and behaviour which determined the way men lived and reacted to one another and their localities. Analogies with most of the Polynesian cultural features, and no less with the Micronesian, can be found somewhere or other in the New Guinea-Solomons-New Hebrides area. Nor are the differences in conformity with physical type. If black fuzzy people in the Solomons chew betel-nut as a stimulant, while the Polynesians drink *kava*, what of the fact that the brown 'Malays' in the East Indies chew betel-nut, while the dark Fijians drink *kava*?

Cultural evidence of a general character cannot therefore be considered either to support or oppose the view that the Polynesians came from somewhere in Micronesia, or the view that they came from somewhere in the New Guinea-Solomons-New Hebrides area, or any combination of these views.

The truth of the matter therefore is that neither the theory of accidental migration across the larger gaps, nor the general cultural evidence, nor the patterns of the winds and currents, can throw any final light on whether the Polynesians came from some point or points in the New Guinea-Solomons-New Hebrides area, or from some point or points in Micronesia, or from some point or points in both. The geography, in relation to the meteorology, is compatible with either or both views, since sustained westerlies and north-westerlies occur from time to time in the Western Pacific. The capricious character of accidental migration in this broken island-studded area does not allow of any firm conclusions on these grounds. Whether or not a trail of migration sufficiently definite to form a conclusion can be established by linguistic comparison is an open question. It cannot be assumed that any definite course of migration from island group to island group into Polynesia ever occurred, since accidental infiltrations may have by-passed intermediate groups.

The approaches to Polynesia were in historical times full of mixed strains, dialects, and cultural features. There must have been long-standing variations in these broken geographical areas.[44] Yet the Polynesians themselves showed a broad similarity throughout their widespread islands. It was natural that the earlier theorists should seek to explain this by a theory of comparatively massive purposive migration. In the light of accidental settlement there can be only one explanation, and that is that the Polynesians were dispersed from a suitable local centre. Nor does one have far to look, for the islands of Tonga and Samoa are just across the threshold of Polynesia from the approaches from the west, and the linguistic evidence shows that the Tonga-Samoa area was an early ancestral Polynesian speech area. In early times accidental migrants, in whom brown straighter-haired people apparently predominated, came into the Tonga-Samoa area and set up the Polynesian language, culture, and people, some of whom were in due course carried progressively by accidental voyages to Eastern Polynesia and the farther Polynesian islands. It was only because Western Polynesia formed a bottleneck between the approaches to Polynesia and the eastern area, and was itself highly suited to the development of the Polynesian people and culture, that their broad uniformity occurred.

The Tonga-Samoa area was well-suited to such a rôle. Cook and John Williams have left graphic pictures of the two main groups at the time of European contact.[45]

The fact that the Tongans were the main voyagers makes it probable that they provided many of the early settlers who were carried to Samoa and other parts of Polynesia. Tonga was in a good situation to develop the maritime arts and so have the widest contacts in the western area, as well as to provide many accidental migrants in consequence. But since deliberate contact existed between Tonga and Samoa, the cultures continuously affected each other.

The main Samoan islands form a large land mass with plenty of room to expand. Savaii and Upolu are only ten miles apart, and comprise 1,200 square miles. Many of the ancient and medieval states of Greece and Italy were no bigger, and were less fertile. Every form of sea-food abounded. For six months in the year the breadfruit gave a source of fresh food of the highest quality, and could be preserved by fermenting. The *taro* patches, which were the only cultivation the Samoans needed to do, and then only to save themselves the trouble of going into the mountains after yams, gave copious food for the rest of the year. There was also the plaintain and the banana. There were pigs and fowls, to say nothing of rats and dogs. Not all these were there when the first people arrived, we may be sure, but Samoa had abundant food resources from the start. To the east of Savaii and Upolu, at a distance of about forty miles, another high fertile island, Tutuila, was in historical times in constant touch with the bigger islands, and we may conclude that from an early date it was closely associated with them. To the east of Tutuila, separated by another gap of about forty-five miles, were the small islands of Manua. The early missionaries found that these were rather of the nature of outliers which were harried by the other Samoans. But since people who are frequently raided contributed to a common stock through the abduction of their women and the absorption of conquerors, Manua may also be regarded as having contributed to the matrix of the Polynesian culture.

The Cooks, the Tahiti-Tuamotu area, the Marquesas, Hawaii and New Zealand were worlds apart from Tonga-Samoa, and from one another, apart from occasional accidental arrivals. They derived their basic affinity of culture, including that more abiding cultural feature, basic vocabulary, from the western homeland. Yet the inhabitants of all these groups had common cultural features, including basic words, which were different from those of Western Polynesia. The only reasonable explanation is that these features were developed in an early centre of settlement somewhere in Eastern Polynesia, and were dispersed from there. It would be difficult to conclude otherwise than that this centre was somewhere in the central islands, and that the wide dissemination of these Eastern Polynesian cultural features took place because the maritime arts were developed for local inter-island voyaging, leading to many accidental voyages. This is a very different thing from saying that all the other groups with an Eastern Polynesian culture got it directly from the Tahiti area, or that the Tahitian islands were necessarily the first part of Eastern Polynesia to be peopled.

The presence of negroid and brown people in the Pacific Islands has rightly been considered by many theorists to call for explanation. Yet it cannot be said that the conventional views of the methods of migration of the Pacific peoples have been reconciled with the facts. Those who have accepted the logic of their assumption of fairly massive settlement of a planned character have been obliged to think in terms of separate migrations of varying racial types. In this they are consistent with their suppositions, for it would be unrealistic to think that the colonizers would go round enlisting migrants from different places and strains. Yet it could not be doubted that in due course the differing types had in many parts got mixed up. The only feasible explanation appeared to be that there had been strata of population, some older and some not so old. But when the cultural stratification that one might expect to find if dual or multiple colonizing movements had occurred in the areas in question is looked for, it is conspicuously absent.

In recent years the interpretation of Polynesian cultural differences as being the result of separate migrations of differing peoples, whether dark or brown, has been opposed by Professor Piddington.[46] In the light of accidental migration, it is doubtful if any well-defined cultural strata representing separate migrations existed anywhere in Micronesia, Fiji, or Polynesia.

So long as the notion of deliberate settlement of the Pacific Islands persists, no progress can be expected in solving the puzzles of the negroid and brown people who were cheek by jowl in many of the Pacific areas, or of the cultural affinities which were so obviously independent of such differences. The attempts to explain the facts eventually dissolve in chaos. Dark men who, when convenient to the theories, are supposed to have been stay-at-homes round whom the 'Malay-Polynesians' of Micronesia and Polynesia sailed to their new homes under the impulse of their innate voyaging instinct, become far-ranging colonists when this view is considered to be enforced by the facts of Fiji. On other islands such as Yap, people of different physical types were found together, and yet no evidence of cultural difference can be found to correspond with the thought that they came there as colonists at different times.

The thought of massive waves of migration, or even ripples, in the Pacific Islands, either in ancient times or late, is against all the evidence. When piecemeal settlement over a long period of time by accidental voyages is substituted for the notion of deliberate settlement, the facts of the Pacific become capable of comparatively simple explanations. The physical differences in various islands, coupled with the community of culture that characterized the various areas, would arise from the random selection of differing types by the winds and currents, followed by the development in Western Micronesia, Fiji and Western Polynesia of contact areas which dominated the cultures of the areas near them and immediately beyond them, irrespective of physical type. No one lot of new arrivals would have sufficient impact to dominate the existing culture or language, but would be absorbed.

It is doubtful if any significance attaches to the presence of people with blood group B in Western Polynesia and New Zealand, but not in the farther parts of Eastern Polynesia.[47] If a few people with or without blood group B arrived in an area before the population built up, these people would have a significant effect on the blood group constitution of the later people.

Since the Fijians had access by sea to all the islands in their own group, but had a barrier in the gap to Tonga-Samoa, it is not surprising that they retained cultural and physical differences. One might also expect that the Western Fijians, having expanded in the two fertile main islands, would come to dominate all the group by diffusion and conquest. In doing so the Western Fijians may have mixed with and conquered proto-Polynesians on some of the eastern Fijian islands, or the Tongans may have infiltrated among existing dark people in these islands.

The Micronesians also showed a broad similarity of culture over a wide area.[48] But since the Caroline area was more diffuse than Fiji, or than the Tonga-Samoa homeland of the Polynesians, there was more differentiation of language, culture, and physical type.

In the light of accidental migration, the earlier affinities of the various Pacific peoples may be hard to trace.

It cannot be said that the peoples of the Pacific came solely through the Malay land bridge. Many probably came directly from the Asiatic mainland or Formosa into the Philippines-Celebes-Moluccas-New Guinea area. In the light of accidental settlement, land bridges lose a lot of their significance everywhere.

It would also be an unwarranted assumption to derive the Australians solely from the New Guinea area. Many or most may have come by accidental voyages with the north-west monsoon from anywhere between Java and New Guinea, losing their maritime arts on the isolated land mass of Australia.

Some indication of the difficulties is given by the use of the term 'Malay' as a comparatively meaningless cloak for diversity in the Pacific area. The remnants of Magellan's expedition in the early sixteenth century told of how they found 'Moros' or Moslems in the Moluccas at the threshold of the Carolines, together with 'Gentiles', as the Spaniards called the non-Moslem peoples. Elsewhere in the East Indian area the Spaniards drew the same distinction between the Moslems and the Gentiles, commenting that the 'Moros' were comparatively late arrivals in the Moluccas.[49] The ethnic backgrounds of the area, either in early times or late, may not lend themselves very easily to any confident generalizations.

Radioactive carbon dating may throw some light on the accidental settlement of the Pacific Islands. This method of dating early human occupation depends on the fact that all living organic matter contains ordinary and radioactive carbon in a fixed and known proportion. On the death of an organism, plant or animal, its component of radioactive carbon begins to decay at a known rate, half of it disappearing in about 5,600 years. It is thus possible to take organic material from a site of human occupation – charcoal, bone or shell – and by calculating in the laboratory the extent of decay to arrive at an approximate date for the settlement in question. The method has limitations when applied to the early occupation of the Pacific Islands. The discovery in the field of the sites of earliest settlement would be a matter of chance and time, particularly where the process to be dated is one of accidental settlement leaving a minimum of evidence in its initial stages. The earliest accidental migrants may well in some places have been men who did not leave a continuing settlement. What radioactive carbon dating can do is to show that accidental voyages were occurring from a potential source area of continuous settlement at the time of dating. The earliest human occupation which has been traced so far by radioactive carbon dating in the Marianas is somewhere round 1500 B.C., and in Hawaii is between A.D. 825 and A.D. 1185[50] – the latter agreeing significantly with Dr Elbert's conjecture from the linguistic evidence. These dates may not be very far away from the broad time depth of the settlement of the Pacific Islands. If so it could scarcely be said that the reputed proto-Polynesian and Polynesian colonizers of Micronesia and Polynesia were in any hurry. What would be needed would be a theory of how the settlement of the Pacific had taken so long. Piecemeal accidental migration with slow population build-up over a very long time would supply the need.

CHAPTER FIVE

# The Traditions

*

AN account of the traditions and geographical notions of the Caroline Islanders was recorded by Cantova at the time of European contact. It contained no ideas of origins from any farther islands. The missionaries in the Philippines who interviewed the other accidental voyagers who had come to Samar found that they thought they were the only people in the world.[1]

When Kotzebue and Chamisso questioned the Marshall Islanders on their knowledge, they found that apart from their own local geography they had only a few shadowy names derived from accidental voyagers.[2]

R. H. Codrington, the foremost nineteenth-century authority on the New Hebrides, Banks, and Santa Cruz Islands, stated that the whole world of the Banks Islanders was bounded by the other islands close to them.[3]

These facts are hard to reconcile with the view that the Gilbertese and Polynesians, who lived in the islands beyond the key points in the Caroline and New Guinea-Fiji chain, had traceable memories of the colonization of their islands through either area.

Hudson's and Hale's inquiries in the Gilbert Islands in 1841 do not support the idea that the Gilbertese made voyages to distant parts either at that time or any other. They found that some of the islands had contacts only with the other islands which were within a short distance of them. So discontinuous was the voyaging that two Europeans who had been living for several years in the Gilberts did not know the other was there.[4] Later tales of visits to Polynesia in ancient times are slim evidence in the face of such facts.

If theories of origins are to be founded on such traditional evidence, then the traditionalists must accept the logic of their own method. The Ellice and Tokelau Islands lie between Micronesia and the main Polynesian islands. The Ellice Islanders had traditions that they had come by accidental voyages from Samoa in comparatively late times and had found their islands uninhabited.[5] It has been suggested that the earliest Samoans came from the Gilberts through the Tokelaus, and that later Polynesians came from Micronesia to Tahiti and thence to Samoa.[6] This would avoid the Ellice Islands and the difficulties of their traditions. Further trouble, however, develops beyond the Ellice and Tokelau Islands, for the Samoans did not think they came through the Tokelaus or Tahiti or anywhere else, believing themselves indigenous in Samoa,[7] while the Tahitians did not have any recognizable traditions of derivation from the Gilberts. It might furthermore seem strange that the colonists of the Ellice Islands, like the later Samoans from whom they thought they came, should have come from Micronesia on a 2,500-mile detour through Tahiti when the Ellice Islands are next door to Micronesia, and that the Tokelaus should not have been occupied by the migrants until eventually people with a Polynesian culture showing close linguistic affinities with Samoa should have arrived.

The view that separate accidental migrants came to the Gilberts and Samoa disposes of these difficulties, and vindicates the traditions of the Ellice Islanders that they came in later times from Samoa, even though the traditions themselves may have been late ones.[8]

Whether any of the traditions of the Pacific Islanders are derived from memories of first settlement is not of great importance, since it was the end-product of continuing accidental dispersal that determined the character of the peoples and cultures. The traditions which contain recognizable place-names of homelands and which were recorded early enough to be considered reasonably free of derived European knowledge can be numbered on one hand. Any or all of these older traditions could have been brought by later accidental voyagers after the time of original settlement.

On the other hand the older traditions give some clues

to the places from which the streams of accidental migrants came.

In order to avoid any suspicion that such traditional names as suit a particular case are being selected, they will be taken from the earlier European traditionalists who used data recorded in the first period of contact. The chief of these was Abraham Fornander, a man of considerable attainments who spent nearly forty years in trading and public service of various kinds under the old Hawaiian monarchy. He says that for thirty-four years he collected the Polynesian traditions of origins through his contacts in Hawaii and the other groups. Fornander published his interpretations of the traditions in the seventies and eighties of the nineteenth century.[9] Fornander's method was applied by S. Percy Smith and others to the traditions of New Zealand, Rarotonga and other places.

The interpretations of the Fijian and Polynesian traditional names which are offered in this chapter are made in the light of accidental settlement and not as evidence for it.

In Fiji, Tonga, and Samoa the name for the heaven to which spirits returned was Bulutu (Pulutu, Belotu, Burattu). Since the Pacific Islanders had no writing, the Europeans who recorded these names represented the sounds in various ways. Fornander connected this traditional name with the island of Buru in the Moluccas.[10]

One of the southern islands in the Gilberts is Beru or Peru.

Quiros, in his accounts of the Spanish contacts with the people of the Duff Islands to the north-west of Fiji in 1606, tells of a traditional tale about a land named 'Pouro' where precious metals were found.[11]

The Bulutu tradition occurred in Samoa, but was not regarded as the name of a homeland. The Samoans considered they had originated in Samoa itself, which is not so fantastic a conception as it might seem to be on a literal view.

Whether Bulutu was an actual place, and if so where, will never be known, for there are too many candidates for selection. The supposed resemblance to Buru is somewhat contrived. In any case Bulutu was envisaged as an ethereal spirit world rather than a place of origin.

All that can be said, therefore, is that Bulutu was a traditional name throughout the Fiji-Tonga-Samoa area.

In Tahiti and all the other groups to the east of Tonga-Samoa, including Hawaii and New Zealand, an ancient traditional name for a homeland was Hawaiki. This was certainly an Eastern Polynesian pre-European traditional name, being recorded at the time of Cook's first voyage in the Tahitian islands as well as New Zealand.[12] Again the name was spelt by the early explorers and missionaries in varying but unmistakable forms – Avaiki, Hawaii, Heawie, Heavai, Owaii, Heawije. The spellings were arbitrary, being renderings of the spoken word.

The main Samoan island is Savaii. This is the Samoan dialectal equivalent of the Eastern Polynesian name, Hawaiki. The Samoan 's' is pronounced lightly and there is a check before the final letter. It will be found that the sound changes as described are orthodox Polynesian linguistics.

In the Samoa-Tonga area Bulutu is an ancient traditional name, but Hawaii is not. In Eastern Polynesia Hawaiki is an ancient homeland. On one side of the gap is Savaii, the main island of Samoa. On the other side the equivalent of Savaii is the name of a place of origin which is not known directly. Throughout the rest of Eastern Polynesia the name appears and reappears as the name of a homeland. The explanation of this name as a symbol of dispersal from the west becomes a reasonable *prima facie* assumption.

That the Hawaiki of the Raiatean area of the Tahiti Group was considered by Tupia to be Savaii in Samoa appears to be shown by the information recorded in Forster's chart and accompanying notes. 'Oheavai' is placed with tolerable accuracy in association with 'Ouporroo', these names being the Tahitian dialectal equivalents of Savaii and Upolu. In one of the notes Tupia gave, Oheavai was described as much larger than Tahiti, and called the 'father of all the islands.'[13] Presumably the Tahitian word was 'fenua', which was the word for their own islands. Fenua-ara, the island cluster in the extreme west of the Tahitian islands, means 'way of the peoples' and may be connected with the same traditional view of derivation from the west. The interpretation of Tupia's 'Heavai' as Savaii was made by Hale, and Gill said there could be no doubt that the traditional name was derived from Savaii.[14] A Raiatean chant recorded in or about 1817 described 'Havai'i' as the 'birth-place of lands', from which rose Vavau and the eastern islands.[15] All these facts fit in with the view that Savaii had become the symbol of a western homeland which was not directly known.

Such a general name for this homeland as Hawaiki throughout Eastern Polynesia, New Zealand, and Hawaii was no doubt the result of many involuntary journeys across the vital gap from Western to Eastern Polynesia. In Raiatea the traditional name was apparently re-identified from time to time with Savaii. Elsewhere it was merely a vague name. It was natural that the name of the largest island in Western Polynesia should become the main symbol of the Polynesian homeland in the west.

In the Cooks the traditional names are significant of the dual stream of migration from west and east. The western Rarotongans, as has been seen, had a tradition that they came from a homeland named Manua somewhere to the west. John Williams identified it with the nearest island of Samoa which bears this name.[16] Again the tradition may reasonably be regarded as recording the fact that many Rarotongan ancestors were conveyed from Samoa during the long centuries of the Polynesian dispersal. The other Rarotongans believed that their ancestors had come from Tahiti.[17] Since they inter-married freely, the distinction is academic. One may see in the Cook Islands traditional names, symbols of the fact that accidental voyagers came both from Western Polynesia and Tahiti, keeping alive the knowledge of the names.

Williams,[18] and later Gill,[19] believed that such traditions were evidence of earlier deliberate contact in the central belt, but since their own writings clearly show that there was no contact in their day, the occurrence of the names is obviously no less consistent with knowledge derived from accidental voyages. Gill found what appeared to be echoes of the Makea Karika chiefs of Rarotonga in Samoa, with traditions of exchanges of visits, but since Williams himself had taken Makea of Rarotonga on a visit to the Samoan chiefs,[20] and many Rarotongans and Samoans had in the meantime passed between the two, the existence of this later derived knowledge is too obvious for such late data to be of value. Indeed, one Rarotongan, having heard of Chief Malietoa of Samoa, had changed his name to Malie and gone to Samoa to claim kinship with the chief.[21]

Avaiki and Kupolu were other traditional names in the Cook Islands. They are too reminiscent of Savaii and Upolu for the identification to be open to doubt. The form Kupolu is close to the Tongan form of the word. Again they mean no more than that accidental voyagers no doubt on occasion came direct from the west to the Cooks, as one family did in Gill's time. Again they are valid signposts of the directions from which the streams of accidental voyages took their courses rather than records of settlement. The fact that Tahitian names also occurred in the Cooks shows that in the case of these islands it was a twofold process.[22]

Fornander and his followers could not accept the view of Hale and Gill that Hawaiki was derived from Samoa. They could not by their own logic think that the Eastern Polynesians whom they imagined as going back and forth in earlier times over thousands of miles could have had an unknown homeland in Polynesia itself. The original homeland represented by the name Hawaii was removed to Java or somewhere near it, and before that to Saba in Arabia, or elsewhere in Asia.[23] They interpreted the name as meaning 'Little Java'. But according to George Turner the Samoans believed that their equivalent name, Savaii, was derived from the name of an early settler.[24]

In Hawaii Fornander found that in addition to the traditional name of Hawaiki or Hawaii, after which the main island had been named, there was also Katiki.[25] This is the Hawaiian dialectal equivalent of Tahiti. One might think it obvious enough that Hawaii and Katiki were relics of the earlier Hawaiian sojourns in Western Polynesia and Tahiti, being again symbols of the course of the migrations.

Fornander accepted that the Hawaiki of the New Zealanders was Savaii in Samoa.[26] Fornander's followers in New Zealand were not however content to leave it there. For it was – and is – obvious that the main Maori ancestors came from Eastern Polynesia. So the circle was squared, and the Hawaiki of the Maoris was shifted to the Tahitian area,[27] while the Hawaiki of the original Polynesians was left where Fornander had placed it, in the East Indies or Asia or both. All the Eastern Polynesians, however, had the same basic tradition of Hawaiki or Hawaii, and the fact that the New Zealanders remembered the tradition is precisely what one would expect from their Eastern Polynesian derivation. By putting Hawaiki back in Savaii, and bringing the supposed original Hawaiki or Hawaii back to the same area, the whole pattern falls into place, and accords with slow accidental migration from west to east and thence to Hawaii and New Zealand.

Another ancient and general traditional name in Eastern Polynesia and the other places populated from it was Wawau.[28] The archaic chants of some islands have been said to contain it, and Porter found that it was the name of a homeland of the Marquesas.[29] The biggest island in the northern Tonga area is Vavau. It appears in Forster's chart, where it is identified as a pre-European Tahitian name by being reversed from north to south, and as the Tongan island by being placed in association with the other western islands. Later Europeans made many identifications of the Eastern Polynesian traditional name of Vavau. Again it does not seem necessary to go past Tonga for its origin. It was between Vavau and Samoa that some of those longer journeys took place, during which the Tongans told Cook that canoes were occasionally lost and 'never heard of more'. Apparently some of these voyagers were conveyed from time to time to Eastern Polynesia with the names of Vavau and Savaii on their lips.

In the Marquesas islands, a long way to the east of Western Polynesia, with all the Cooks, Tahitian and Tuamotuan islands in between, Fornander's informants reported that in addition to Hawaiki and Vavau, the islanders had about a dozen or more other traditional names. They had the lists worked out in order like an itinerary, through which their ancestors had journeyed to the Marquesas.[30] Such lists gave an opportunity to the theorists who followed Fornander for some speculations, although any noticeable resemblance between the traditional names and those of known islands was slight indeed. The truth is surely simple enough. Not all the Marquesans could have come originally from the same islands to the west by accidental voyages, since such islands are very numerous. Many of the Tuamotuan islands were inhabited temporarily from time to time, and their names changed. When the early people on the Marquesas got together it is reasonable to believe that they found Hawaiki and Wawau as common traditional names, and an assortment of other island names. The views of multiple origins that thus arose were no doubt sustained by similar later voyages from many points to the west and south.

The chaos to which the traditions were reduced by the notion of deliberate colonization is shown by the fate of the most celebrated Polynesian story, that of the coming of the first Hawaiian ancestors. The tradition said that the homeland was to the west, as indeed it was when the Hawaiian ancestors were in Eastern Polynesia. Fornander, however, brought the Hawaiians direct from the west in the teeth of the prevailing winds – a feat of voyaging which the early Spaniards were unable to do. Since Katiki in the Hawaiian tradition was a great land near the traditional homeland, Fornander shifted Katiki to the west as well.[31] Later theorists rejected Fornander's logic on this point, identifying

Katiki with Tahiti. This gave some of them the opportunity of bringing the Hawaiians from the Marshalls, others from Tahiti, and others still from both.[32]

Having removed both Bulutu and Hawaiki out of the Pacific Islands, Fornander and his followers found themselves in further difficulties. The Polynesians were remarkably similar to one another, so in their western homelands they must have been similar too. For how otherwise could they be imagined as having retained their similarity in such widely separated island groups as Hawaii, Central Polynesia, New Zealand, and Easter Island? Having thus enforced on themselves the notion of a lot of early people like the Polynesians from Java to Polynesia, they could not merely leave them there as a uniform people without tracing their uniformity to earlier sources. So the Fornander school, and the modern heirs of the deliberate settlement notion, had to look for still more distant homelands for their homogeneous Polynesian-like people, and are still doing so. Fornander found the proto-Polynesians in Saba in Arabia, others have found them in America, and others in the Caucasus.

Fornander's data were secured by reasonably objective methods. He says that he soon found that the only way to get old Hawaiian material was through Hawaiian associates,[33] who secured traditional data that a European would never have got. The traditionalists of a later age were not so objective. Sir George Grey, who collected many Maori traditions between 1848 and 1854, had said that at that time the old-time chiefs and priests were a fast vanishing race.[34] Such gleanings as could reasonably be regarded as pre-European had already been picked up by that time. Anything after 1850, when the entire Pacific had been traversed by the Europeans, could not possibly be regarded as free from the incorporation of later derived knowledge. For folklore, while it remains unwritten, is never static, but goes on merging new experience and knowledge by progressive assimilation. From 1770 on thousands of Polynesians moved around the islands as sailors on European ships, and in due course migrants from other island groups came to be established all over the Pacific. The later traditional material is full of Hebrew stories derived from the early missionaries. It would be no more illogical to suggest that the Polynesians were Jews than that the later stories recorded pre-European origins or deliberate long voyages. Old residents of Honolulu in the nineteenth century saw thirty whaling ships there at one time.[35] The Polynesians made good sailors and were in great demand. Moreover, the way news got around was surprising. The Tongans in the southern islands told Cook about previous European visitors to the islands to the north.[36] Andia heard in Tahiti the names and descriptions of New Zealand, Tonga, and other islands visited by Cook himself on the second voyage.[37]

When therefore the Pacific Islanders incorporated later knowledge in their stories, they were doing what all makers of folklore do, and a very proper procedure, too, for it gave colour to the traditional history. They did the same thing with the Christian stories, embodying them in their own tales. All European folklore was evolved in the same way. The later stories are just as much traditions, and just as genuine, as the earlier ones, for anything that is handed down from one generation to the next is a tradition. But nothing that was collected after the mid-century could even begin to rank as a pre-European tradition. There was a late Rarotongan tradition that Tangiia visited Rapanui (Easter Island) thousands of miles away, but an ethnologist has shown that Rapanui was not an old-time native name for Easter Island,[38] being a late invention. There is a similar case of the incorporation of the names Pangopango and Hamoa in late New Zealand traditions,[39] whereas such names were entirely unknown in the older material; J. B. Stair, an early missionary in Samoa, got pages and pages of late traditions of this type from a Rarotongan migrant to Samoa,[40] who knew his geography of the Pacific well enough to take the early Rarotongans to every part of it. This was no more wilful deception than was Homer's *Odyssey*.

The systematic collections of Polynesian traditional

material, such as those of Grey, White, Laval, Fornander, and Smith, were all secured after 1845. A customary method was to send notebooks to intelligent young natives educated in the church schools, and get them to write down the material as it was dictated by the older men. These scribes were adherents of the austere Christian doctrines of the day, which regarded heathenism and all its works as anathema. The older Polynesians regarded their lore as mystical and not to be divulged to commoners or outsiders. Grey and others prided themselves on having the confidence of the old priests and chiefs, but just how much of the older material they got, how much was withheld or lost at that time through missionary influence, and how much was stream-lined to European taste, either by the scribes or the European editors, is doubtful. A whole chapter could be written expos-ing obvious later knowledge in all these collections, and chapters to that effect have in fact been written by some of the later traditionalists themselves. Their method of reject-ing the unlikely stories and accepting the possible ones does not seem either objective or judicial.

The later theorists who, in the final decade of the nine-teenth century, sought new data, were therefore too late. Furthermore, they had their theories in the first place and went in search of facts to support them. This is revealed again and again by the quoting of informants as saying that they did not remember such and such an event. In that case how could they know they did not know it? The revelation of leading questions or fore-knowledge is apparent. Any-thing can be proved by the methods of the older tradition-alists, which is to say that nothing can.

It is on such material, gathered between 1890 and 1910 by deliberate searches in Rarotonga, Tahiti, and New Zealand, that the current and oft-repeated views that the traditions of various islands corroborated one another on the subject of long voyages is based. All of this material, with the exception of one account is no less consistent with one-way voyages than deliberate two-way contact. The excep-tion was the account secured from a Rarotongan informant[41] in the late nineties of last century, who, on being asked if he remembered traditions of ancient migrations from Raro-tonga, said he had been told when a boy that the New Zealand colonizing fleet from Hawaiki had sailed from Raro-tonga, and that one of the canoes had called in on the way back to Hawaiki. The informant remembered being told that some preserved moa had been brought back from New Zealand by an explorer who had preceded the fleet, and added some circumstantial details which recapitulated Maori traditions about the doings both of the explorer and the fleet. He did not, however, remember the names of such and such a canoe – a plain proof of leading questions. He did, however, know that the name for New Zealand was Aotea-roa. This highly necessary name for New Zealand as a whole first appeared in Grey's collections in the mid-century,[42] although the name Aotea had greater antiquity. Bishop Williams, an authority on the Maori language, went on record later to the effect that 'Aotea-roa' was unintelligible to the older Maoris themselves, and that the usual rendering, 'Long White Cloud', was bad Maori. Other Maori scholars have continued to debate its meaning without reaching any decisive result.[43] No hint of such Raro-tongan traditions was recorded by Williams or any of the other early missionaries, although Williams himself had visited New Zealand[44] and lent a willing ear to the other Rarotongan traditions of contact with Tahiti. Previous inquirers who knew the Maori traditions had visited Raro-tonga and sought out material. Seventy-five years of frequent contact between Rarotonga and New Zealand had gone by. The fact that the method and its results are not acceptable as evidence does not mean that the interviewer or the informant did not ask and answer the questions in good faith.

In Tahiti the equivalents of the Hawaiian names of Olopana and Ru'utia, who made voyages to far places in Hawaiian tradition, occurred in old lore. In due course it was found that two learned men in the South Island of New Zealand remembered traditions of the Maori equivalent of the name of Olopana and his wife.[45] The discovery had no significance as evidence of deliberate contact, for it would be surprising if the Hawaiians, Eastern Polynesians, and New Zealanders did not have the same traditions and the same heroic ancestors, since they came from the same islands. This is, however, just as compatible with accidental voyages as deliberate ones. Two or three other cases were found where the heroic early forefathers of widely separated groups had the same name.[46] That Whiro and Toi and Koropanga appeared in the traditions and genealogies of a number of islands proves that the islanders were of common stock with common traditions before being parted, if indeed any proof is needed. But it throws no light on the manner of the parting. One might wonder, however, why the fact that Maui was much the most widespread traditional ancestor among the Polynesians should have received so little publicity, since he was considered by a number of widely separated groups to have been an ancestral visitor or resident. Arbitrary decisions to include some early ancestors in the reconstructions and leave others out are again a rejection of the traditions rather than a use of them as a foundation for a valid theory.

Such are the supposed grounds for the claim that the traditions of various islands confirmed one another on the subject of long voyages. The suggestion that the pre-European traditional data of New Zealand contained specific mention of Rarotonga was not accepted by Sir Peter Buck, an acknowledged authority on the Maori traditions.[47] Neither was the notion that Olopana's wife had left Tahiti, for Buck considered that the Hawaiian historians had adapted the story from Tahiti to Hawaii.[48] Thus the temples of the older traditionalists were undermined by a more objective modern one, but the devotees still worship in the ruins.

The Pacific Islands' traditions which were recorded at the time of first European contact, or which contain internal evidence that they dated from pre-European times, are so few that they can be stated in a few pages. Those among them which contain recognizable place-names of origin can be given in this paragraph. Cook's associates on the first voyage stated that 'Heawije' was a general traditional name of origin in the Tahiti area and New Zealand.[49] 'Oheavai,' shown in Tupia's data to be Savaii, was described as 'father of all the islands' by Tupia. Williams found that some of the Rarotongans had a tradition of origin from Manua. The Cook Islands traditional name of Kupolu is so like the Western Polynesian form of Upolu that it must surely have come direct from Western Polynesia. There is Porter's statement that a main tradition of origin in the Marquesas referred to Vavau, which it is difficult to believe came from post-European times, since there was no reason why it should be picked out above more obvious islands. There is the Hawaiian tradition of origin from Hawaii and Katiki, the pre-European character of the names being shown by the fact that the homelands, together with Katiki, were placed to the west instead of the south. The New Zealand traditional names Rangiatea, Kuporu, Waerota and Nukuroa[50] are indicated to be derived from pre-European times by the fact that the New Zealanders themselves did not identify them with any specific islands.

The only bits of the traditions of origins, whether ancient or late, that the general reader now sees are those which appear to give an historical account of deliberate discovery and settlement. Of the extracts which have thus become the conventional traditional canon, nine out of ten are taken from very late data. This editing was essentially a European practice, for the old Polynesians took their traditions in their full-blooded form, which was the way they were meant to be. Very few of the old traditions of origin make the slightest appearance of being historical. Nearly all of them describe the ancestors as being transported by the gods, or riding on sea-birds, or swimming, or simply that they just 'came from Hawaiki'.

It can scarcely be described as scientific or objective to take a few late extracts which appear to suit one's case, and discredit the rest as nonsense. Such a method is in fact based on a rejection of the traditions. When the traditions are reviewed as a whole, it becomes very plain that the manner of transport by which the ancestors were described as coming was mystical and figurative. William Colenso, a missionary who was also a scientist of note, lived for thirty-five years among the old-time Maoris. When the Europeans in New Zealand started their editing of the Maori traditions in the sixties, Colenso advised the people of that day not to take the traditions of the origins as literal history, saying that the Maoris did not do so themselves, but preserved all the miraculous events intact. Sir George Grey himself did not regard them as realistic history.[51]

Most folklore contains elements which are explanations or reconstructions. Since it is impossible to decide which are reconstructions and which may have had some basis in fact, it would be no less misleading to quote the large numbers of traditional accounts of arrivals by accidental voyages as to quote the few late ones which have some semblance of deliberate colonization or long voyages about them. But the mode which was actually chosen by the story-tellers was for the most part neither deliberate nor accidental cruising, but supernatural transport.

The Europeans have robbed the Pacific Islanders of their heritage of pre-European tradition. By picking out the bits that suited their case and discarding the rest, they have destroyed the real appeal of the folklore. One may imagine how the tables might have been turned if Omai had applied to the folklore of the Londoners the sort of treatment that the later Europeans meted out to the Polynesian stories. He might then have reported to the Tahitians as follows: 'These people have a tradition of an early heroic character named Santa Claus. Claus is an old Nordic name. "Santa" appears to be a corruption of the Roman "sancta" meaning "holy". There are the usual miraculous elements in this tale. Holy Claus is depicted as proceeding across the skies in a curious conveyance, drawn by eight fabulous quadrupeds. Claus was also reputed to have been a generous fellow, giving away things for nothing. From what we know of these European people, we may discount this as invention. He was no doubt a trader. It would appear that "holy" Claus was a merchant who visited Rome.'

As soon as the vain effort to squeeze out of the traditions more than was ever put into them is abandoned, the stories can stand forth unashamed in all their original detail and appeal. It would not be regarded then as a matter of any great consequence that Kupe discovered New Zealand and found it uninhabited, but that his immediate associates in the homeland to which he returned came down to the new land and found large numbers of people there.[52] It would not be an occasion of undue worry that a later New Zealander said that his people had sailed by Antares,[53] which might have taken them to Australia. The Polynesians were making stories and poetry, not writing history. Let the navigators sail by any star they like, as Santa gallops across the sky at midnight. No undue scepticism has arisen over the fact that midnight is in a lot of places at different times, and that Santa Claus's sledge must have been very fast to have covered Christendom in one night. The fact that Maui appeared as an ancestor in many islands need not be offered as an objection to the claim of each group separately that he was their ancestor. The only mistake that can be made in such matters is to rob Santa Claus of his reindeer because they do not have wings, or to put Antares in its right place, in which case Santa Claus falls flat on his face and the navigators are lost for ever.

All maritime peoples, particularly those living near great oceans, had folklore of voyages to unknown lands far across the sea. The Celts had their Avalon, the Arabs their Sinbad who visited the Land of the Great Roc, the Greeks their Ulysses who came upon the island of Circe, the Peruvian Indians their land which Tupac Yupanqui visited, the Romans their Islands of the Blest. Dare one include the Thule of the Greeks, or the Vinland of the Norse, when the inveterate determination of later peoples to read history into such stories by hook or by crook has enforced on modern believers the creed that Tule was Iceland and Vinland Nova

Scotia? The only reason why the Vale of Avalon has escaped identification is because its similarity to the Hudson Valley is not yet specifically proved, and in another 500 years Mark Twain will be quoted to complete the demonstration. The Great Roc became the dodo of Madagascar when the bones of this extinct bird were found there, although the other places visited by Sinbad are not yet certainly identified, and the Old Man of the Sea still rides backs without being equated to Peking Man. The Land of the Great Roc may find a rival for its identification in New Zealand, for the bones of the extinct moa, which was undoubtedly a bigger bird than the dodo, can outmatch that evidence, and there was also an ancient eagle which, unlike the dodo, could fly.

The Polynesians were one of the most imaginative and poetic of peoples. Why should their folklore be singled out above that of all other peoples for the dreary process of being reduced to an unconvincing realism, let come what may? The story-teller, who takes his environment for his material and thereby imparts a substratum of reality to his stories – maritime peoples have sea stories, land people have Lands of Ophir – must always escape beyond the bounds of known space if his story is to acquire the elusive quality of romance. When the earth is reduced to a marble, the story-tellers go to Mars.

Some of the islands in Tupia's data are echoes of legend. We have already seen that 'Moenatayo' was an echo of the Mangaian tradition of Tiaio the shark-god, which is not recorded elsewhere, and which clues up with the name Ahuahu, the old name for Mangaia. Tupia also mentioned an island with ships so big that the *Endeavour* was small in comparison. Lest the Europeans think that this was a sign of primitive unsophistication, one may recall that in Columbus's time there were islands with unicorns and sirens.

Another legendary name in Tupia's material is that of Rarotonga (Rarotoa). John Williams says he had heard of Rarotonga long before he found it.[54] Its existence was known to him from a Raiatean tradition. The tradition said that two priests had come to the central part of Raiatea from a district on its farther side, bringing a sacred drum for the gods, and had been killed. The gods were so wroth at the sacrilege that they detached the home district of the dead priests from Raiatea and transported it to the south as a distant land. The name Rarotonga means 'under the south'. In due course Williams found Tumutevarovaro and identified it with the Rarotonga of Tahitian legend.

That Tumutevarovaro was not identified by the Raia-teans themselves with their traditional Rarotonga is shown by Tupia's data, in which both Tumutevarovaro and Raro-tonga are shown, the former in somewhat the wrong direc-tion, and unmistakable with such a distinctive name, and the latter to the south (displaced from south to north in the European representations), as the tradition said it was. It may possibly be connected with Tonga. That the 'Rarotoa' of Tupia was 'Rarotonga' is shown by the fact that the same word 'tonga' for 'south', is also rendered in Forster's chart as 'toa', this being the Europeans' version of the Tahitian spoken word.

Tupia was a priest-chief of Raiatea who might be expected to know the sacred lore of that area better than anybody. He put Rarotonga in the quarter where, accord-ing to Williams, Raiatean tradition said it was after the gods had removed it, and showed Tumutevarovaro as a separate island. If then the Rarotongan traditions of contact with the Tahitian islands are historical, one might think it strange that the Tahitians should not have known that Tumutevarovaro and Rarotonga were identical. It is on the traditional data secured from the old priests that the theory of deliberate voyages is reputed to be based. Yet here is Tupia, the foremost priest-chief of his time, as the conven-tional theorists of the nineteenth century said when they quoted his data as evidence of long voyages, describing Rarotonga and Tumutevarovaro as two separate islands. Williams's arbitrary identification of Tumutevarovaro with the Rarotonga of Raiatean legend therefore falls to the ground.

Those peoples whose origins have been traced, either in

whole or in part, to Rarotonga, meaning the old Tumute-varovaro, therefore may be from elsewhere. William Wyatt Gill was led to believe that Manihiki and Rakahanga and Tongareva in the northern Cooks were peopled from Tumu-tevarovaro, meaning the modern Rarotonga because 'Rarotonga' was their traditional place of origin.[55] This is still the conventional view. This did not accord with the opinion of the missionary who was carried to Manihiki by the winds and currents in Williams's time. It seems that the tradition was either not pre-European or was an echo of the traditional island of Tahitian folklore.

Rarotonga is mentioned in a New Zealand tradition recorded by Sir George Grey.[56] On such evidence the pic-ture of migrations by way of Rarotonga to New Zealand was based. Since Maori sailors from New Zealand, as well as chiefs who visited far places as the guests of the British, could have brought the name at any time in the previous twenty years, this name is not necessarily pre-European. If it were, it might have been derived from the Tahitian tradition, although not necessarily from the Tahiti Group itself.

Whether Rarotonga had become attached within the Cook Islands as a name for Tumutevarovaro may be an open question. William Wyatt Gill said later that Rarotonga was an alternative name to Tumutevarovaro on the island itself, and connected it with Tonga.[57] This may well have been the case, although there is no clear evidence of it. Williams asked the people of Aitutaki and Atiu if they knew of any islands south of them. If he asked them whether they knew an island 'raro tonga' it would not necessarily mean any more to them than that he was inquiring after an island to the south. The Aitutakians knew of Tumutevarovaro from accidental voyagers and from people brought by a whaling ship. Tumutevarovaro was the last of a number of islands discovered in those parts, and since other islands had been revealed by such traditional information, it was natural that Williams should make his identification of the legendary island with the last to be found, since he had traversed all the other parts where the unknown traditional island might be. Gill's much later statement that Rarotonga was an alternative name may reflect Williams's christening of the island. Buck, in dealing with the late traditions of Manihiki, which appeared to show connexions with Rarotonga, expressed his suspicion that some elements in them might have arisen from later contact.[58] The suspicion must apply generally to all traditional names which are not shown to be pre-European by some independent evidence.

Atea, the name of a primal source of mankind, appears throughout Eastern Polynesian tradition. Sometimes it is a place, sometimes a first man, sometimes both. The theory that the Polynesian stories reflected memories of origins from the East Indies and Asia was considered to derive support from interpretations of this name. The Rarotongan legendary place 'Atia-te-varinga' was identified with an Asiatic origin because 'vari', which meant 'mud' in Rarotonga, was supposed to be connected with the eastern word 'padi', meaning 'rice'.[59] William Wyatt Gill had already said that in Mangaia 'vari' meant 'the very beginning', that Vatea and Vari were connected in Mangaian tradition as a primal demi-god and mother, and that in his opinion the Rarotongan word 'vari' had the same origin.[60] Wakea, the Hawaiian equivalent, was a demi-god. Tupia put an island 'Adeeha' to the west of Tahiti, as we have seen. This may be an echo of the general Eastern Polynesian name.

The legend of Atea does not appear in Samoa. If it was a land of paddy-fields farther to the west, its existence was apparently not known to the Samoans. That Atea and the gods Tu, Tane, and Rongo, were religious concepts developed in Eastern Polynesia and not brought from Western Polynesia appears plain.

Fornander and his followers show little sign of having studied the recorded evidence of the early Europeans in the Pacific, which is full of data on what the old-time Polynesians said about their beliefs. Fornander himself says that there was no public institution in Hawaii in which he could get background information on the Pacific.[61] Relying on

1a. Atiu. Cook's ship's boat went in to the shore, much as this boat is doing. Among the islanders at the water's edge Omai met three fellow countrymen from Tahiti.

1b. Tongan Sailing Ship. Drawn by John Webber, artist on Cook's third voyage. George Vason, who lived among the Tongans at the end of the eighteenth century, accompanied over 250 warriors in a large double canoe.

2. These Voyagers had Instruments: Cruiser at Niue.

3. Drinking Ceremony in Eastern Fiji (*Photo Public Relations Office, Fiji*).

4a and b. Storm in the Pacific (*Official R.N.Z.A.F. photographs*).

5. *Feʻi* Banana Gatherers in Tahiti.

6. Hawaiki.

7. Hawaiki.

8. Eastern Polynesian Double Canoe. Drawn by John Webber, artist on Cook's third voyage.

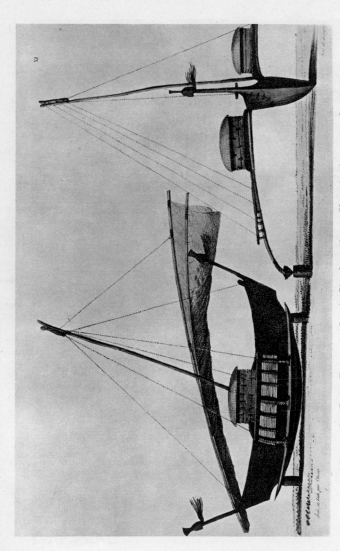

9. Micronesian Prau. Drawn by Louis Choris, artist on Kotzebue's voyage, in 1817.

10. An Eden without an Eve: Norfolk Island.

11. Some Colonies Lasted Longer: Modern Maoris of New Zealand in traditional dress and setting.

12. An Early New Zealander: Moa-hunter buried with adzes, whale teeth and moa egg, reconstructed with actual grave materials by Canterbury Museum, Christchurch, New Zealand (*Photo Albion Wright*).

# A CHART
### representing the
## ISLES of the SOUTH-SEA
#### according to
### the NOTIONS of the INHABITANTS of
## O-TAHEITEE
### and the Neighbouring Isles, chiefly
#### collected from the accounts of
## TUPAYA

Opa-tooe-rou

Tatahaieta

Ohe Tootera

o-Heeva-roa, Teohoooi
o-Heeva-potto  o-Nateya
Waitahoo or Whattare-oop, Whattare-teah
o-Otto  o-Terowhu
Te-Manno o
Neeo-heeva o  o-Haneanea

o-Rima-roa
o-Heava-toutou-ai

o-Mateiva Oura o-Teohoow
o-Anna  Waltoi
o-Fatai Raitea
o-Iah  o-Whateva

Hitte-tamaroo-eirre

Oiratah o
Toometoa-rearo  Hitte-hamea-tane
Maeatta o-Whao
Mannua  o Ouropoe
Eito-nooe
o Moutou

Opa-toa

o-Ururutu

o Wooreeo
o-Ahoua-hou  o Mpggeha
o-Weeha  Whennua-oora  Mourooa  Iuhai
o-Papatea  Bonabor  o-Iah
Labu-a-mannoo  o-Huaheine  o-Heeva-nooe
Einoo o  o-Raia-teah  o-Taheitee
Moe-no-tayo  Ohteroa
Te-Toopa-tupp-tahou  Ohtee-roa
Ohteavai  Oporroo  Wouwou
Te-Errepoo-opo-matte-hea  o-Tootoo-erre
Te-Ororo-Mativatea  o Ouowhea

o-Toomo-papa
o-Ahourou  o-Fai-havai  o-Rima-tarra  o-Adeehu
o Earatea
o Toutepa
o-Reeva-vai
Taimuna

Terraati
Tootera
o-Hitte-potto
o-Hitte-toutou-atu
o-Hitte-toutou-nea
o-Hitte-toutou-rera
o-Hitte-taiterra
o Te-Am-roo-hitte
o Te-Atou-hitte

o-Rinaatena

their imaginations for their reconstructions from the traditions or rather those parts which appeared to fit their theories, the traditionalists elaborated the myth of long voyages and deliberate settlement, going far beyond the Polynesians themselves in doing so.

The last thing that can be concluded is that the traditions of the Pacific Islanders should be disregarded. Rather should they be restored to their unedited pristine form. The picture that they then give is very different from the suppositions which were based on select extracts from the later and more sophisticated material. There may be those who would still wish to think otherwise. If so, what will they believe? For every interpretation of traditional evidence in favour of one view, another interpretation has been made in favour of another. The Hawaiian traditions have been variously interpreted as implying derivation from the Marshalls or Tahiti or both. The Marquesan evidence has been supposed to support origins from Vavau, and on the other hand from America. Some of the New Zealanders are reputed to have said their homeland was to the west, and others to the east. The most ancient and widespread tradition of origin of the Eastern Polynesians did not say they came from either direction, but from the god Tangaroa who appeared as an egg and canoe. In such circumstances the bewildered may consider themselves entitled to think that the most ancient and general traditions were the most likely to reflect the truth. The logical conclusion is that the Samoans were indigenous and the Eastern Polynesians came from an egg and a canoe. [62] The supernatural character of Polynesian tradition is obvious in everything except the late European editing of it.

No Polynesian need be in the slightest degree disturbed about the impact of the accidental settlement conclusions on his genealogy or his tribal history or his tribal canoe. Obviously the Polynesians had ancestors, and obviously they came in canoes. The only thing that needs to be revised is the manner of their arrival, which was by accidental voyages which only the hardiest could survive, rather than by

supernatural means or their equivalent, deliberate navigation over great distances without instruments.

Here is a Polynesian travel tale which has its appeal and
meaning, provided one does not edit all the life out of it in
an attempt to represent it as history. It was collected by
William Wyatt Gill on Aitutaki, and is given in his English
translation, in which he said he tried to preserve the archaic
appeal of the original.[63] It has been abbreviated somewhat.

In the fairy land of Kupolu there lived the renowned chief Rata,
who resolved to build a great double canoe, with a view of exploring other lands. Shouldering his axe, he started off to a distant
valley where the finest timber grew. Close to the mountain stream
stood a fragrant tree, where a deadly combat was going on
between a beautiful white heron and a spotted sea-serpent ...
The beautiful bird was living but very much exhausted. Its unre-
lenting foe, sure of victory, was preparing for a final attack when
Rata chopped it to pieces with his axe, and thus saved the life of
the white heron ... From the branch of a distant tree the heron
watched the labours of Rata throughout the livelong day. As soon
as the chief had disappeared in the evening, the grateful bird
started off to collect all the birds of Kupolu to hollow out Rata's
canoe. They gladly obeyed the summons of their sovereign, and
pecked away with their beaks until the huge logs were speedily
hollowed out ... It was almost dawn ere the work was completed.
Finally they resolved to convey the canoe to the beach close to
Rata's dwelling. To accomplish this each bird took its place on
either side of the canoe, completely surrounding it. At a given
signal they all extended their wings, one to bear up the canoe, the
other for flight. As they bore the canoe through the air they sang,
each with a different note ... On reaching the sandy beach in
front of the dwelling, the canoe was carefully deposited by the
birds, who now quickly disappeared in the depths of the forest ...
Rata speedily provided his bird-built canoe with a mast and
sail, and then summoned his friends, and laid in food and water
for his projected voyage. Everything being now ready, he went
on board ... The crafty Nganaoa, seeing the canoe start without
him, ran to fetch an empty calabash, knocked off the top, and
squeezing himself in as best he could, floated himself off on the
surface of the ocean, until he got a little ahead of the canoe ... A
voice now issued from the calabash. 'O Rata, take me on board

your canoe!' 'Whither away?' inquired the chief. 'I go,' said the poor fellow inside the calabash, 'to the Land of Moonlight, to seek my parents ...' Rata now asked, 'What will you do for me if I take you in?' ... (Nganaoa promised) to destroy all the monsters of the ocean which might infest their path ...

Swiftly and pleasantly, with a fair wind, they sped over the ocean in quest of new lands. One day Nganaoa shouted, 'O Rata, here is a terrible foe starting up from the main.' It was an open clam of fearful proportions ... In a moment this horrid clam might crush them all by suddenly closing its mouth. But Nganaoa was ready ... He seized his long spear and quickly drove it down into the fish ...

Again they pursued their voyage in safety. But one more great peril awaited them. One day the brave Nganaoa shouted, 'O Rata, here is a great whale!' The enormous mouth was wide open, one jaw beneath the canoe and the other above it. The whale was evidently bent on swallowing them up alive. Nganaoa, the slayer of monsters, now broke his long spear in two, and at the critical moment, when the whale was about to crush them all, he cleverly inserted both stakes inside the mouth of their foe, so that it became impossible for it to close its jaws. Nganaoa nimbly jumped inside the mouth of this great whale and looked down its stomach, and lo! there sat his long lost father Tairitokerau and his mother Vaiaroa, who had been swallowed alive when fishing by this monster of the deep. (The monster swam to the nearest land, where, on reaching the beach, father, mother, and son walked out through the open mouth of the whale.)

The island proved to be Iti-te-marama, or Moonlight. Here the canoe of Rata was drawn up on the beach, and for a time they all lived pleasantly. They daily refreshed themselves with its fruits and fish, adorning their persons with fragrant flowers. At length they longed for the land of their birth in Avaiki, and they resolved to return. The canoe was prepared and launched. Food and water were laid in. The great sail was set up, and at length the brave navigator Rata, with the parents of Nganaoa and the entire party started once more. After many days, but without further peril, they eventually reached their original homes in the lands of the sun-setting.

Those who wish to see history in this typical Polynesian folk tale will note that Rata pushed off to seek new lands. They will, if they believe in deliberate long voyages, remove

Avaiki and Kupolu to a great distance west, in order that its mysterious character may be sustained, since the later Aitutakians did not know quite where it was. William Wyatt Gill believed less spectacularly that some voyagers from Samoa had brought the legend with them. On the Samoan island of Upolu, which is near Savaii, a long low rock was still called Rata's canoe in Gill's day. Gill himself had found on Mangaia a 'numerous family' who had been blown across the vital gap from Western Polynesia to the Cooks, and quoted this as an example of the dispersal of people and traditions from west to east.

What light does Cook throw on the traditions? When he left the Tahitians to go north in 1777, he asked them if they knew of any islands in that direction. They said that they did not. He then discovered Christmas Island, and later Hawaii.[64] Christmas Island is one of the equatorial islands, others of which have signs of early Polynesian occupation on them. They are therefore quoted as staging posts in supposed deliberate voyages between Tahiti and Hawaii. Since, however, the evidence for the voyages is based on traditional evidence, why is it that the Tahitians had no such traditions of their erstwhile colony Hawaii, and the islands in between, to offer Cook? On the other hand the Hawaiians did have Katiki, the equivalent of Tahiti, as a traditional name. Accidental one-way travel from Eastern Polynesia to Hawaii explains these things. The belief that the Tahitians went on two-way voyages to Hawaii is hard to reconcile with them.

Cook tells of the difficulty he had in finding out from the Tahitians details of what the Spaniards from Lima had done on their visit to Tahiti, as proved by a cross with a date on it which the Spaniards had erected over the grave of a ship's commander who had died there. Cook had considerable difficulty in finding out from the Tahitians just what had happened. Most of the details seemed to have been forgotten by them, despite the fact that the Spaniards had been there for two years, and all sorts of varying answers were given to his questions.[65] This seems to indicate that the Tahitians were not very interested in recording prosaic history. Why should they have been? They were story-makers, not historians. Yet 150 years later European traditionalists were finding out facts about the pre-European period by interrogating the later islanders.

That the suppositions of long voyages and deliberate settlement were based on interpretations of the traditional evidence has been freely conceded by the traditionalists themselves. The heirs of these suppositions have included most people who have written about the Pacific migrations in the last eighty years, although few before that. The belief that the sun went round the earth was not more vociferously nor unanimously expounded than has been the myth of deliberate settlement over the past half-century. Recent writers have not, however, followed the methods of their predecessors in picking out bits of the traditions and discrediting the rest. The recounting of them by Sir Peter Buck[66] and others has preserved the fact that they were full of the miraculous, even when telling of long voyages. But as soon as one restores them to their proper form, they cease on the very face of them to be historical. The picture they give is that few of the Polynesians came to their homes by prosaic canoe voyages, whether deliberate or accidental, but for the most part by being conveyed by the gods, or by sailing on the backs of fish or animals, or by the aid of priests who quelled the storms and the serpents who beset the way. So in these latest days the deliberate voyage theory has come to be a view without any evidence at all, least of all the traditional evidence.

The true traditionalists are those who wish to see the Polynesian traditions restored to the form in which they were before the Europeans edited them. When this is done, the older data give some indirect clues on the pre-European background. Those areas whose inhabitants were derived from an extended area themselves did not have any clear-cut traditions of origin or any recognizable place-names in them at the time of European contact. This applied to the whole of Micronesia, Melanesia, and Western Polynesia. It could not be otherwise, since the islanders were derived by multiple voyages from diffuse source areas. On the other hand the Eastern Polynesians, having come through the Western Polynesian bottleneck, had traditional names derived from Western Polynesian islands, while the Hawaiians, Cook Islanders, and New Zealanders had further traditional names from within Eastern Polynesia itself. In the case of Raiatea and the Cooks, the situation of the Western Polynesian homelands was vaguely known from continuing accidental voyages. In all the other Eastern Polynesian groups, as in Hawaii and New Zealand, the traditional names had become vague symbols, all relationship to any actual islands having been lost or obscured.

# CHAPTER SIX

# Accidental Settlers from Three Kingdoms

*

IF deliberate voyages happened in early Polynesia, why did they not happen in Cook's time or in the century following him? There is not one authentic record of a deliberate long voyage, as compared with the many accounts of accidental voyages. Thus in later times, when the populations had increased, there was no deliberate colonization across the larger gaps, even to the many sparsely settled or uninhabited islands which might have been expected to relieve population pressure. Yet in earlier times it is supposed there was. Those who suggest that when the main islands had been colonized the long voyages were abandoned, do not explain the changes in incentive which might have caused this to happen before the colonization of all the suitable islands had occurred.

If in fact the Polynesians ranged the ocean in earlier times, but stopped doing so in later, they went through a development which was the precise reverse of that of all other maritime peoples. Those who colonized invariably passed through a subsequent phase in which their maritime arts were retained for trade and war.

Take for instance war. Almost all the islands of Polynesia which were in reach of one another in historical times were continually at war. The Tahitian islands were involved in war on a dozen separate occasions, some of them lasting for years, in the first quarter-century of European contact. The Tongans were in the same condition of continual conflict. As soon as the Polynesians heard of any new islands from the Europeans they wanted to go and conquer them, and some of them did.[1] The islands which were isolated by distance were the lucky ones.

Now with such opportunities and incentives for war as

deliberate long voyages would have given, how is it believable that the Polynesians would have given them up? Nothing is more certain than that the local character of the warfare was not the choice of the local Napoleons themselves, but enforced on them by the fact that they, like all primitive navigators, were limited by the inescapable facts of navigation without instruments. The range of the wars was in fact precisely the same as the proved range of their cruising.

Coming now to trade, and the distribution of the useful livestock, plants and cultural items – or rather their lack of distribution – we find that further golden opportunities were apparently passed up by the voyagers who were supposed to have been far-ranging colonists at one time and stay-at-homes within their own islands later.

Take for instance the pig. The pig is the most valuable Polynesian commodity. Pork and Polynesians are indelibly associated in the minds of those who read about the old feasts, or for that matter the modern ones. The pig undoubtedly came into Polynesia through the New Guinea-Fiji chain, being a native of Asia and the East Indies. It came in man-made vessels because it could not otherwise have crossed the long gaps, or at any rate not all of them. It did not come through Micronesia because the Gilbert and Ellice and other atolls were unsuited to it. These are truisms which everybody has accepted. The later theorists who considered that the Polynesians had come solely through the Caroline chain could not bring the pig with them, and therefore pictured the Polynesians as getting it from Fiji later.[2] Wherever the Polynesians came from, it does not necessarily follow that the pig arrived with the first settlers. Suffice it to say that sooner or later it became established in Polynesia.

The pigs reached most parts of Polynesia. The high fertile islands were ideal for them. Being omnivorous, they ran wild in the forest uplands where they lived on roots, tubers, rats and fallen fruit, while on the coast they lived a domestic life with man on a diet of plantains, coconuts and offal. If the pigs on the coast ran low, there was always the reserve in the hills. When Cook's two ships stayed at one of the small Hawaiian islands in 1778 for a protracted period, large supplies of hogs were brought to them.[3] At the time of discovery pigs flourished in Samoa, Tahiti, Rarotonga-Atiu, the Marquesas, and Hawaii. They must have been long established in Samoa and Tahiti, since they had got to the farthest islands beyond them.

The presence of the pig on these islands is no less compatible with accidental transfer than deliberate importation. Since there is no evidence that they came in the earlier canoes which crossed the longer gaps, they had the whole span of man's time in the Pacific to get to the farther islands.

The conventional reconstruction envisages the hypothetical deliberate colonists as intentionally taking livestock on board their vessels to their new islands during the period of settlement which is reputed to have lasted over several centuries.

Now all that was necessary to establish the pig was one farrowing sow. Why then did not Mangaia and Aitutaki have the pig, which was in fact introduced by the early missionaries?[4] These are high warm islands right in the middle of Polynesia, where the erstwhile deliberate voyagers are reputed to have made their traverses over several centuries. Pigs flourished on Samoa, Tahiti, and the other conventional colonizing islands, and had got as far afield as the Marquesas and Hawaii. The people of Mangaia and Aitutaki had known the pig existed, because William Wyatt Gill narrates how the Mangaians knew the name for pig, 'puaka', but did not know what it looked like, while Captain Bligh of the *Bounty*, the discoverer of Aitutaki, found they knew of pigs there, but had none themselves, although they did have the fowl.[5] It will be suggested that the pigs had disappeared since the old voyaging days. If so, why did they not get some more from Rarotonga or Atiu, only 110 to 150 miles away? For curious as it may seem, those islands had the pig at the time Williams made contact with them.

A number of islands suited to the pig which did not in

fact have it could be mentioned, including Mangareva and Easter Island, the latter of which nevertheless had the fowl. The Mangarevans had a tradition that they had the pig up till the seventeenth century,[6] which may well be the case. One might wonder why they did not re-import it thereafter. The older theorists used to quote Tupia as testifying to Polynesian long voyages at the time of discovery. Nowadays the voyaging is ante-dated to a remoter period.

Another curious state of affairs existed on Niue, the isolated island which Cook found between Tonga and Eastern Polynesia. When John Williams made contact with Niue and offered the islanders some cooked pork, they had no knowledge of animal food of such a nature and thought he was giving them some form of human flesh. This naturally perturbed them, since the thought that he might want to replenish his supplies at their expense occurred to them. Williams had a pig killed to convince them.[7] Niue, because of its position, is a port of call of the theorists who consider the Polynesians traversed the Pacific on their voyages, without however being able to credit them with enough initiative to introduce some breeding stock or even establish a tradition of it. And if the pig had died out on Niue since the days of long voyages, no tradition of it remained.

These facts are hard to reconcile with the idea of deliberate voyaging in early times or late over the bigger gaps, even in the Polynesian heartland of Samoa, Tahiti, and the Cooks. On the other hand they fit in with accidental voyages. If any of those who came on Niue remembered the pig, the memory did not stay with their descendants. The pig never got to Mangaia or Aitutaki, or did not survive to historical times, but the people either remembered it or heard about it from later arrivals. Yet it was just alongside them in Rarotonga, Atiu, and Mauke, which were in contact with one another. Capricious distribution by accidental voyages explains these things. The islanders had to be content with what luck gave them over the centuries, when some canoe passing between its home islands with an item of livestock aboard was blown away and came on an island which lacked the pig or fowl, or a canoe of exiles brought some breeding stock.

The rat does not mean a great deal in this debate. As Cook conjectured when he saw the broken canoe and the rats on the desert island, the rat was a stowaway who got everywhere, and multiplied rapidly where the food supply was good. When Williams came to Rarotonga there was a plague of rats.[8]

The Polynesian dog got most places too, being man's constant companion, and so liable to accompany him on accidental voyages. The dog even got to far New Zealand and Hawaii. He was well adapted to survive accidental voyages, but did not have a high survival value when living with man on islands where there was no wild game in the interior, being a competitor of man for animal food, as well as being eaten himself. When, therefore, times of famine arose, the dog was likely to be a casualty, except in the bigger islands where he ran wild in the interior. Elsewhere he was sometimes considered more of a nuisance than he was worth. Mariner tells of how the chief of one of the Tongan islands had all the dogs destroyed for this reason.[9] The dog's absence from the Marquesas and other islands does not therefore mean a great deal.

New Zealand had the dog, but not the Polynesian pig or fowl, at the time of first European contact. The botanical evidence shows that the climate of New Zealand was warmer than it is today up to the thirteenth century or thereabouts. On the other hand when Cook took down some Polynesian pigs and fowls on his way to New Zealand in the eighteenth century, they died on the way.[10] The absence of the pig and fowl is therefore probably without significance. This may account for the contrast with Hawaii. The pig, dog, and fowl reached this farthest group in the Polynesian dispersal. No doubt pigs and fowls started on accidental voyages to New Zealand, but could not take the climatic change on such journeys in the later centuries of the dispersal.

On the evidence of accidental voyages it is not necessary to imagine that the dog, pig, and fowl invariably accompanied man. For it is abundantly obvious that canoes which were left at the water's edge were frequently borne away in sudden storms. Many tales of storms, in which just about everything movable was swept away, have been put on record. The Polynesian canoes were no doubt much like those of fishing people everywhere, with fish offal, coconuts, and the like below decks, and the early accounts show that pigs, dogs, rats, and fowls wandered around everywhere. Canoes which were swept away with livestock aboard probably arrived on distant islands more than once in the several thousand years of the Polynesian dispersal. Nor can the possibility be ruled out that human beings died of exposure, leaving the canoes to the livestock. This may have happened in the case of those islands which had rats but no sign of earlier human inhabitants.

It is not possible to conclude that when human beings first arrived in early times in any group any livestock accompanied them, or that any came for centuries afterwards. The dog, the pig, and the fowl may have come separately at widely differing dates to those groups which had all of them. Only one or two individual dogs, pigs, or fowls were necessary to establish each livestock item in a whole island group. Over many centuries the highly fertile groups could scarcely avoid getting them. Yet the significant gaps here and there are eloquent of the lack of system or design.

The useful plants of Polynesia have been repeatedly used as evidence of the purposive colonization of the farther Pacific Islands.[11] Much play has been made with the useful plants of Polynesia which are reputed to have been conveyed to the farther islands by deliberate colonists, particularly the seedless varieties of *taro*, *kumara*, breadfruit, and common banana, as well as the coconut. Seedless varieties could not have been propagated across great distances of ocean by winds and currents. The coconut is reputed to have been vulnerable to long immersion in sea water owing to rotting of the eyes.

Where it is necessary to invoke human agency to explain the occurrence of such plants on distant islands, the facts are no less compatible with accidental transfer than deliberate. It is rather the omissions of plants and livestock that are significant.

The *taro* and *kumara* were particularly suited to be transported on accidental voyages. They could be propagated from parts of the tubers, which were resistant to long exposure.

The two useful plants which could not be grown from seed, or from fruits, tubers, and other portions of the plant which were used for food, were the seedless banana and the seedless breadfruit. Seedless varieties of fruit were developed by man without any great design by selection of those which had fewer pips or were more vigorous. There must have been many instances where people transferring these desirable plants between local islands or round the coasts were blown away in storms, or where deliberate exiles set out with them. Banana sprouts and breadfruit shoots were unsuitable for food on the accidental voyages themselves, probably ranking even after one's mother-in-law.

It has been said that the coconut could not have come over great oceanic distances without man's agency. If this were so, the presence of the coconut on distant islands would still be particularly compatible with accidental transfer. The coconut was food and drink on canoe journeys, and it is probable that half the canoes that were lost at sea during the Pacific dispersal had coconuts on board. Exiles could also easily transfer them.

The yam and the sugar-cane were two other useful plants which were well suited to accidental transfer, being propagable from parts of the plant which were used for food.

The remainder of the useful plants which were found on the farther Pacific Islands could be grown from seed, pips, roots, and other easily transportable parts of the plant. If, therefore, human agency were necessary to explain their presence on any or every island where they occurred, there would be no difficulty in accounting for their transfer by accidental voyages of canoes blown away in storms, or by canoes of exiles.

The occurrence of useful plants on distant islands is therefore in no case evidence of deliberate colonization or two-way contact any more than of accidental settlement.

There are a number of cases where it is a moot point whether human transfer, whether accidental or deliberate, is necessary to explain the facts.

That the factors which lay behind the occurrence of seeded and seedless varieties of plants were complex is shown by the following evidence. Seeded varieties of *taro* and *kumara* occurred on Hawaii.[12] Seeded varieties of breadfruit were found at the time of European contact in Samoa and Tahiti.[13] Since seeded varieties of plants could arise from seedless ones which had been neglected, as well as from seed brought by man himself, such occurrences are not evidence that wild varieties existed. What they do show is that each set of local facts needs to be examined on its merits,[14] for seeds, rather than seedless plants, may have been transported in the first place, or may in some cases have been dispersed within the islands themselves by natural agencies, including hurricanes or rafts of vegetation floating in the sea. The only varieties of common banana and of breadfruit that occurred on Hawaii at the time of European contact were seedless.[15] This is evidence that they were transported to Hawaii itself by human agency, probably by exiles,[16] possibly by people carried away while transferring plants locally. Yet since seeded varieties of breadfruit occurred in Samoa and Tahiti, how can one be sure that breadfruit was not transferred to other islands in some cases by seeds? The facts of the breadfruit do not lend themselves to any confident generalizations. When Moerenhout visited Pitcairn in the early nineteenth century, he was told by the Tahitian wife of one of the mutineers who came there in the *Bounty* that when they arrived they found some 300 breadfruit trees, but they could not propagate them as in Tahiti, the only way in which they increased being by spontaneous shoots.[17] Moerenhout in another passage traces how there were many flourishing varieties of large breadfruit tree on Tahiti, but that, as one moved south to cooler parts, on Mangareva there were only two or three small varieties, on Pitcairn there was this non-propagable variety, and on Rapa there were none.[18] When Williams made contact with Rarotonga there were only seedless varieties of breadfruit.[19] On the other hand on Kapingamarangi the breadfruit was seeded.[20]

By far the greater number of the useful introduced plants were seeded wherever they occurred. It is not therefore possible to be quite sure when they were transferred locally by natural agency or when by man. Obviously the useless seeded plants were not the result of horticultural expeditions, either intentional or involuntary.

That the eyes of coconuts rot when they float in water for long periods[21] is no doubt true. The question is how long it would be before the myriads of coconuts which were adapted to float in sea water all without exception lost their germinating power. The ability of cyclones to hustle them along is something that can scarcely be proved or disproved. Furthermore, if a raft of vegetation with a coconut tree uppermost was eroded and committed to the currents, there seems to be no reason to believe that the nuts would ship more water on long journeys than on the short journeys in the sea itself which they were certainly adapted to survive. Much of the vegetation on the eastern islands and Hawaii was of East Indian origin.[22] The course that the winds and currents imposed on the men and the pigs may throw some light on that of some of the plants. The latter had the advantage of a few million more years to get to the farthest islands. But even if it could be proved that all the coconuts on every island in the Pacific had got there in human vessels, it still would not be evidence that they arrived with deliberate colonists using purposive navigation.

A reasonable view of the way in which the useful introduced plants spread through the Pacific Islands is that they were dribbled along piecemeal over 3,000 years from group to group and from island to island, for the most part by transfer across the longer gaps in human vessels, aided locally here and there to an unknown extent by natural agencies.

Useful plants were not the only ones that were introduced in pre-European times by man. A large number of the non-indigenous plants in south-eastern Polynesia at the ends of the lines of settlement were East Indian weeds.[23] Presumably they came by unconscious human agency with earth in canoes, or with useful plants that were being transported, or with vegetable trash, or on rafts of vegetation, or by hurricanes, or by birds, or by any combinations of these. Useful plants with small seeds could have been conveyed across some of the gaps in the same way. The one method that cannot be invoked for the weeds is purposive transfer by colonists.

Few of the multifarious vegetables of the Asiatic and East Indian regions were passed along progressively to the farther islands by the navigators who are reputed to have plied back and forth over the longer gaps. No potatoes or maize were conveyed through Easter Island and Pitcairn to New Zealand from the American habitat that yielded the cotton and the *kumara*. If it is thought unreasonable to have expected the ancient voyagers to have been so systematic, some strange omissions occurred within the islands themselves.

The botanical evidence shows that the *kumara* was introduced into New Zealand.[24] Yet according to George Turner the *kumara* was not established in Samoa until European times.[25] Nor is there any record of its having been in the Cook Islands, which the Tahitian colonists of New Zealand have been described as using as a staging post.

The *fe'i* banana, which formed the main food reserve, had been a long time on Tahiti, because there were a large number of local varieties. Yet in Hawaii, Tahiti's reputed colony, the plant, which does well in suitable locations, is considered to have been of post-European introduction. That bananas of other sorts got to Hawaii by man's agency is apparently shown by the occurrence of the seedless banana. In pre-European days all the varieties of the common banana in Hawaii were seedless.[26] The reasonable conclusion is that the seedless varieties of common banana were transferred to Hawaii by people who had been blown away while transferring plants between local islands, or by exiles.

No doubt many useful plants were in fact conveyed from time to time over the longer gaps in the Pacific by man. There is no evidence that deliberate voyaging was necessary to such transfer. On the contrary the distribution of useful plants was much what one would expect from their relative suitability to accidental transfer, while the absence of some of them in important groups is against the thought that there was any system or design.

Those who like a touch of whimsy may enliven these themes by the thought that human beings carried away with coconuts and other useful plants may not have survived to plant them out, and many a canoe might have rotted on a deserted shore with strange outgrowths comparable in the botanical world to the rats which Cook found with the broken canoe on Palmerston Atoll.

Livestock and plants were not the only commodities which got to islands in canoes. Some of the most fascinating chapters in the long story of the Pacific have been concerned with the discovery on various islands of multitudes of material relics of the past – adzes, fish hooks, spear heads, harpoons, canoes, necklaces, bowls and the like. For the most part they fit in with the general culture of the particular island or group in which they are found. Yet many relics of distinctive types have been found on islands where they have little relation with the local culture, but rather with that of some island group at a distance. The evolution of the differences between the cultures of Western and Eastern Polynesia, and of the various areas of the eastern cultures – Tahiti, the Cooks, the Marquesas, Hawaii, New Zealand – was assisted by the subsequent isolation in limited contact areas. Had deliberate contact been possible, the differences would no doubt have been less. But since the isolation of the various areas was transcended by a series of later accidental voyages, one would expect that these later arrivals would take with them articles and techniques which did not quite fit in with the culture which had developed in their new homes.

In Western Polynesia a few adzes of a distinctive late eastern type have been found.[27] They are quite unlike the others in the area. Since we have seen a number of examples where accidental voyagers were borne to Western Polynesia from the eastern islands, these adzes, or the technique of making them, could have come with similar arrivals in earlier times.

Some ornaments of distinctive Western Polynesian type have been found in Mangaia.[28] Since Gill observed an actual instance of the conveyance of accidental voyagers from Western Polynesia to Mangaia, this also fits in with the proved facts of what was possible with accidental voyages.

The people of the Chathams, 500 miles east of New Zealand, had a culture which showed affinities with the 'moa-hunter' culture of southern New Zealand, the stone adze-heads which have been examined by the archaeologists being similar. However, a number of adze-heads which are typical of those of the North Island of New Zealand have been found in the Chathams. Such adzes might possibly have come with later accidental voyagers, arriving in the same manner that Hale was told of.[29]

The examples are limited to those which were matched by an accidental voyage in historical times, on Cook's principle that an actual demonstration that something could and did happen is worth a 'thousand conjectures of speculative reasoners'. But if one extended one's reasonable surmises to include those instances where exotic cultural features are explicable by accidental voyages in later times after the cultures had become differentiated, one could no doubt fill a volume.

As with the animals and plants, however, it is above all the presence of useful arts or relics on one island or group, and the absence of the same arts from others which were within the supposed range of long voyages, that is most significant. The experts in material culture have built up a formidable body of evidence on the cultures of the islands of

Polynesia. It shows that there were many apparent anomalies of this kind.

Harpooning[30] was practised in the Marquesas, but not in
the rest of Eastern Polynesia, at the time of European contact. Harpoon heads have been found in the moa-hunter
sites of New Zealand, showing that harpooning went on
there in early times. They have also been found in the
Chatham Islands. The distinctive thing about harpooning
was that the harpoon head had a long rope attached to it by
which big fish were played after the harpoon had been thrust
into them from the bow of a canoe – an exciting way of
getting a lot of food in one effort.

Why then are there no traces of harpooning in the
Tahitian islands or other parts of Eastern Polynesia besides
the Marquesas? It has been suggested that the art of harpooning was introduced to the outer islands – New Zealand,
the Chathams, and the Marquesas – by the Tahitians, but
that the art disappeared from Tahiti itself in later times.

If the thought of long traverses between Tahiti and the
outer islands is given up, the difficulty of the absence of
harpooning in the Tahiti-Tuamotu area would seem to be
capable of an alternative explanation, namely that the New
Zealanders and the Marquesans developed the art of harpooning separately in their own islands, and that the accidental voyagers from New Zealand who established in the
Chathams the 'moa-hunter' type of culture that the archaeology reveals took the art of harpooning with them there
too.

The Maoris perfected spiral carving beyond anything
that was devised elsewhere in Polynesia,[31] including the
hypothetical centre of deliberate colonization, Tahiti. The
Easter Islanders had an unique bird cult, and devised
strange hieroglyphics on wooden tablets.[32]

The correlation of these localized arts with the culs-de-sac
of the Polynesian dispersal is obvious. It is reasonable to
think that such facts are explainable as developments after
one-way settlement, and that the reason why the culture
items were localized was because they were not diffused to

other islands by later voyages, apart from the transfer of harpooning to the Chathams.

Another cultural anomaly, on the theory of two-way settlement and long voyages, is the wide divergence that existed between Western and Eastern Polynesia. It does not matter whether one supposes the Western Polynesian cultures came from the Eastern Polynesian or the Eastern Polynesian cultures came from the Western Polynesian. These areas are only 700 to 1,000 miles apart, yet their cultures were sufficiently different for de Bougainville and his Tahitian interpreter to conclude that the Samoans and Tahitians were different people with a different language.[33] It was in due course realized that their cultures, including their languages, were basically related. Yet the divergence between them had developed to such a point that scholars in historical times have been able to determine which other islands derived their culture from either area in the settlement period. Thus there is general agreement that the Ellice Islands, Rotuma and Uvea derived their cultures from Tonga-Samoa. It is no less generally agreed that New Zealand and Hawaii derived their languages and general culture from the Eastern Polynesian area. It is, however, a basic tenet of the deliberate settlement view that New Zealand and Hawaii derived their Eastern Polynesian features from two-way contact in the hypothetical period of Polynesian long voyages. How then could the Eastern Polynesian type of culture be recognized so clearly in New Zealand and Hawaii at distances of 1,500 to 2,000 miles from Eastern Polynesia, whereas so great a divergence had occurred between Samoa and Tahiti, which are so much nearer to one another? If deliberate voyages were making the colonization of the more distant islands possible, one might expect that contact was at the same time occurring between groups nearer at hand. In that case the clear-cut divergence which occurred between such important groups as Samoa and Tahiti becomes anomalous. When one adds to this the fact that the Tahitians themselves, in the light of Tupia's data, knew of the existence of Samoa but showed no sign of knowing their supposed erstwhile colonies Hawaii and New Zealand, the mystery becomes greater still. Indeed, on the view that the Polynesians were able to establish two-way contact at any time with New Zealand and Hawaii over thousands of miles of stormy ocean, contact over a mere 700 to 1,000 miles should have been maintained indefinitely without the marked difference in language which developed. Autourou the Tahitian could not converse with the Samoans and thought them a different people from himself. Tupia and Omai had no difficulty in understanding the New Zealanders.

All the facts are what one would expect from slow movement of population by accidental settlement. The Western and Eastern Polynesian cultures would begin to diverge as soon as Eastern Polynesia was accidentally settled from the Tonga-Samoa area, because there was in the nature of things no close contact. The building up of population in Eastern Polynesia would be slow at first as compared with what it was later, for such would be the nature of increase from small beginnings by accidental settlement. But when the population in the Eastern Polynesian area was increasing by leaps and bounds in later times, long after the first beginnings of population in the area, the divergence between Western and Eastern Polynesia would be well advanced, and numbers of accidental settlers would be dispersed from Eastern Polynesia to New Zealand and Hawaii. Thus there would be a closer correspondence between the Eastern Polynesian cultures and those of New Zealand and Hawaii than between any of these and Western Polynesia, as was indeed the case.

Almost the first comparative impression of the Pacific Islands cultures which was reached by the early explorers was the close correspondence of the Eastern Polynesian, New Zealand, and Hawaiian dialects as compared with those of either Western Polynesia or Fiji or Micronesia or America. It is an impression that has been amply confirmed by later studies, including comparisons of basic vocabularies. The only view that can explain these facts is that New

Zealand and Hawaii were settled later from Eastern Polynesia than Eastern Polynesia itself was from either Western Polynesia or Micronesia or America or anywhere else. Reconstructions of settlement by deliberate long voyages and two-way contact cannot be reconciled with these facts. The difficulty is not in explaining how the currents or winds could have brought vessels from any given direction, but of how sea-rovers could have mounted colonizing expeditions to some areas and then suspended contact for so long that the great divergencies which occurred between them developed, while at the same time contact was maintained between other and more distant groups for so much longer that they showed close affinities.

A concept of primary west-east settlement by occasional westerlies, with slow increase of population in each main group, followed by accidental settlement of the peripheral groups and islands of the Pacific, is compatible both with the divergencies and affinities of language and general culture that existed.

Not every writer on Polynesia in the past eighty years has failed to see the wood for the trees. Professor Piddington has quoted with approval a suggestion by Dr E. S. C. Handy that the cultures of Polynesia can best be explained by the thought that sporadic accidental movements occurred over several millennia. Dr Handy does not document his hunch by detailed research, and is prepared to concede that the Maori movements to New Zealand may have been exceptional. Professor Piddington supports Dr Handy's main generalization by citing Gill's accounts of accidental voyages.[34] Perhaps others have entered similar reservations both recorded and unrecorded. Such realists will no doubt be gratified to know, if they do not already, that their suggestions have the powerful support of Cook, Anderson, Dibble, Lang, Hale, Turner, and Pritchard, who saw things for themselves in the early days of European contact.

# CHAPTER SEVEN

# The Lonely Islands

*

OUTSIDE the main natural groupings of the Pacific Islands are a great number of scattered islands. Apart from those which are so close that they are regarded as one cluster, few were in touch with other islands when they were discovered.

The islands outside the main groups are full of lessons for our themes.

Very challenging is the evidence from the most isolated islands in the Pacific, the equatorial islands[1] of Palmyra, Washington, and Fanning. These three islands, unlike most of the other atolls in the mid-Pacific, have a fairly good rainfall and a substantial cover of vegetation in their middle areas.[2] They are also out of the worst storm areas. Yet they were all three uninhabited at the time of discovery. On the other hand the atolls of the northern Cooks, several hundred miles to the south – Tongareva, Manihiki-Rakahanga, Pukapuka – were inhabited, yet they were much less fertile and were in the hurricane area.

Why did the early colonists who are supposed to have populated the less fertile atolls in the hurricane area fail to colonize permanently the more fertile atolls to the north? It cannot be said that the latter were less fertile in earlier times, because the botanists consider that the coconut groves and undergrowth in the interior were long-standing. Survival on the more fertile islands outside the area of natural hazards should have been more feasible, yet it was on the less desirable ones that continuing colonies were found.

It cannot be argued that these more fertile atolls were off the beaten tracks of the deliberate voyages which were supposed to have occurred, for they were right between the central belt of islands and Hawaii. Fanning and Washington in fact have signs of early human occupation, although not Palmyra. They have accordingly been quoted as staging posts in the hypothetical early voyages between the Tahitian islands and Hawaii, although Palmyra was unaccountably not included in their itineraries. Yet, as we have seen, when Cook asked the Tahitians whether they knew of any islands to the north, they had no knowledge of any, although it is supposed to be on traditional knowledge gained from early voyages that the conventional theories are based. If some of these islands were used as staging posts, why were they not continuously inhabited like the less fertile ones to the south? Palmyra indeed was one of the more desirable islands to choose either as a staging post or as a home if one had an option, yet it had no relics of human habitation.

If one looks at these facts from the point of view of accidental settlement, they fall in line with what one would expect. Whereas the atolls to the south are in the course of the prevailing winds and currents from the whole of Eastern Polynesia, the only group of high fertile islands which are a likely source of accidental voyages to Palmyra, Washington, and Fanning are the Marquesas. Therefore one would not expect that so many canoes would come on these northern islands, nor that the chances of surviving the voyages would be so good. The atolls to the south are strung out from east to west across the line of the prevailing south-east trades, while Fanning, Washington, and Palmyra are more or less in line with the direction of the winds and currents. Accidental voyagers could not pick out the more fertile atolls to the north, which never became the scene of a continuing colony because no canoes with women happened to be borne upon them, or stayed to leave descendants.

Palmyra had no signs of human occupation. Washington had a few indistinct lines of coral blocks. Fanning, however, had quite a few remains, including coral structures, fallen into ruins, as well as several raised graves with human bones and ornaments. In the light of accidental voyages Fanning is one of the most interesting of islands. The clues are known in reasonable detail. An enclosure of coral blocks, marking the outlines of a rectangular building, was reminiscent of some Tongan structures. A basalt adze was found. It must have come from a high volcanic island, for basalt does not occur on low atolls. The adze resembled Tongan or Samoan types. No tools of the local tridacna shell, such as were used on most inhabited atolls in the absence of supplies of suitable stone, have been located. Some fish-hooks which were of indeterminate ancestry, but in some respects not unlike Western Polynesian ones, occurred. On the other hand drilled porpoise teeth, which were used both in the Marquesas and Hawaii for ornaments, but not in Western Polynesia as far as is known, were found in a tomb.

On this set of facts it has been conjectured that the Fanning Islanders came from Tonga, and later left Fanning. Their coming was thought to have been not earlier than the sixteenth century, on the ground that a Tongan structure dating from that century, according to the genealogies of the chiefs whose forefathers built it, had L-shaped corner stones like the Fanning structure.

The question then arises as to why the distinctive Marquesan or Hawaiian feature of drilled porpoise teeth should have occurred. There seems to be no good reason to take account of the supposed Samoan or Tongan affinities rather than the more distinctive Marquesan-Hawaiian one. On the other hand it is scarcely likely that Tongans were contemporaneous with Marquesans or Hawaiians there since both types of relics were found in close association.

The following alternative reconstruction is suggested. A canoe with men only, or without women of reproductive age, was blown off the Marquesas at a time when the culture there was more like the Tongan than in later days. The wanderers had the rare luck to be borne on Fanning by the prevailing winds and currents, which come from the Marquesas to the equatorial islands with no islands in between. They had a few basalt adzes on board. These lasted them out, without their having to make tools out of the unfamiliar tridacna. In their strange new world they fashioned blocks out of the coral and made a house. They found the coral

easier to cut than their native stone, had basalt adzes to do it
with, and even devised right-angled corner-stones which are
stronger than separate blocks. One corner did not in fact
have a right-angled block, as if they learned as they went
along. The island was attractive enough to hold them for the
rest of their lives. Their occupation may have lasted for the
fifty years or more that the younger men still had left to
them – more than enough to account for everything on the
island. After a while the old men began to die. They were
buried reverently, and the drilled porpoise ornaments that
had come with them were buried with them. Finally the last
survivor died. The wooden material rotted, and the bones of
the man whom nobody remained to bury mouldered away,
but the tombs retained the bones of his companions and the
ornaments buried with them. No sign of disaster is found
and none is necessary to explain the disappearance of the
inhabitants. No deliberate migration away from the island
occurred.

Other involuntary visitors may have come to Fanning
before or after the people who left the main Fanning
remains. Among them may have been a canoe with women
whose occupants decided not to stay. Yet the relics seem to
be compatible with the view that there was only one phase
of occupation over any length of time, and by no great
number of people. The coral blocks showed no sign of later
interference or reinstatement before European times. Roll-
ing such blocks into position would not require any great
number of men. The absence of tridacna tools, coupled with
the presence of the basalt adze, fits in with the unique and
temporary nature of a hypothetical arrival of a canoe with
men only who lived their lives on the island. The occurrence
of the basalt adze accords with an origin from the Marquesas, from which come the prevailing winds and currents.
The presence of the drilled porpoise teeth also agrees with a
Marquesan derivation. The fact that the adze and fish-
hooks were not of quite the same form as later relics from the
Marquesas is in conformity with the fact that the Marquesan culture was not static, which is true of all cultures. If the

Tongan resemblances are significant, they would fit in with the possibility that the incident happened at a time when the Eastern Polynesian cultures had not become greatly different from those of the Polynesian homeland in Tonga-Samoa.

In 1777 Cook and Anderson passed to the east of Fanning, and later died in the North Pacific. The ghosts of Fanning were still undisturbed, except it be by the ghost of Anderson himself, the ever-curious investigator who saw and heard the truth in Tahiti. Finally came Captain Fanning, who unlike his ancient predecessors was on a two-way passage with instruments.

The most centrally situated island in the Pacific is Star-buck, midway between the central belt and Hawaii, and between the Ellice Islands and the Marquesas. It is therefore well situated to have been a port of call on the hypothetical traverses which are presumed to have taken place. Here ancient voyagers could find refuge, or refresh themselves on some of the birds and fish. Yet Starbuck is in fact one of the few islands in Polynesia with no signs of previous callers.

Malden Island is another challenge. It is an island, uninhabited at the time of European discovery, which had unmistakable signs of early occupation over an appreciable period. Malden is different from the other atolls in the mid-Pacific region in that there is clear evidence that a canoe with women aboard must have arrived, for rubbish heaps which could only have accumulated over a long time, together with numerous structures, graves and house sites, make this plain. Nor is it difficult to conjecture why they disappeared. Little hollows for collecting water, some with the dippers still lying in them, were found all over the island, and the island itself is in the hurricane area. Thus too little water in times of drought, and other natural hazards, made life there precarious. In some such way the island became depopulated, and no other canoe with women aboard ever happened to come on the island again to leave descendants.

THE LONELY ISLANDS

On the chain of isolated equatorial atolls stretching from Malden and Starbuck to Palmyra, we thus see eloquent evidence of the hit-or-miss nature of accidental settlement, while the facts are inexplicable on the basis of deliberate voyaging. Starbuck, the one nearest to the central belt, had not a sign of having had human visitors. Nor had Palmyra, a particularly desirable atoll if one had a choice. Jarvis also had no sign of occupation. Christmas and Washington had fragmentary signs of human beings, left there perhaps by involuntary callers who pushed off in the hope of seeing human kind again, or became unburied skeletons which rotted away. On Fanning a definite episode can be traced, which is consistent with the conclusion that men only lived out their lives. On Malden alone did a canoe with women aboard clearly arrive and stay. Which of the two last-named colonies was the happier is not revealed by the archaeology.

South of these mid-Pacific atolls, a string of inhabited atolls, the northern Cooks, run more or less from east to west a few hundred miles north of the central belt of Polynesian islands.[3] As we have seen, Williams and Gill give accounts of accidental voyages in historical times from the central islands to one or other of these atolls, as well as between the atolls themselves, in both directions. The obvious source of population for them is from the Marquesas, the Tuamotus or Tahiti, from which come the prevailing winds and currents. On the other hand voyages from Western Polynesia with the seasonal westerlies cannot be ruled out. It is not surprising therefore to find that they have an Eastern Polynesian type of culture for the most part, intermixed with Samoan-type elements in the more westerly ones.

Manihiki and Rakahanga have been a bit of a puzzle to scholars. They are different from the other northern Cook atolls and from Tahiti, with which on the deliberate voyage theory it is natural to think they would be most closely associated. The dialect was however more like the Tuamotuan or Maori than Tahitian, and the appearance of the islanders was more reminiscent of the Tuamotuans. It will be remembered that John Williams heard this from the wife

149

of his native missionary who was driven to Manihiki in the storm.[4] William Wyatt Gill, thinking that the Manihikian tradition that an ancestor came from Rarotonga referred to Tumutevarovaro, started a belief that the island was populated from the Cooks. Since the evidence is against the view that the name Rarotonga referred primarily, if at all, to Tumutevarovaro, the modern Rarotonga, the way is open to ask again where the Manihikians really did come from. It can then be noted that the nearest island of the Tuamotus to Manihiki is Manihi, that Manihiki could mean Little Manihi, and that Moerenhout, an early visitor to Manihi, commented on the exceptionally strong current from the east which flows past Manihi.[5] With these clues to go on, and the knowledge that Williams's native missionary, who knew both Tahitians and Tuamotuans, considered the Manihikians were like the latter, it seems reasonable to conclude that this is another puzzle which accidental settlement can throw light on. That does not mean to say that Tuamotuans from the Manihi-Takaroa area of the Tuamotus were necessarily the only accidental voyagers who were borne on Manihiki, or even the first. All that the cultural evidence and the place-names and traditional names can show, where they are distinctive enough for any presumptions to be made from them, taken in conjunction with the geography in relation to the winds and currents, is the broad source area from which most of the people came. Such evidence all agrees with primary west-east settlement through the central belt followed by predominant east-west settlement to the more isolated islands.

Moving west through this string of inhabited atolls, we come past Pukapuka to the three northern islands of the Tokelaus, namely Fakaofo, Nukunonu, and Atafu, which Horatio Hale said in 1841 were in touch with one another, but not with other islands. Yet he found they knew the name Pukapuka.[6] Since this is the name of the island immediately to the east, whence come the prevailing winds and currents, there is no mystery about this knowledge, despite the fact that the Tokelau Islanders visited only their own islands.

In George Turner's time a canoe of Manihikians was taken by the winds and currents past Pukapuka to the Tokelaus. William Wyatt Gill recorded another accidental voyage from Manihiki past the Tokelaus to the Ellice Islands, and William Pritchard, who lived in Samoa in the mid-century, gives an account of the finding at sea near Samoa by a European ship, of accidental voyagers from Tongareva 800 miles away to the east.[7] The same process had obviously been going on for centuries. When some accidental voyagers from another island were accepted, not only did they remain for the rest of their lives as commemorators of the name of their own island, but also they provided one more link in the cultural nexus which arose as the result of a number of such incidents.

Pukapuka marks the changeover from the predominantly Eastern Polynesian character of the string of inhabited atolls. It shows mixed Eastern and Western Polynesian features,[8] being in easy reach of accidental voyagers from both areas.

Hale found that his Samoan interpreter could converse fairly well with the Tokelau people. Again this is in conformity with the geography in relation to the prevailing winds and currents, although there are many evidences of Eastern Polynesian influence also.[9]

The older records are against the view that the Tokelaus were in deliberate contact with other groups. The Samoans, according to Dillon, went to Tonga only in Tongan vessels, while Turner recorded that they did not go outside their own islands.[10] The name 'Toggelao' in Cook's list of islands from the Tongans must surely refer to the Tongan island of Tokolu, which was a prominent landmark, although the Tokelaus were probably also known to the Tongans from the accidental voyages which occurred from the Tokelaus to Uvea.[11] Swains Island, the low atoll 200 miles north of Samoa and about 100 miles south of Fakaofo, which was uninhabited in the early nineteenth century, although intermittent accidental settlement may have occurred, was an inadequate landmark. Late stories of deliberate voyages to and from Fiji, Tonga and Samoa in early times have against them the powerful evidence of Hale's unequivocal statement that Fakaofo was in touch only with Nukunonu and Atafu. On the other hand authenticated accounts of accidental voyages to and from these areas exist.[12] Knowledge of the names of some of these other islands, and derivation of some of the Tokelau ancestors from them, are again what one would expect from accidental settlement and continued dispersal from them. Predominant derivation from the western areas of Polynesia, and in particular Samoa, is in line with the evidence of the basic vocabularies.[13]

On the more isolated islands of Polynesia the predominant knowledge of the names of islands to the east, whence come the prevailing winds and currents, is matched by known accidental voyages. Thus a varying selection of the northern Cooks were known to the peoples of the islands to the west, arising from similar incidents in the past. Other instances were the Rarotongan knowledge of Tahiti, the Aitutakian knowledge of Manihiki, the Rapan knowledge of Mangareva, the Tikopian knowledge of Tonga and Rotuma, the Atiuan knowledge of Tahiti, all matched by accidental voyages in historical times which were no doubt not the first.[14]

North of the Tokelaus are the low atolls of the Phoenix Group – Hull, Gardner, and Sydney. They were uninhabited at the time of discovery, although there were signs of early visitors as well as the inevitable rats.[15] Yet some of them have been able to support a population in modern times, since they are in the area where the rainfall is appreciable, as with Fanning and Washington, and Palmyra. They have been used by the Gilbert Islands officials to relieve the pressure of population there.[16] The Gilbert Islands were much congested at the time of European contact. The fertile Phoenix atolls several hundred miles to the east of them, which were used later to relieve their over-population, had not been colonized by them. Yet it is said that the Tahitians were Gilbertese deliberate colonists who by-passed the Ellice Islands and Samoa which were alongside them, and then doubled back and colonized Samoa and the Ellice Islands after a 2,500-mile circuit. In historical times contact even within the Gilberts was circumscribed.[17] All these facts clue up with the evidence of Kotzebue and Chamisso that the Marshall Islanders neither visited nor were visited by any other islanders outside their own group, although they knew all the Marshalls themselves with the exception of Taongi, Eniwetok, and Ujelang.[18] Similarly Hudson and Hale found no sign of any knowledge of the Marshalls in the Gilberts.[19]

So much then for the lonely islands north of the central belt. There is a great pathos about the human signs on the arid uninhabited ones. Did some of the people who in Porter's stories were reported to have set out for the delectable traditional islands to the west[20] strike one of them? This would be less than Paradise, being not 15 feet above the sea, with little more than sea-food to live on.[21] The thought of the breadfruit which was to give shade and food in their new home would be tantalizing indeed. Perhaps they were just fishermen who for the most part came on these equatorial atolls. On most of them it would seem that involuntary migrants built a fireplace and then went off again, or a canoe with an adze, and perhaps some skeletons, rotted on their shores. Only on Fanning and Malden were some apparently tempted to stay and leave their buried bones for us to find. It cannot be too strongly emphasized that the people who settled both Polynesia and Micronesia were wanderers who had lost their way in the trackless wastes of the vast Pacific Ocean, not castaways.

South of the main Polynesian islands are some more lonely outposts. When we come to them we are in a different type of world from the atolls. For these southern islands are high islands in the sub-tropical areas, where hurricanes did not strike with devastating force, and where rainfall was more adequate. They were on the edge of the zone of variable winds to the south of them. Such were Easter Island, Pitcairn, Rapa, the Kermadecs, and Norfolk Island.

Easter Island, 1,450 miles from the nearest habitable

land, had a flourishing colony when it was discovered by the Dutchman Roggeveen and a succession of European explorers. Yet it has a European name, despite the fact that most of the inhabited Polynesian islands are known by their native names. The Easter Islanders appear to have had no pre-European name for their island.[22] Apparently the supposed ancient colonists did not devise one to differentiate their island from the other islands with which they were supposed to be in contact.

Westerlies are a feature of the meteorology of the Easter Island area at a certain time of the year. To the south is an extensive area of variable winds. One need not look any farther afield than accidental voyages from Polynesia to account for the clear-cut Polynesian character of the Easter Island culture. There is nothing on Easter Island which could not be the result of a few accidental voyages from any of the eastern islands stretching from the Cooks to Mangareva and the Marquesas. The culture, including the language, is essentially Polynesian, if the congruent evidence of the experts can be believed.[23]

Easter is the only island in the Pacific with no inhabited ones to the east of it from which a backwash of accidental voyagers could have come. It is therefore a test case of whether origins can be traced in detail. The island is so isolated, and the direction from which its Polynesian culture and language could have been acquired is so restricted, that one might expect to find a correlation with the cultural features of the place or places of immediate origin if such were possible anywhere. The ethnologist who did the main study of Easter Island considered that the culture showed analogies with New Zealand, the Tuamotus, Mangareva, the Marquesas and Hawaii. Predominant early settlement and continuing later diffusion from Tahiti and the nearer Tuamotus is no doubt the reason for the scattering of Eastern Polynesian cultural affinities over so wide an area. It does not follow that the accidental settlement of the outlying groups was directly or exclusively from any particular area of Eastern Polynesia. The basic vocabularies of large numbers of islands cannot now be traced owing to depopulation or because the occupation of atolls was often temporary or unstable, and the missionaries propagated a standard dialect in some areas, including a number of the Cooks and Australs, so that precise linguistic relationships were obscured. The Tuamotus were an area of changing population movements and conquests, and yet a suitable region for accidental voyages. The possibility of multiple voyages with women before the population filled up from the first one cannot be ruled out even in the case of small detached islands.

It may possibly be significant that it was with Mangareva, according to the general cultural evidence, that the Easter Islanders showed the greatest affinities.[24] This could be explained by the assumption that the Easter Islanders and Mangarevans came from some place or places unknown, and that they mutually affected each other by later accidental voyages between them, arising from the winds which blow in both directions seasonably in the zone in which both Mangareva and Easter Island lie.

No firm conclusions can be reached on the immediate origins of the definitive settlers of Mangareva and Easter Island, except that in both cases they were Eastern Polynesians.

Wherever the Easter Islanders came from within Eastern Polynesia, the appreciable divergence of the basic vocabulary from those of the Tahiti-Tuamotu area indicates that the Easter Islanders and the people of the main area had not been in contact for a very long time, at least so far as sharing a common speech was concerned. Over the centuries the Easter Islanders collected a number of the useful plants and livestock items which it is reasonable to suppose percolated from the west through the Tahiti-Tuamotu archipelago. They had the fowl, rat, banana, *taro*, sugarcane, yam, and paper mulberry. On the other hand they lacked the pig and dog, and had few trees.[25] They were so isolated, and so restricted are the directions from which involuntary settlers could have come, that the arrival of canoes with women must have been rare. While advents of canoes with women would be of primary importance in the peopling of the islands, it by no means follows that later canoes with men only did not have a decided influence on the cultures, particularly by introducing food plants and livestock.

Next we come to that most mysterious of Pacific islands, Pitcairn.[26] This high fertile island is situated about 150 miles from a chain of deserted atolls, some of which have fragmentary signs of human visitors, and one of which, Ducie, has none whatever. The nearest land with any continuity of occupation is again Mangareva, some 350 miles north. Pitcairn is however well within striking distance of accidental voyages from a host of low atolls to the north, east, and west of the Mangareva area.

When the *Bounty* mutineers arrived on Pitcairn, they broke up some old ruins of structures left by Polynesian predecessors. There were however many relics which were buried beyond their reach, and from the remnants of the structures later archaeologists have been able to describe what the originals must have been like.

There were three lots of stone works, at least one of which was associated with burials. Included in the burials were bits of pearl shell which must have come from the islands to the north. There were numbers of adzes made of the local stone, many of them well executed, in which one type predominated, but with others comprising many different features of construction. Some of the adzes bore resemblances to those of far-off places, including Hawaii and Samoa. There were some crude rock drawings, and some well-executed stone images, both medium-sized and small, of typical Polynesian style. There were also about 300 breadfruit trees.

Again it is impossible to pin-point where the early people on Pitcairn came from, except to say that everything is again Polynesian. It happens however that the late traditional material of Mangareva collected by Honoré Laval, a nineteenth-century missionary, contains references to

Mataki-te-rangi, a traditional island which one of the early chiefs of Mangareva is described as colonizing, planting the breadfruit. Mataki-te-rangi is described as being 'like Petania', or 'in truth Petania'.[27] This was the late Mangarevan name for Pitcairn, after both islands had been discovered by the Europeans. On such evidence the theory that Pitcairn was colonized by Mangarevans has been based, which shows the lack of real evidence of where the early people on Pitcairn came from. When Laval's material was written down for him by an educated protégé, Pitcairn was well-known to the Mangarevans from visits in European ships. The comparison of Mataki-te-rangi with Pitcairn shows it.

The breadfruit trees on Pitcairn[28] may have arrived independently of the coming of the people who made the stone works and were buried in association with them and the relics. There is no clue as to whether the plant came before, after or with such other people.

The temporary character of the Polynesian occupation of Pitcairn has been considered a matter for which no firm explanation is apparent. The absence of continuing settlement when so many poor atolls had been permanently occupied is certainly a puzzling business if one thinks in terms of deliberate long voyages.

Again the suggestion is hazarded that there were no works or relics which cannot be explained by one or more accidental voyages of people who merely lived out their lives on the island. Since Pitcairn is within 400 to 500 miles of many inhabited islands to the north, some arrivals may have been of canoes with fishermen. The pearl shell which was found in the graves, like the porpoise teeth in the Fanning burials, came with them as a precious memory of home. They found themselves on a fertile island, which gave an attractive diet as compared with that of the atolls, confined as that was for the most part to coconuts, pandanus, and fish. Unlike those who came as temporary visitors on so many of the atolls, but like the Fanning Islanders on their relatively fertile one, they decided to stay. They built stone

platforms from the abundant natural stones. They could all
have been built by a few men in a year, as compared with
the many years that remained to the younger ones
when they came on their new world. If they came from a
Tuamotuan atoll it may well have seemed that the gods had
been even-handed, taking away the society of their kind with
one hand, and giving plenty and security with the other.
They made adzes from the local stone. They buried the old
men with funeral gifts of the exotic pearl shell, until finally
all were dead.

There are no signs on Pitcairn to show whether or not
more than one lot of exiles may have stayed there. The
number of relics that are reputed to have been recovered
from Pitcairn may be misleading, since the attributions of
many early relics in the Pacific collections are uncertain.
One might well think it probable, however, that a number
of separate incidents occurred in the case of this high fertile
island so near the Tuamotus. Some of the people who came
there may have stayed only until nostalgia for a more gre-
garious existence impelled them to try their fate on the sea
again.

The Pitcairn relics had the signs of great age upon them,
and were subtly different from those of later times in the
central islands.

Why should there have been a large number of differing
adze types on Pitcairn, bearing resemblances to numbers of
types in far distant islands? The adzes comprised rough
ones as well as better-executed ones. An explanation that
comes to mind is that they may represent experimentation
by atoll-dwellers who were not used to basaltic stone, or
by people of some island where the stone was of different
character. Such migrants would presumably have Polynesian prototypes in their own islands, and yet be obliged
to experiment with the new material. Some of the resemblances to other types may therefore have been accidental.

The fact that the trips to Easter Island, Pitcairn, and
other detached islands were one-way passages from unknown islands, and yet that the culture should be considered

by the experts to be clearly Polynesian, makes it obvious that the culture areas were wider than the spheres of deliberate contact which were the dispersal sources.

It is evident from the signs of temporary occupation without graves on many of the uninhabited isolated islands that migrants did not always elect to stay. One might even think the evidence was sufficient to create the impression that it was seldom that they did. Fanning, Malden, and Pitcairn appear to be the only ones which had burials but were uninhabited in later times. It would be wrong to conclude from this that the lonely islands had not had many visitors through the centuries. The broad impression one would get from all the facts is that an island had to be more than ordinarily attractive, or very isolated, to encourage involuntary exiles to accept their fate. Gill's 'numerous family' who got carried away to the uninhabited atoll of Nassau, and then to the uninhabited atoll of Palmerston, apparently elected to try their fate and go on, rather than land or stay on a deserted atoll. One of Dillon's stories throws light on this. He relates how the Tikopians used to destroy any coconut saplings each time they visited one of their uninhabited satellite islands, in order to discourage accidental migrants from staying there.[29] The correlation of burials and signs of temporary occupation on Fanning and Pitcairn with the relative fertility of those islands may therefore be considered significant.

Rapa is a high island, small in extent, some hundreds of miles from the nearest islands in the central belt, on the southern fringe of Polynesia. When Moerenhout visited it he described the islanders and their way of life as being much the same as those of Tahiti and the other islands in its neighbourhood.[30] It does not follow that the first people came from the Tahiti area, or any of the later ones, for the broad sharing of Eastern Polynesian cultural features throughout so many islands makes it impracticable to pin-point the origins of the Rapans. Yet the linguistic evidence shows that all these islanders must have derived their cultures for the most part from a common speech area in

Eastern Polynesia which was also a source of many accidental voyages. It could have been somewhere else than the
Tahiti area.

Despite its isolation and smallness, Rapa was one of the
few lonely islands which had a continuing colony. Again this
is probably a reflection of its relative attractiveness. Yet
Rapa was not sufficiently attractive to hold all the migrants
that came there against their will. It will be remembered
that Ellis tells of the exile from Mangareva who was found
by the early missionary on Rapa. Moerenhout, who used to
organize pearl shell diving expeditions, and who is therefore
a mine of information on the outlying southern islands,
gives some more information about this accidental voyage.[31]
Seven people, including women, were driven on Rapa. They
thought they had come from the south-east instead of the
north-east. They had traversed the 600 miles from Mangareva in quick time, and had no idea of the distance. When
they had rested and re-fitted their raft, some of them, despite
the hospitable endeavours of the Rapans to dissuade them,
waited for a following wind from the north-west and then
pushed off to the south-east, where in fact no land lies until
the polar ice. One can only conjecture how many human
dramas were finally extinguished by the ocean during so
many years of human sacrifice to the storm. Better to be
carried to the ends of the Pacific, to New Zealand, or
Hawaii, and know there was no hope of return.

The other islands of the Australs are strung out to the
north-west of Rapa. Again they showed signs of the predominant derivation of their culture from the central islands
of Eastern Polynesia. They also had probable indications
that there had been a certain amount of cross-settlement
between them. Tubuai had culture items which were
reminiscent of those on Raivivae. Rapa and Raivivae were
alike in not practising tattooing. The early missionaries
thought that Tubuai had been peopled from Rimatara.[32]

That romance exists in plenty in the Pacific dispersal is
shown when one lets one's imagination play on the facts.
That many a happy ending to a long ordeal occurred is

shown by the presence of the Pacific Islanders on the farther islands. A specific tale of chivalry and romance is recorded by Moerenhout from Rimatara. A Tahitian lady who had been converted to Christianity was the sole survivor of an accidental voyage to Rimatara, an isle which Moerenhout and others describe as somewhat of an earthly Paradise. She became the bride of a local chief, converted him, and inspired him to defeat his enemies.[33]

The last outposts between the central Polynesian islands and New Zealand are the Kermadecs and Norfolk. They lie about half-way between, at a distance of 600 to 800 miles. They are high fertile islands, and yet were uninhabited at the time of discovery. Nor did they have any of the stone works or house enclosures or burials which on Fanning and Malden, and Pitcairn show that people stayed and lived their lives out. Yet, as on so many of the lonely islands, they have fragmentary remains which show that people have been there.[34] An adze or two, and traces of fireplaces, have been found – mute signs, perhaps, of some involuntary celibates who, like others who left traces on the atolls, went off again in the fond hope of seeing once more the faces of their friends.

In these five isolated islands to the south – Easter, Pitcairn, Rapa, the Kermadecs, and Norfolk – we again see that capricious distribution which is so understandable with accidental settlement and so mysterious from the point of view of deliberate voyaging at will. Easter Island, the most isolated, yet a biggish fertile island, got men and women who decided to stay. Pitcairn, the least isolated, got settlers who left stone works and burials but no descendants. Rapa, a small island in the oceanic wastes, but again fertile, held accidental migrants who left descendants, and also at least one later lot who, despite every inducement, decided to go off again. The Kermadecs and Norfolk, although large and fertile, merely had callers who did not bestow their bones for later visitors to find.

Finally there are those islands with Polynesian cultures far to the west of Polynesia, on the eastern fringe of the New

Hebrides and running up to the Caroline chain – Rennell, Tikopia, the Duffs, Kapingamarangi and Nukuoro.[35] Their distribution is in accord with the direction of the prevailing winds and currents, and yet is entirely capricious from north to south. Rennell is even tucked away on the other side of the New Hebrides-Santa Cruz area. It is impossible to reconcile these facts with any valid theory of deliberate colonization, with maintenance of two-way contact. On the other hand the facts fit in well with capricious piecemeal dispersal by accidental migrations, not necessarily always direct from Polynesia, since when one little settlement arose on an isolated island, such as Tikopia or Kapingamarangi, other little settlements could have come from them by accidental migration. It is clear that thousands of accidental voyagers must have been borne to these western areas with the prevailing winds and currents. Turner found that Sualo and his companions from Tonga and Samoa had established themselves in the New Hebrides.[36] The first accidental voyages that were recorded in the Pacific were of Polynesian canoes, which Quiros was told had been borne to the Duffs.[37] The Polynesian outliers cannot be explained as pockets of early migration left by the Polynesian ancestors coming from the west. The cultures, including the vocabularies, are too close to the Polynesian cultures of the main islands for such a view.

# CHAPTER EIGHT

# Early Man in New Zealand

*

NEW ZEALAND, being large and isolated, lends itself to the possibility of reasonable conclusions about the arrival and development there of man.

The archaeology of New Zealand[1] shows that man and the moa, a large wingless bird which is now extinct, existed together in earlier times. Moa-hunter settlements with accumulations of split moa-bones, remnants of fishing tackle, human burials, shark tooth necklaces and other ornaments, adze-heads and the like have been found at a dozen or more river mouths in the South Island.[2] The relics of moa-hunter type, since they were contemporary with the moa, must have been derived from the earliest settlers. They were found both in the North and South Islands.[3]

Modern experts in material culture have not found any evidence of elements in the later Maori culture which could not have developed progressively from the moa-hunter culture. The moa-hunter relics are matched by similar ones in the central belt of islands to the north.[4] On the other hand there are distinctive elements in the Maori cultures of historical times which are not matched by similar late elements in the central islands.

Could there have been a fairly massive arrival of migrants in New Zealand at a later date? Its possibility is precluded by the nature of accidental settlement, which was of necessity by isolated canoes at infrequent intervals. On the contrary later arrivals when the population had built up would have less impact, being a handful of accidental voyagers coming on just one place in an extended coast-line which was already peopled by the descendants of the early arrivals.

In the light of accidental settlement it is necessary to

think in terms of a formative period, in which every canoe with women aboard, coming on a part of the coast which was still unsettled, was vitally significant in the formation of the culture and people, forming a little knot of settlement which in due course expanded.

Could there have been only one canoe with women aboard which arrived in the formative period? Theoretically there is no evidence that this could not have occurred. Men only might have arrived from time to time later, giving new blood. It might have been many centuries after the first continuing colony arose before another canoe with women aboard arrived. In Samoa today the rate of population increase is equivalent to a doubling of their numbers every twenty-one years.[5] Let us suppose that in early New Zealand, with an abundance of food, plenty of room to expand, and a healthy climate, but with more natural hazards and less infant welfare, the population doubled in fifty years. Then if six women had survived an accidental voyage to New Zealand in A.D. 900, the population in A.D. 1150 would be only 384, by A.D. 1350 it would be 6,144, and by A.D. 1550 it would be 98,304. This population could therefore theoretically have been built up from six women in seven centuries, with new blood coming occasionally by canoes of men only, which must have predominated greatly in the early accidental voyages in Polynesia. Nevertheless, it is open to doubt that that was the whole story in the formative period. The evidence of Hawaii and Easter Island is against it. These places must have been less likely to receive accidental settlers than New Zealand because they were at the ends of the Polynesian lines of settlement, whereas New Zealand, as soon as the central belt was settled, was in line for such incidents. Yet Easter Island had obviously collected some accidental settlers in early times, and Hawaii had had some people by A.D. 1200, and probably long before.[6]

Could there have been a number of knots of settlement from widely separate parts of the central belt? We cannot say that this was not so in the earlier part of the formative period. The evidence of the early relics shows that most of the types found by the archaeologists in New Zealand can be matched in one part or other of the central belt. Whale-tooth relics which call to mind Fijian religious practices occur, but if they were made by western Fijians one would expect pottery, since the archaeology of Viti shows pottery at the early levels of occupation, and there was clay in New Zealand.[7] Furthermore, one can never be sure with accidental voyages whether small finds of relics do not merely record transient occupation, possibly of men only, as on so many of the uninhabited islands. The peoples of the central belt were too alike, the processes of early cultural change are too uncertain, and the nature of early accidental settlement too capricious, for the conclusion to be reached that any part of the Polynesian central islands did not furnish accidental settlers to New Zealand in the formative period.

What can be said, however, is that at an early date a common culture was evolved, and that the main component in the culture was unmistakably Eastern Polynesian. This comes as the unavoidable conclusion from the linguistic affinities of the later peoples,[8] coupled with certain facts about the archaeology. The relics of moa-hunter type occur in both islands, and their distribution shows that this arose from widespread diffusion. Internally one or more knots of settlement originating from Eastern Polynesia and merging with a minority from Tonga or Samoa may have given the culture its obvious Eastern Polynesian character, but elements other than Eastern Polynesian are undetectable on present evidence.

The whole picture given by the objective evidence, there-fore, taken in conjunction with the nature of accidental settlement, is one of expansion from small beginnings in which Eastern Polynesians predominated. An appreciable population had been built up and had spread within the moa-hunter period, meaning by this the early period during which moas were still being hunted somewhere in the country in appreciable numbers. The moa-hunters were essentially Eastern Polynesians and ancestral to the later Maoris.

Why then is the conventional picture of the arrival and development of man in New Zealand so different? The idea that earlier inhabitants preceded waves of deliberate Maori colonization still reigns supreme. This arises from the erroneous interpretations which the later Europeans placed on the Maori traditional material. When these are revised, the Maoris achieve their true antiquity, and an end is made of the questions of whether the later arrivals were absorbed by the greater numbers of the earlier peoples, or whether they managed to kill most of them off, or just what did happen.

What did the old-time Maoris themselves really say about their origins? The first records of the Maori traditions were made by Cook and his associates. Cook said in his journal that the Maoris in the north had a tradition that their ancestors had come from islands to the north of New Zealand.[9] Hawkesworth, who wrote a contemporary account of Cook's first voyage incorporating material from Cook and his associates, said that there was a general tradition in New Zealand and the other Polynesian islands that their ancestors had come from 'Heawije'[10] – obviously Hawaiki. The islands visited by Cook on this voyage were confined to Eastern Polynesia, apart from New Zealand itself.

Samuel Marsden was the next visitor to New Zealand who made extensive contacts with the Maoris and left detailed accounts of his experiences. He set up the first New Zealand Mission, and on his voyages between 1814 and 1837 he journeyed extensively on foot in the hinterland of the north, having long talks with the foremost Maori chiefs and priests. He left only one note on their beliefs of origin, which gives cold comfort to the deliberate settlement school. He said that he 'could not learn that they had any traditions amongst them from whence they came'.[11]

J. S. Polack, a European resident of the north of New Zealand from 1831 to 1837, has left some notes on the traditions of origin at that time.[12] He said that some of the tribes had a tradition that a gigantic bird had laid a large egg on the ocean, from which emerged a canoe with a woman and a man and a boy and a girl, who discovered New Zealand and peopled it from end to end. The Bay of Plenty Maoris had a tradition that their ancestors were divinities with the appetites of men who had arrived in a canoe and planted the *kumara*. The East Cape Maoris and the Maoris farther south of them, according to Polack, had somewhat differing views of their origins. Polack had no axe to grind in supporting or opposing any particular theory. The tradition of the egg and the canoe was indeed a particularly ancient Eastern Polynesian one which got as far afield as Hawaii.[13] Yet how often does one hear of it in the edited versions of the traditions?

Another objective glimpse one gets is the account of Horatio Hale, the American ethnologist who visited the north of New Zealand in 1840. He says that the Maoris there had traditions that they had come from Hawaiki in four canoes.[14] Hale placed credence on Polynesian tradition where he found it elsewhere in his travels. Yet apparently he did not hear anything from the Maoris which disagreed with his conclusion that they had come to New Zealand by accidental voyages.

Cook, Marsden, Polack, and Hale all got their information on the traditions of the Maori origins in the north of New Zealand. Their records show plainly that there was no general canon and that the traditions were not static. The fundamental Eastern Polynesian tradition of creation from the egg and the canoe had apparently been lost somewhere round Hale's time.

Edward Shortland, a graduate of Cambridge who became an authority on the Maoris and their language, worked among them in the forties as Protector of Aborigines. He recorded the Maori tribal canoe traditions at that time. He says they were all of one-way voyages, with one exception. This was the Wanganui tribal story of Kupe's discovery of New Zealand and return to Hawaiki, which Shortland said was 'so mixed up with the fabulous and marvellous that it can scarcely be believed to have any

foundation in truth'[15] – a comment which does not detract
in the slightest from its value as folklore.

The older Maori traditions therefore are not in conflict
with the facts of accidental settlement or the course of the
Polynesian dispersal. The people came on one-way voyages
from Hawaiki, as they undoubtedly did from Western to
Eastern Polynesia, and then to New Zealand. All the
peoples who came from Eastern Polynesia had the same
basic tradition of Hawaiki. The fact that they had been
conveyed by the winds and currents to farther islands did
not efface this tradition from their minds, nor change the
truth of the claim that they had in fact come from Hawaiki.
That, however, was not the only ancient Polynesian tradition that the Maori ancestors brought with them to New
Zealand, for when Daniel Tyerman visited Raiatea in 1823,
he was told of how Taaroa (Tangaroa) had existed as an
egg and a canoe and had peopled the world.[16]

By Hale's and Shortland's time Maori chiefs and sailors
had been going all over the world for thirty years. Within
New Zealand the more sophisticated Maoris from the whaling ports, armed with European muskets, had penetrated
the hinterland of both islands.

The Maori traditional material which was recorded after
Shortland has little value as evidence of pre-European
knowledge. This does not mean that the later material did
not contain an abundance of pre-European tradition. The
trouble is however that we have no means of knowing
whether identifiable place-names and other references were
included as the result of later derived knowledge. In no
sense was such inclusion in some way deceitful or improper.
Oral tradition, while it remains unrecorded, is never static.
There is no need to argue whether later derived material was
in fact inserted. Sir Peter Buck, himself of Maori blood,
spent many pages of his main book on the Maori in revealing all sorts of borrowings, confusions and inventions in the
later material.[17] What of it then can be taken as certainly
derived from pre-European material?

At the late date of 1848 to 1854, the first systematic

collection of Maori traditions and chants as at that time was
made by Sir George Grey. He says that at that time the old
chiefs were a fast vanishing race. After the publication of
Grey's book, the Europeans started extracting from what
they regarded as credible their reconstructions of the supposed deliberate colonization by the Maoris. In these earlier
days most of the editing of the Polynesian traditions was
done by Europeans, not Polynesians, since they did not have
writing. The first formal historian of New Zealand, Thomson, worked out a supposed historical canon in this way,[18]
and it became the sport of Europeans associated with the
Maoris over the next fifty years to collect further additions.

It was when the making over of the material by the
European editors in the sixties was well under way that
William Colenso, one of the few early European residents
who had lived among the Maoris and were still alive,
sounded his warning against taking bits and pieces from the
folklore and neglecting the fact that it was impregnated with
the miraculous. He pointed out that the traditional material
which was being used was in modern language, as compared
with some of their songs.[19]

John White's collections, which were published between
1886 and 1891, embody painstaking work over a long
period. White recorded the traditional material of his time
on a regional basis, and in an objective manner. He commented that the accounts of the folklore varied not only
from place to place, but also within the same area.[20]

That the appearance of historical detail in the European
extracts from the Maori traditions which have become the
conventional renderings derives from the European editors
and not from the Maoris of former times is best shown by
reading the traditions in their un-edited form. Take for
instance the traditions of the bringing of the *kumara* and
the lizards. Almost every European who has written about
the Maori in the last fifty years has recounted the tradition
of the bringing of the *kumara*, because it is reasonable to
believe that it was in fact introduced by man. But who now
recounts the tradition, recorded by White, that a special

canoe brought the lizards including the *tuatara*? This has been dropped because the scientific evidence shows that the lizards were in New Zealand for hundreds of thousands of years before man. As for the *kumara*, a number of representatives of leading tribes whom White interviewed each stated that it had been brought by his own ancestors, and repudiated the claims of the others.[21]

Some later Europeans acquired exclusive property in some traditions secured by an educated protégé from late Maori sources, and withheld them for fifteen years while they edited them. They then published them after the turn of the century in the form of a running account and commentary. It mentioned earlier dark people called Maruiwi, from which a suggestion of migrations of 'Morioris' from the Melanesian area, preceding the main colonists, was evolved by these editors.[22] Bishop Williams, a foremost expert on the Maoris, criticized this view,[23] as have Sir Peter Buck[24] and many later writers. There is no reason either from this evidence or any other to think that there was such an earlier migration, although there is ample evidence that the Polynesians, like all the other people of the Pacific, were not of uniform appearance. Nevertheless, as we shall see, there was a good reason for the persistent and widespread Polynesian notions of earlier inferior people, who appeared also in the tradition of the Manahune in Tahiti and elsewhere.[25]

Sir Peter Buck, a master in the field of material culture, was an heir in the twentieth century of the deliberate settlement school, not a promoter. Buck, by refusing in his accounts to disguise the fact that the later traditional material was full of borrowings and internal contradictions, and by repeating many traditions with the miraculous elements preserved instead of edited out of them,[26] has done more than anybody else to bring the traditional material into proper perspective.

Another outstanding Maori thinker and leader who was apparently coming to the conclusion that the later records could not be regarded as a complete coverage of the early history of the New Zealand peoples was Sir Apirana Ngata. In a late paper he agreed that the traditional canoes could not explain all the facts and that earlier canoes must have arrived. He also suggested that where two canoes were described in the traditions as arriving together – citing the Tainui and the Arawa, from which nearly half the Maoris traced their origin – a feasible explanation might be that they were the two parts of the same double canoe.[27] One of the things which set Sir Apirana to thinking along these lines was the remarkable parallelism of the canoe traditions. Sir Peter Buck commented at length in his own writings on these coincidences and similarities, which occurred even in the canoe traditions of tribal divisions which dated their arrivals a number of generations apart. A Maori chief in a Land Court dispute in the nineteenth century heaped scorn on his opponent's head because he could not remember the canoe his ancestors came in,[28] but it seems probable they both had many ancestors in common.

What then of the tribal divisions of historical times? How did they arise, and what is the bearing of the tribal histories, canoe traditions and genealogies on the arrival and development of the people?[29]

The tribal history in each case equated the arrival and commencement of the tribal division to the arrival from Hawaiki of the chiefly families of historical times, from which all the free men derived their origin. The founding ancestors were the fathers of their people and usually gave their names to the tribal division or the tribes which made it up. All the arrivals were described as having taken place on the northern parts of the North Island, whence the tribes at once set off to the various parts of New Zealand which in historical times were the tribal territories. The arrivals of the tribal ancestors in their various canoes were calculated by the European reconstructionists as having occurred in the twelfth and fourteenth century, because the count-back of the generations in the chiefly genealogies, calculated at twenty-five years to a generation, established those dates.

Now the evidence of countries with tribal divisions shows

that where a land area is divided into inhabited valleys by ridges which separate the people and yet are not impassable in themselves, tribal divisions and war will tend to develop. It happened in Scotland, the Balkans, and New Guinea. It happened in the Marquesas and Rarotonga. It even happened in Rapa, a tiny little island divided geographically by ridges, where internecine warfare developed.[30] Equally obviously however this cannot happen until people to fight with have in fact been established at a distance. There is no evidence that in New Zealand there were later irruptions of people from abroad in substantial numbers after the first arrivals had expanded, and there could not have been, for accidental voyages are invariably of isolated canoes. The conclusion to which one is forced is that the tribal divisions developed in later times with the expansion of the people into the more distant parts of the country, and with the loss of the feeling of common affinity that occurred after they had been partially isolated for a number of generations. Thus the moa-hunters had not attained to specialized war-weapons, but later institutional warfare developed, and had obviously been the practice for a long time when Tasman and Cook visited New Zealand.

In the light of this it is obvious that the chiefly families of historical times were those which had emerged from a long period of expansion, inter-marriage, alliances, conquests, and absorptions. Yet nowhere in the whole body of Maori tribal history is there any genealogy of a defeated previous family. All the surviving ones are of the families which were still in power in historical times.

These processes, including the dominance of the final successful families and the omission of the earlier genealogies, are shown in the following example. In 1843–4 Edward Shortland was told by the chiefs in the south of the South Island of how the Ngatimamoe had been defeated several centuries earlier by invaders from the north, and of how eventually a new tribe was formed from the merging of the older remnants with the invaders. This new tribe, the Ngaitahu, were so called from Tahu, the progenitor of the chiefly families of the invaders. 'I found', says Shortland, 'that all the families of the present day, of any consideration, traced their origin to the Turanga, or Poverty Bay sources – as being the conquering side, and therefore the more honourable – and neglected altogether the Ngatimamoe sources, beyond the time of their conquest'.[31]

None of this means that any given tribal canoe tradition does not embody an actual memory of an early arrival. Least of all does it mean that any genealogy is affected. The only things that need to be revised are the manner of arrival, which was by isolated one-way passages, and the times of arrival, which in many cases must have been long before the emergence of the historical lineages. Even the dispersal of the canoes to various parts of New Zealand is valid as a figure of the expansion of the tribes, and it cannot even be said that any given canoe did not in fact go prospecting for unsettled country after arrival on the north coast. The last thing that can be concluded from the evidence, however, is that the tribal divisions represented the primeval state of man in New Zealand, or that most of the people arrived by purposive migration in the twelfth and fourteenth centuries. No old-time Maori ever claimed that, for each Maori had his own tribal history. The generalizations from the tribal histories, and the calculation of the supposed dates of the supposed late deliberate migrants, were the work of Europeans.

The Maori tribal divisions were of course very real in later times. They became in fact the dominant feature of the country. No Maori could or should give up his tribal canoe, which is as fundamental to the tribal differentiation as the rose of England or the thistle of Scotland. Nobody can challenge the authenticity of any tribal canoe, since any or all of them may embody the memory of an actual arrival of a component of the Maori people. This cannot however overshadow the fact that their blood, like their culture and traditions, was inextricably intermingled. To an objective observer the community of blood and culture in the Maoris was and is much more pronounced than their divisions. This community was derived from the earliest times, and was continually sustained thereafter by war and marriage. None of the Polynesian tribes was ever an exclusive caste, but intermarried freely with other tribes, and the continual warfare mixed them up as much as friendly alliances. Warfare throughout the ages has always been a potent agent for mixing people, because it forces them into offensive and defensive association, and because conquerors absorb or are absorbed by the conquered.

What became of the conquered parties in the incessant New Zealand warfare? There is ample evidence that in many cases they continued to live among the conquerors as commoners. Shortland's example of the defeat and absorption of the Ngatimamoe by the Ngaitahu is a case in point. When some ancient tribe or part thereof was absorbed by another, the chiefly genealogy and tradition of origin of the party that was defeated would be replaced by that of the party that prevailed. Nor, as the case of the Ngatimamoe shows, would the people within the tribe who were predominantly derived from the conquered segment be likely to preserve its memory. The Maoris considered that defeat in war was a disgrace. This would mean that the earlier history of the Maori people would tend to be foreshortened and forgotten. All these factors may also explain the persistent Polynesian notions of former people of a somewhat alien and inferior character as being memories of elements which were defeated and absorbed. Thus the Tahitian Manahune were described as previous people from whom the chiefs did not trace the lineage, but who still survived as commoners. The word 'manahune' meant commoner. It seems likely that 'Maruiwi' or 'Moriori' was a Maori word with the same background.

An enticing field of speculation is opened up by the question of where the accidental voyages which took place to New Zealand started from.

The main European traditionalist in New Zealand, S. Percy Smith, in the late nineteenth century propounded the view that the later traditional canoes which were reputed to

have come to New Zealand – the Fleet – derived from the
Tahiti Group, and stayed in Rarotonga for some time before
going on to New Zealand. This was based on the correspondence of Tahitian and New Zealand names, and the
occurrence of the phrase 'seed of Rangiatea' as an ancient
explanation of their origin among some of the tribes on the
west coast of the North Island, coupled with the mention
of Rarotonga in late New Zealand tradition. 'Rangiatea' is
the Maori dialectal equivalent of Raiatea.[32]

Sir Peter Buck, while unwilling to accept that Rarotonga was a pre-European New Zealand traditional name,
considered also that the Tahitian islands, including Raiatea,
were the main homeland of the later Maoris, citing the fact
that Havai'i, corresponding to the Hawaiki of New Zealand
tradition, was an old name for Raiatea, the temple Taputapuatea (meaning 'Sacred Atea') at Opoa in Raiatea being
considered to have been a source of New Zealand religious
ideas.[33]

The full proverbial expression 'We are seed scattered
hither from Rangiatea' is a distinctive and striking one, and
more in character with an accidental voyage than a deliberate one. It was obviously a pre-European saying, for it
was spread over a wide area among a number of the West
Coast tribes at least as early as the late eighteenth century,
being remembered by chiefs such as the renowned Raupa-
raha from their youth.[34] These tribes had the general
traditional name of Hawaiki, and had this arresting phrase
as well.

It has been seen that the traditional names of other
islands in the rest of the Pacific were in marked accord with
the direction of the winds and currents in relation to the
geography.[35] If then Rangiatea is a recognizable place-
name in an area or areas from which it is reasonable to
believe the winds and currents would have brought accidental voyagers to New Zealand, it would be a reasonable
conclusion that the New Zealand traditional name derived
from accidental voyages from those parts. Furthermore, if
any of the Maoris were part of the seed of Rangiatea, all of

them were, for all the Maori peoples came to be of common blood, and all their traditions were intermingled. Wherever Rangiatea was, or what it was, it was representative of general Maori tradition, like Hawaiki.

Where, and what, was Rangiatea? The exclusive identification of it with Raiatea depends on the assumption that it could not have been anywhere else. But Maretu, a Rarotongan who is telling of happenings in his own lifetime at the time of European contact in the early nineteenth century, in a description of the warfare of tribes and sub-tribes in Rarotonga, says that Rangiatea returned to the Ngatangiia part of Rarotonga. From the context Rangiatea were apparently a sub-tribe of Ngatangiia. Furthermore Maretu states that Taputapuatea in Rarotonga was burnt when Christianity was introduced.[36]

Other facts which appear to associate the New Zealand traditional names at least as closely with the Cook Islands as anywhere else, are the following. Smith, at the time when he identified Rangiatea with Raiatea, put on record that Waerota and Nukuroa were ancient New Zealand traditional names, the origin of which could not be identified at that time. Maretu states that Vaerota was a sacred place in Rarotonga, while Gill put on record that Nukuroa was an alternative name for Mitiaro. Smith also stated that Kuporu was another old traditional name. This is closely allied in form to the Rarotongan Kupolu, which Gill identified with Upolu in Samoa.[37]

The other New Zealand traditional names – Tawhiti, Hawaiki, Wawau – could have come from anywhere in Eastern Polynesia, including the Cooks. The same applies to all the New Zealand place-names, although Bishop Williams considered Maketu, on the east coast of the North Island, to be an un-Maori-like name, and Maketu is reputed to have been a place-name in Mauke.[38]

It would therefore seem that there is no necessity to look any farther afield than the Cooks for the immediate origin of every recognizable New Zealand traditional name or tradition of origin. The Cooks, particularly Rarotonga-

Atiu-Mauke, where most of the voyaging was done, are a natural source area to look to for some of the accidental voyages to New Zealand.

Again it is necessary to say that these traditional names are neither evidence that elements in the New Zealand population did not come from places other than the Cooks, nor evidence that the first settlers came from there. The concept of first settlement is in fact of no great importance as compared with the end-product of mergings of accidental settlers during the formative period. All the traditional names could have been established by later arrivals, including men only. While there is no evidence that any canoe ever came direct from Tahiti to New Zealand, there are ample signs of Tahitian influence in the Cooks. A distinction between the Cooks and Tahiti is in fact somewhat academic. Many Tahitians no doubt went into the formation both of the Rarotongans and New Zealanders. Smith and Buck were both right in a figurative sense at least, in the same way that the names are symbols of the flow of migration from Western to Eastern Polynesia and back to the Cooks and New Zealand. Nor can the possibility of other voyages from the Australs or Tuamotus or other places farther afield, including Tahiti itself and the Tongan area, be dismissed.

The language evidence does not throw any more light on the immediate origins of the New Zealanders than that they were predominantly Eastern Polynesians, and that the period when the speech was established in New Zealand was many centuries ago at about the same time as in Hawaii.[39] Since the effect of later changes in Eastern Polynesia and internal conquest in New Zealand cannot be precisely known, it would seem best to leave it at that.

Can the supposed part or parts of New Zealand where the first knots of settlement established themselves be traced, and so throw light either on origins or the early development of the people?

The traditions of the historical tribes said they dispersed from the north of the North Island. This may well be a figurative picture of the expansion of the northern tribes in later times, but cannot be taken as necessarily applying to the early arrivals, for Shortland's evidence that the genealogies of some tribes had displaced those of others no doubt applies no less to the tribal traditions.

The fact that a comparative profusion of early relics has been found in the South Island, but few in the North,[40] has tended to create an impression that in the moa-hunter period the human population was mostly in the south. The relics in the South Island have however been found mostly at river mouths where the moas could be cornered, and the sand which in due course covered them was a good preservative. Away from the beaches the relics of occupation would rot away a good deal more quickly. Quite apart from moas there were many choice birds and fish on which the population could be built up in either island.

Remains of moas, with bones obviously split by human hands, have been found here and there in parts of the North Island. Yet no intensive moa-hunter sites with accumulations of split bones, human burials and relics comparable to the dozen or more in the South Island have been found in the North Island. The experts agree that moas throve in the tussock country extending from Wellington to the East Cape. In this area numbers of remains of moas which died natural deaths in swamps and caves have been found to prove it. This country is indeed much the same as the moa country across the straits in the north-east of the South Island and south of it on the plains, where the most striking finds of moa-hunter sites have been made. No sign or possibility of any natural cataclysm such as earthquake, fire, or flood whereby the moas in the North Island could all have been reduced without extinction can be imagined. Indeed the moas are known to have roamed both the North Island and the South for millions of years, and had adapted themselves to every natural threat that nature could devise in that time.

The following explanation may possibly fit the facts. It is known that the rat and dog were in the country before the moas were extinguished in the South Island, because their remains have been found in the moa-hunter settlements there.[41] There can be no doubt that canoes with men only predominated greatly in the accidental voyages of Polynesia. Women did not ordinarily go in fishing or war canoes.[42] The chances that the first canoes which were borne to New Zealand established continuing human colonies are therefore small. On the other hand there are at least five Polynesian islands which had rats but not human beings at the time of discovery, and there were no doubt therefore many more in earlier times. Presumably the rats got there in canoes with men only, or in derelict canoes which were blown away without human beings or whose occupants had died of exposure. The scavenging possibilities of rats and dogs in such canoes will be obvious. The chances that rat colonies were established in New Zealand before the first canoe with women aboard arrived are therefore high. The rat multiplied astronomically where the food supply was good and no natural ground enemies existed. The dog was also man's constant companion, and was no less well-adapted than the rat to survive accidental voyages either with men or without. When the dog got to islands with game in the interior he was well suited to going wild like the rat. Williams tells us this had happened on Savaii and Upolo.[43] In historical times there were large numbers of wild rats and dogs in the interior of New Zealand.

While it is reasonable to believe that rats were able to make onslaughts on moa eggs, since the moas in the North Island were mostly of the smaller species, $2\frac{1}{2}$ to 3 feet high, laid their eggs on the ground, and were unused to vermin, the result might be a great reduction of moa numbers, but not necessarily extinction. While one might also believe that dogs could have run moas round and picked off the chicks or weaker birds, the same would apply to them. Some objective evidence on the impact and also the limitations of rats is given by their history in the Cocos Islands in the Indian Ocean. These islands were uninhabited until well into the nineteenth century. When they were colonized, it was found that the rat had become established on one atoll only, but not on any others nearby. On this atoll it had pro-liferated in countless thousands. The rats had learned to open ripe coconuts, which are less vulnerable and no smaller than moa eggs.[44] If the hypothetical first rat or dog colony was established only in the North Island, it would seem that the water barrier of fifteen miles and more separating the two islands would confine their expansion to the North Island until eventually a human colony arose somewhere in the country and provided transport for the rats or dogs or both across the strait. So when human beings were estab-lished, at which time their numbers would be sparse, there would be only moas enough in the North Island for the men to hunt them piecemeal to final extinction, with no oppor-tunity or incentive to set up moa-hunter camps at the river mouths. On the other hand the moas would still abound in the South Island, so that overt traces over an appreciable period would be left by the hunters.

The same effects might possibly have arisen if rats or dogs had in fact arrived with the first continuing settlers, since the greater rate of increase of the animals might have meant that they would out-run the men and reduce the moa in the North Island before the human beings got to the South. In that case one or two semi-intensive moa-hunter sites might exist in the North Island. Yet the discovery of such sites would be no evidence in itself of primary settlement in the North Island.

By the same token it is not necessary to consider that a great period of time would be required to extinguish the moa even if the access of the human beings, rats or dogs had been in fact delayed in the case of the South Island, since the rats and dogs might have out-run the men there also with the same destructive effects on the wild life.

These speculations on the relationship of man to the moa in early New Zealand may show that alternative views of the facts seem possible, and that no firm conclusions on the regional development of human occupation can be made from the present evidence.

Nor can one derive any conclusions about where the early

population might have developed from the supposed relative climatic attraction of the North Island, for when the early people were still hunting moas, the climate in the South Island, as in the North, was apparently several degrees warmer than it is today, and had been so for many centuries prior to the fourteenth century.[45]

The idea that the first landings or settlements were confined to the north coast of the North Island, or that settlement there was necessarily predominant, has no evidence to support it other than that geographically it is nearer the central belt of Polynesian islands. No conclusions from that can be made where accidental settlement is concerned, since the approaches with the variable winds cannot be regarded as localized in this way.

The truth therefore is that we can have no firm view on where the first landings were made or the early people established themselves.

On the other hand the archaeology of the moa-hunter period throws much light on the character of early settlement in New Zealand. The vital early chapters in the story of the Maoris have been left suspended in mid-air as if they did not really belong, while the Maoris that really mattered have been supposed to have been later deliberate migrants. There never was any evidence for this view, even in the older traditions of the Maoris. No cultural items necessarily deriving from a supposed later phase of migration can be traced. There may have been differing elements in the early population derived from separate original settlement from different parts of the central belt of Polynesian islands, and each phase of moa-hunter archaeology may not necessarily reflect a homogeneous culture in very early times. There is, however, sufficient evidence to show that the moa-hunter period as a whole was essentially the first period in the slow and progressive evolution of the Maori cultures of later times.[46]

In later times the population increase in the North Island apparently went forward at a greater rate. The extinction of the moa is not an adequate reason. It seems reasonable to believe that the relative suitability of the north to semi-agricultural development and increase through *kumara* cultivation had something to do with it. In no sense is this evidence that the *kumara* had not been in the country for centuries previously. Nor can the possibility that in fact more knots of settlement from canoes with women, or earlier ones, sprang up in the north be dismissed. Another factor may have been that later canoes from islands in the central belt where increase of population had in the meantime caused a development of the martial arts, gave the northerners an advantage over the south, although the thought that there could not have been a quick adaptation throughout the country is not necessarily a sound one.

The conclusions on the origins and development of the New Zealanders are far from negative. The evidence shows that they were mostly Eastern Polynesians, and the earlier derivation of the Eastern Polynesians has been traced by what it is hoped is a persuasive body of evidence. Few people have as good a knowledge of their derivations as that evidence appears to establish for the Maoris.

The Chatham Islanders were also much the same people as the people of New Zealand, being for the most part derived from them through a series of accidental one-way voyages. The older culture of the Chathams, from the evidence of the relics, is still increasingly being shown by the archaeologists to have been derived from the older culture of New Zealand.[47] This agrees with the pattern of the winds. It cannot be said that accidental voyagers from New Zealand were the only ones that ever came to the Chathams, for the same winds and currents that peopled New Zealand may have taken voyagers from the central belt direct to the Chathams. Indeed on general grounds it seems distinctly probable. But the formative culture was evidently derived from early New Zealand. When the first settlement of the Chathams occurred cannot be known precisely, for the same reasons as in New Zealand and the other islands. Again the genealogies are of no help because displacement in the constant wars both in New Zealand and the Chathams cannot be traced. The fact that the Chatham Island genealogies[48] appeared to date the arrivals there before the arrivals in New Zealand is without real significance.

There is not one iota of evidence that any voyager ever got back from the Chathams to New Zealand in pre-European times. The thought that the Chathams could have been colonized from New Zealand or anywhere else by two-way voyages becomes a flight of fancy in the light of the local meteorology of the area and the copious evidence of the inability of the Polynesian vessels to make sustained voyages against variable or adverse winds. Cook's ships were sometimes obliged to traverse hundreds of miles and spend days and weeks in order to recover their courses in New Zealand waters. When John Williams, having taken a passage in a sailing ship, was in sight of the New Zealand coast, his ship was blown 300 miles to leeward,[49] which is more than half-way to the Chathams. The romanticists who have taken the Polynesians across the oceans by deliberate voyages have not tested their theories by going in double canoes from the Chathams to New Zealand. If ever they did, it would be of the nature of a rehearsal for the trip from New Zealand to the central belt of Polynesian islands. If the Chatham Islanders had been far-ranging colonists in earlier times they had forgotten their origins in later, for their traditions gave no clue to the place or places which colonized them in the first place, despite the fact that it is on supposed traditional evidence that such theories are based. The dog did not get to the Chathams.

None of the evidence reviewed in this chapter makes the slightest difference to the appeal of the later Maori folklore, but rather enhances it. These stories were evolved, like all true folklore, in response to a need. We have it from Colenso that the older Maoris did not treat their lore as literal history.[50] Henry Stowell (Hare Hongi), a Maori scholar whose recollections went back to the seventies of last century, and who said of himself that from his earliest years he was instructed in the Maori lore by its outstanding masters, stated that there was no fleet, and, speaking of Kupe and others, said that their canoes, and they themselves, should not be included in the subject of ordinary human migrations. He considered that later leaders who were described as having come in traditional canoes were New Zealand-born ancestors round whom fables had been woven.[51] Sir George Grey stated that some Maori chiefs denied that the tradition of Kupe referred to anything more than the discoveries made by the early Maoris when coasting to the various parts of New Zealand.[52]

It would seem that the early New Zealanders, when they were projected on those distant shores, achieved as near an approach to the ideal state in which some romantic writers have imagined early man as human beings ever got. They hunted moas, pigeons, and other succulent birds, caught masses of cod, groper, shark, seal, and porpoise, had a very good stone for their adzes, were free of natural enemies, and even had a better climate than the Europeans inherited in later times. The scenery was magnificent, with high snow-clad mountains and swift rivers everywhere. Innumerable birds raised a tuneful chorus to the rising sun, as they were still doing when Cook's associate Banks noted the fact in his journal centuries later.[53] An occasional shaking of the earth reminded them of the wrath of the gods, and sacred mountains flashing fire were their visible embodiment. The New Zealanders were the survivors of a long succession of accidental voyagers from the East Indies itself, and were healthy, hardy, and optimistic, taking life as it came, as their forebears who were borne to distant islands had done many times before them.

If a monument of the origins of the Maoris, suitably placed, and compounding all views, had to be devised, a solution would be simple enough. The obvious place is somewhere on the north-east coast, looking towards the central belt of Polynesian islands. A double canoe, with high carved stern posts, might be an appropriate form for the monument to take. A suitable inscription might be somewhat as follows, being a highest common factor of all opinions: 'This monument is a symbol of the arrival of the

Maori ancestors in New Zealand. The cultures which the Maori peoples so impressively adapted to their new environment were brought from Eastern Polynesian islands lying far to the north-east of this coast.'

CHAPTER NINE

## The Extent of Deliberate Early Voyaging

\*

THE character of the earlier voyaging in all the farther
islands of the world can be established from the evidence of
the early explorers and observers, or rather from what the
islanders themselves told them. It is in fact the whole story
of man's oceanic voyaging outside the land-locked seas and
gulfs before the days of navigation instruments. The picture
that emerges is a fascinating one when viewed in ascending
order of the voyaging. It shows that the extent of contact
was determined by the environment.

All the solitary islands that became inhabited lost the art
of off-shore voyaging. They had to, because there were no
islands within reach to go to. This applied no less to large
solitary New Zealand than to small solitary Easter Island.
The navigation on all these isolated islands consisted of
coastal cruising and visits to islands which were in sight
from the coast. The Chatham Islanders, who came farther
by sea than any other people in history in getting to their
final homes, eventually gave up canoe voyaging altogether.
and were reduced to raft-like vessels because of lack of suitable timber.[1]

The solitary inhabited islands which were thus worlds
to themselves were Easter Island, Rapa, Raivivae, Tubuai,
Mangaia, Tongareva, Pukapuka, Niue, Chatham, New
Zealand, Ocean Island, Nauru, Kapingamarangi, Kusaie,
Taongi, Ujelang and Eniwetok.

Some of these islands had quite a good information
service from occasional involuntary arrivals. These islands
were the ones that were in the stream of accidental contacts
from the east. To a certain extent the service was reciprocal
where westerlies blew. The classical examples were most of
the Cooks and Australs, which, as we have seen, had tradi-

tional names and recognizable islands both to east and west. At the other end of the scale were Easter Island and Chatham, which were at the end of a cul-de-sac, with only the vaguest notions of an outside world.

The evidence on the voyaging of Kusaie is noteworthy. This island, as the map will show, is right on the direct line from the Western Carolines to the Gilberts at the threshold of Polynesia. It has therefore been an inevitable notion oj the reconstructionists of Micronesian voyaging, and so of Polynesian, to imagine that Kusaie was a link. If so things had certainly changed since the old days. When Lutke, the Russian explorer, visited Kusaie in 1827, he said that the islanders never went outside the reefs, and that since they did not have any opportunity for voyaging, they did not use sails.[2] Chamisso heard no reports of contact with Kusaie from either the Western Caroline or the Marshall Islanders whom he and Kotzebue questioned in 1817, and said that there were 15 degrees of longitude between the Western Carolines and the Marshalls of which nothing was certainly known.[3]

On the small isolated islands the degeneration of off-shore voyaging was manifest in their vessels. Nevertheless the correlation of the basic designs of their canoes with those of the areas from which the evidence of basic vocabularies shows they came, is remarkable. Kapingamarangi and Nukuoro, south of the Carolines, had unmistakable signs of peopling from Polynesia and not the islands which were so near to them on the north. Their canoe designs were of Polynesian type, and yet unlike one another in a number of ways. Nukuoro was within the Western Caroline contact area in Kotzebue's time.[4] The only reasonable explanation of these facts is that the contact area developed after the settlement of Nukuoro by an accidental voyage from Polynesia. Yet it is suggested that deliberate long voyagers settled first Micronesia and then Polynesia, apparently overlooking Nukuoro until the Polynesians had developed a distinguishable culture.

Taongi is a lonely atoll some 180 miles north of the main

Marshall Islands. Its native name was Bokak.[5] When Kotzebue and Chamisso made their inquiries of the Marshall Islanders in 1817, they heard of a mysterious island to the north called 'Bogha', which was known to the Marshall Islanders from accidental voyagers from the island.[6] The fact that Taongi was thus isolated, and yet is only 180 miles from the main Marshall Islands, has its significance, as has the further fact that it is on the way to Hawaii. In the light of this it is hard to believe that the two other outlying atolls of the Marshalls, Ujelang and Eniwetok, of which Kotzebue heard nothing from the Marshall Islanders,[7] were ports of call.

Contact within the Cooks was apparently conditioned by the meteorology. It seems strange that the chief of Atiu should have described to Williams how he sailed to Rarotonga, and yet that there should be no evidence that at the time of European contact the Atiuans visited the nearer island of Aitutaki, with the island of Manuae as a link in between. Yet it is compatible with the meteorology that contact between these three latter islands should have been occasional. The winds and currents are not propitious to two-way contact between them. The prevailing ones come strongly from the south-east through these islands, and trips on the return leg would be dependent on awaiting the seasonal westerlies, as in the case of the Tahitian trips from the Raiatea area. But in the latter case the central Tahitian islands offered a good target to the voyagers from Raiatea.

When Cook, after discovering Atiu in 1777, came up to Manuae, the people told him that they were 'tributaries of Teerevatooeah, the chief of Atiu'. This name did not correspond with those of the chiefs of Atiu which Anderson had recorded on Atiu a few days previously. Cook commented that the people of Manuae showed some differences from those of Atiu.[8] John Williams later recorded that during his time the people of Manuae and its twin island virtually annihilated one another by internal fighting.[9] Yet they were apparently exempt from external attack, whereas the people of Mauke and Mitiaro were massacred by the Atiuans. It seems that contact between Atiu and Manuae was in-frequent.

In the case of Aitutaki, Captain Bligh of the *Bounty*, the discoverer of the island, found that they knew the name of the pig there, but had none. Williams found the same.[10] Yet the pig was on Atiu. This is not conclusively against the view that Atiuans occasionally showed up in Aitutaki and got home again, or that Aitutakians did the same in Atiu.

Gill records that the Mangaians knew the name of the pig but had no quadruped but the rat.[11] Maretu, the Raro-tongan missionary, according to Gill, learnt the Mangaian dialect and traditions in order to be able to perform his ministry among them more adequately.[12] Mangaia is well over 100 miles from the other inhabited islands in its vicinity and not in a convenient situation for contact with them. The evidence which points to the isolation of Mangaia contrasts with the statement of the chief of Atiu to Williams that the Atiuans were in touch with Rarotonga. The meteorology would explain why the voyaging was on the Rarotonga-Atiu-Mauke axis across the trade winds.

Rimatara and Rurutu were conveniently placed for sail-ing across the prevailing wind in both directions. William Ellis states that Rimatarans were on Rurutu at the time of European contact, and got back to their own island about ninety miles away.[13] It is not entirely certain whether the visit to Rututu was deliberate.

Rurutu, Tubuai, and Raivivae are in line with the direc-tion of the prevailing wind. One might expect therefore to find that they were not in contact by deliberate voyaging. James Morrison, one of the *Bounty* mutineers, says of Tubuai in 1789: 'They have no sailing vessels and never leave the land except they are blown off as all the islands of which they have any account are at too great a distance for them to hold any intercourse.' Tubuai is situated between Rurutu and Raivivae at about 100 miles from each. Morrison's evidence shows that isolated islanders could have know-ledge of others and yet not visit them, and that vessels were blown away to continue the transfer of names and people to other islands. He tells of how the *Bounty*'s driver-yard, which had been lost at Tubuai, was found at Aitutaki, to which it had drifted.[14]

The extent of contact of that most interesting North Pacific island Ponape, and those in its vicinity, is somewhat in doubt. Ponape itself is a high island with peaks of over 2,000 feet, and would make a good landmark. The Ponape cluster consists of Ponape itself and two small atolls, all within twenty miles of one another. The atolls of Ngatik and Mokil are eighty to ninety miles from Ponape. The vessels of all these islands at the time of discovery showed degeneration from the sea-going praus of the other groups. The vessels of Mokil, which lies between Ponape and the Marshalls, showed in their outrigger attachments advanced Marshallese characteristics.[15] This appears to indicate that Mokil was either settled from the Marshalls instead of the nearer Caroline Islands, or that it was less subject to the influence of the latter than the former, which would be in accord with diffusion from the east by the prevailing winds. An account of a voyage in a small canoe from Mokil to Ponape exists.[16] Such voyages when the existence, direction, and local conditions of wind and current could be known from European voyages are not evidence of two-way contact in earlier times. The extent of the local voyaging in the Eastern Caroline area in pre-European times is not clear. It is however plain that neither the Ponapeans nor the islanders in their vicinity visited either the Western Carolines or the Marshalls. Cantova found in 1721 that his Western Caroline Islanders knew directly all their own islands as far east as Truk, but knew Ponape only from accidental voyagers,[17] while Chamisso stated a century later that the Western Caroline Islanders had knowledge of Ponape from accidental voyagers, but that the geography of the area between Truk and the Marshalls was virtually a closed book.[18] Oroluk, an uninhabited atoll, was the only landmark between Ponape and Truk, some 220 miles from each, and the atolls nearest to Ponape on the east were also far from the Marshalls. Whether the more practised navigators of the Western Carolines visited Ponape is a question which will merit some notice when their voyaging is discussed.

Here we may pause for a moment to consider an ancient mystery. Why did the Easter Islanders make the largest stone statues in the Pacific? Why did Ponape have some of the most celebrated stone ruins? Why did Raivivae have large stone statues too? The art of making them has been supposed by many writers to have been transferred from island to island from the Carolines or the Americas to Easter, and indeed from Asia and even Egypt itself. If so, why were they not on many intervening islands which had suitable stone and larger populations? And why should the biggest be on the most solitary islands? The correlation of larger works with small isolated islands becomes striking when the facts of limited off-shore voyaging and accidental settlements show that they were in fact isolated. Could it be because it was the very outcome of their being isolated, with no interruption from hostile neighbours and no opportunity to attack them, with plentiful time on their hands, and a suitable basaltic stone? Is there anything distinctive about the human form that the thought of imitating it in stone should not spring up independently in a thousand places, including a number of Pacific Islands? Supposing one were the priest-chief of an isolated island with no opportunity of further political or warlike outlets, no external interference, and plenty of willing labour right at hand, what could one organize to pass the next 1,000 years or so, and please the gods as well? Bigger and better statues and stoneworks was apparently the answer on many of the solitary islands. Practically all those with basaltic stone or suitable tuff had them – Easter, Raivivae, Tubuai, Pitcairn, Kusaie and Ponape.

Such a view does not preclude the possibility that there was some local diffusion of these arts by accidental contacts. This may have happened in the case of the extensive stone structures of Ponape and Kusaie, the stimulus for making which may have been diffused from Kusaie to Ponape or from Ponape to Kusaie. Repeated proofs that the islanders showed a remarkable capacity to pick up such information as came their way are found in every part of the Pacific. Amusing evidence of this was found by Lutke on Kusaie. He recorded that when the islanders saw the compass on his ship they shouted out what sounded like the French words 'sacré comment'. Lutke knew that Duperrey had visited Kusaie in 1824, three years previously, and guessed the islanders had picked up the phrase then, but he could make nothing of it. Adolphe Lesson, who sailed later with Dumont d'Urville, Duperrey's second-in-command on the visit to Kusaie, pointed out that this was undoubtedly derived from d'Urville's favourite oath when on the bridge, namely 'sacré gamin', meaning 'wretched fellow'.[19]

Coming up in the scale of voyaging in pre-European times, here and there among the scattered islands outside the main groups were a few minor contact areas. They were the central Gilbert string, Rotuma and the southern Ellice Islands, Atiu-Mauke-Mitiaro-Rarotonga in the Cooks, Fakaofo-Nukunonu-Atafu in the Tokelaus, and Manihiki-Rakahanga in the northern Cooks.

The off-shore element in the voyaging between most of these islands was not great, because the area between them where there were under clear sky conditions no visual indications of land on either side, was small. This applied to the low atolls as well as to the high islands, because in good visibility there were cloud formations over the atolls, and sea-birds in the vicinity. Comparatively short as these journeys were, they were prolific of accidental voyages, as the records of Manihiki-Rakahanga show.

The winds and the currents were the determining factors in early navigation. Nor did they necessarily work together in the same way. The thought that islands which were closer were because of that more accessible is erroneous. Take for instance west-east passages in the Gilberts. These offer ideal conditions for astral navigation, being almost on the equator where a constant overhead star-line can be followed. A sailing schooner once took forty-two days to pass between two islands thirty-five miles apart, another took twenty-three days for a passage of 270 miles, and still another, to come back from the more detached islands to the west of the main Gilbert Islands, eventually went up into the Carolines to do it. These difficulties occurred, not as the result of adverse winds, but in the season when the winds were fitful and the current became the master.[20] What then would have been the position of the imagined sea-rovers when they encountered such conditions in unknown seas?

Each course had thus to be tested separately, and on a seasonal basis. There can be little doubt that much of the local development came from involuntary accidental contacts, followed by purposive journeys.

Dillon found that the Rotumans were in contact with the Ellice Islands, making the trip in single canoes, which were frequently lost on the voyages.[21] These trips involved a gap without intervening islands of about 200 miles, and the relative positions were suitable to sailing in both directions across the trade wind. No doubt the Tongans, being in touch with Rotuma, occasionally went over the same course. When Hale visited the Ellice Islands in 1841, the islanders there described bananas as a product of Rotuma, thereby confirming Dillon's evidence of fourteen years previously that Rotuma was in contact with them. It is therefore all the more significant that Hale found no knowledge of the Gilberts in the Ellice Islands.[22]

Dillon found that the Tikopians, some 500 miles west of Rotuma, had a tradition of an attack by Tongans. Tubou, the paramount Tongan conqueror of Dillon's day, on the other hand, had never heard of Tikopia. The fact that no Tongan traditions of attacks on such distant lands were recorded tells against the conclusion that purposive expeditions made two-way voyages to deliver them. Nor are they necessarily reconstructions of an imaginary character, even though, as in Tikopia, the names of the islands to the east were known from accidental voyagers. The chief of Mafanga in Tonga told Dillon that his son had gone with three canoes to Rotuma to collect tribute some years previously, and had never been heard of since.[23] Lost Tongan marauders may well have raided the western islands. As Cook said, those who were 'never heard of more' in Tonga were no doubt heard of elsewhere on occasion.[24]

The voyages between Atiu and Rarotonga were among the longest that were accomplished outside the main archipelagoes. One gains the impression from the early evidence that it was the Atiuans who were the main voyagers. When Makea of Rarotonga went with Williams to Aitutaki he had not been to sea before, and when coming back he thought it miraculous that Williams could find Rarotonga again.[25] Yet the chief of Atiu had laid the course to Rarotonga for Williams, and told him in detail of his landmarks and procedure of leaving so as to pick up the stars as the landmarks faded from sight. This fits in with the fact that the Atiuans went to the nearer islands of Mauke and Mitiaro and thus had the incentive to keep up their maritime arts.[26] All over the Pacific it was the central islands in the natural groupings that were the main nurseries of those arts. But partial contact means that the cultures affect one another, and there can be no doubt that intermittent exchanges of visits between Rarotonga and Atiu took place, while the pigs had got to all the islands on the Rarotonga-Atiu-Mauke line. They formed a minor contact area with closely related cultures, and it is not surprising therefore to find that the other Cook Islands, as well as New Zealand, showed signs of affinities with them, since it was the contact areas throughout the Pacific that determined the main cultures and the sub-cultures within them. But all these islands were subject to the stream of accidental voyages that went on through the centuries from the eastern area in which the Tahitian contact area was the dominant one.

So much for the islands outside the main Pacific groups. No less eloquent of the true facts than the scattered inhabited islands are the scattered uninhabited ones. It is an interesting thought that had men and women come on either Palmyra, Washington, or Fanning and decided to stay, the European discoverers probably would have found thriving communities on all of them, through the accidental dispersal of people from one island to another. The same might well have occurred in the southern atolls of the Phoenix Group, as well as in the Kermadecs.

Of the main areas of contact, Hawaii offered no great scope for off-shore voyaging, being a compact group of high islands. The southern inhabited ones were all in constant touch, with frequent wars and inter-marriage, and a common culture.

Nihoa, a small uninhabited island 116 miles west of Hawaii proper, had relics of former human habitation which resemble Hawaiian ones. The island of Necker, 155 miles west of Nihoa, had also had earlier visitors, who had left many stoneworks there. The Necker works were strongly reminiscent of those in the central islands of Eastern Polynesia rather than of Hawaii.[27] These again are curious facts on any theory of deliberate visits, for Hawaiian dominance in both islands, if not continuing contact into historical times, might then be expected. In the light of accidental voyages the facts become understandable. Cook picked up some people in a canoe which had been driven off Hawaii in a storm,[28] and no doubt more than one had come in this way to Nihoa. Nor is there any reason why accidental settlers could not have come direct to Necker from Eastern Polynesia itself, as some did to Hawaii.

None of the other islands between the main Hawaiian group and the Marshalls far to the west had apparently been similarly occupied. Voyages of Hawaiian colonizing ancestors from this direction are hard to reconcile with these facts.

The Marquesas Islands form another comparatively compact group and the islands near one another were in frequent contact. Yet it was some time after the southern islands had been discovered and become known to the Europeans before the northern ones, including Nukuhiva, were discovered by accident in 1791. Forster had shown the name of Nukuhiva as a Marquesan island on his chart as early as 1778, although somewhat in the wrong location, and no one realized that this was a clue to the existence of the northern part of the group. The fact that the Tahitians thus had traditional knowledge of the name is again a symbol of the direction of the winds and of the accidental voyages that were caused by them. The fact that the knowledge of the Marquesas shown by Tupia's data was circumscribed, the only recognizable name, apart from those which were known to the Europeans directly, being Nukuhiva, makes it ironical that Forster's Marquesan names should later be quoted as evidence for Tahitian voyages to the Marquesas and thence to Hawaii.[29]

The Santa Cruz-New Hebrides area comes somewhere round this point in a survey of the ascending scale of voyaging in the natural island groupings of the world. Quiros's evidence shows that some of these Western Pacific islands were in contact.[30] R. H. Codrington, a missionary and scholar who lived and worked in this area in the latter part of the nineteenth century, has analysed Quiros's data.[31] Codrington considered that the local names which Quiros heard in the islands north of the New Hebrides did not extend farther south than Vanikoro, the 'Manicolo' of Quiros's information being this latter island, which is still well short of the New Hebrides. Dillon found in 1827 that the only island at a distance which the Tikopians visited was Vanikoro. Cordington says that eleven canoes from Tikopia visited the Banks Islands near the New Hebrides while he was living there, and Santa Cruz-Vanikoro-Tikopia-Anuta were in contact, over gaps of well over 100 miles. Professor Raymond Firth, who made a study of the Tikopian voyaging to Anuta, sixty miles away, in 1929 and 1952, found that the voyagers set their course by landmarks, waited for a favourable wind, sailed by night using horizon stars as guides, and were puzzled when the skies were overcast.[32]

On the other hand Codrington would not have it that the 'Pouro' which Quiros was told of was Bauro, the nearest point of the Solomons to Santa Cruz and the New Hebrides, the distance to Santa Cruz being 230 miles. He said that the pronunciations were entirely incompatible with this. In the same way he considered that the Belotu or Burotu of Fiji, Tonga, and Samoa could not be identified with Buru in the East Indies, as Fornander had suggested. Since Codrington was a first-hand authority on the Melanesian languages, his opinion is entitled to some respect. This gives point to the danger of guesses about the derivation of 'Little Java' (Hawaiki or Hawaii).

When Quiros visited the Santa Cruz Islands in 1595 with Mendana, the Spaniards were 230 miles east of the Solomons which Mendana had visited in 1568, although they did not know it. The Spaniards' knowledge of the Solomons dialect was useless in Santa Cruz. Yet Quiros decided they were near the Solomons because the people and customs were similar.[33]

Further evidence that the Solomons and the New Hebrides area were not in contact is given by Rennell, the Polynesian outlier. Its survival with a recognizable Polynesian character[34] despite its comparative nearness to the Solomons is evidence of the fact that the Solomon Islanders did not range far afield.

The Marshalls in the North Pacific were a contact area with interesting local features. Kotzebue was told by a Marshall Islands chief of how he passed between the nearest islands of the Ratak and Ralik chains which lie more or less parallel to one another. Likiep and Kwajalein are about 105 miles apart.[35] Undoubtedly other islands which were wider apart in these two chains were in direct contact. The two chains offered a wide screen to the voyagers on both legs. Furthermore, there are 867 reefs in the Marshall Islands, and reefs were as good as signposts to voyagers in shallow-draught craft. No wonder there were reports in later days of the study of the swing and variation of local currents and their recording on wooden frameworks with shells and strings.[36]

We now come to the three main contact areas, Fiji-Tonga-Samoa, Tahiti-Tuamotu, and the Western Carolines. Off-shore voyages of several hundred miles occurred in these archipelagoes. The Polynesians and Western Caroline

Islanders share the credit for man's greatest maritime achievement in oceanic areas before the days of instruments, if not indeed at any time. Every man who went out of sight of land in a small boat without instruments on an ocean without coast-lines on either side of him was a hero of the sea whose like may never be seen again.

It is striking that in Cook's list of islands known to the Tongans[37] the only Fijian islands which can be identified with comparative certainty are those which lie on the course between the main Tongan islands and Viti. The nearest islands to Tonga on the west are Tuvana-i-Tholo, Tuvana-i-Ra, and Ongea. Other islands on the way to Bau on the eastern side of Viti are Mothe, Wanggava, and Moala. The following identifications of these islands from Anderson's phonetic spellings will, it is hoped, stand up to examination, 'ko' or 'k' being merely introductory to a proper name in Tongan, the Tongan and Fijian 'l' and 'r' being virtually interchangeable, and the Fijian 'n' before a consonant being lightly pronounced: Tuvana-i-Tholo (Toofanaetollo), Tuvana-i-Ra (Toofanaelaa), Ongea Driti (Kongaireekee), Mothe (Komotte), Wanggava (Wegaffa), Moala (Komoara), Bau (Kopaoo), Viti (Feejee).

It is obvious from Mariner's accounts of Tui Hala Fatai's and Cow Mooaly's trips[38] that a visit to Viti was a very hazardous and long-drawn-out adventure. Getting there with the trade wind would be reasonably simple. Coming home with the undependable westerlies would be the hard part. It was no doubt these factors which held up the expansion of the later Fijians in numbers into the Tongan areas, and allowed the cultures to develop in different ways. The key to the Pacific Islands cultural affinities everywhere is the meteorology.

While the Tongan voyages to Rotuma were among the longest undertaken deliberately by the Polynesians, and also the most hazardous because of the smallness of the target, the conditions permitted of a round course. Cow Mooaly went from Futuna to Rotuma with the prevailing wind, but came from Rotuma to Fiji. Dillon found[39] that some

Rotuman canoes in going to Tonga also went through Fiji, or rather tried to, for they had left Rotuma five months before, and yet had not shown up in Tonga when Dillon left it a few days before hearing of their departure at Rotuma. The voyages between Tonga and Rotuma were rarely undertaken, for Dillon tells of how the Tongans whom he took to Rotuma with him were unwilling to stay there, as it might have been years before they got back to Tonga. Dillon also took with him to Rotuma some Rotumans who had been taken to Samoa in westerlies, where they arrived after a long period of privation. The fact that the son of the chief of Mafanga in Tonga had disappeared with three canoes three years previously while on the way to Rotuma, and that Rotumans had been distributed to Samoa, Fiji, and Tikopia by similar misadventures makes it obvious that it is only in a qualified sense that these voyages can be quoted as instances of successful maritime achievement. In the face of the proved hazards of the voyages in the Rotuma area, the Polynesian ancestors who have been imagined as following guiding stars to unknown islands a thousand or more miles away are shown to be somewhat more than human.

On the trips between Tonga and Samoa, running with the south-east trade wind on the beam both ways gave good sailing, as Pritchard recorded.[40] The intervening knot of islands of which Niuatobutabu, 150 miles from the outlying islands of the Vavau cluster, is the chief, would give a stopover and landmarks. From there to Savaii is another 140 miles. The high mountains of Samoa are visible at seventy miles in good conditions. One may be sure, however, that on many occasions the wind would not permit coming past Niuatobutabu, and that a direct off-shore run of 360 miles in all from Vavau to Samoa, or from Samoa to the Tongan islands, was frequently made. Only when running to a screen of islands was such a voyage possible without instruments. The more one studies the Pacific voyaging, the more obvious it becomes that every course which, considering the geography and meteorology, was practicable, was in fact accomplished.

Of the many anomalies that are associated with the notion of deliberate settlement of the farther Pacific Islands, its relationship to the Fijian voyaging is among the most difficult to explain. The Fijians belonged to the black races who were regarded as comparatively unambitious voyagers. Yet they had got across the 500-mile gap which separated their islands from the New Hebrides. Since they were regarded as being of an earlier race round whom the Polynesians must have come, it would seem strange that, if they had come to their own islands by design, they should not have gone a bit farther and established themselves in Western Polynesia, including the island of Rotuma, which is comparatively near Fiji to the north. The Fijians remained mostly within their own islands. Dillon said that 'no native of Feejee, so far as is known, ever ventured to Tonga, but in a canoe manned by Tonga people; nor ever ventured back to his own island but under the same guidance and protection'.[41] Within their islands, however, they were expert sailors and boat-builders.[42] The theory of deliberate long voyages and colonization would be hard put to it to explain all these facts. When examined in the light of Pacific-wide short deliberate voyaging, with adaptation to local conditions, they become capable of simple explanations. The Polynesians did not in fact go a great deal farther than the Fijians, and where they did, it was because the meteorology and geography happened to favour two-way contact. The Polynesians did not show any more or less ingenuity than the Fijians in getting to the central belt in the first place, because they both came by accidental voyages. Nor did they out-do the Fijians in getting to distant islands, because the peopling of them arose from the fact that the islands were in positions to which the winds and currents bore the Polynesians without design.

The character of the winds in relation to the geography is again the key to the understanding of the voyages in the Tahiti-Tuamotu area. On the journeys where the only course was on an east-west line, the navigators went with the trade winds, and came back in the season when westerlies blew. The Tahitians told Anderson that they did this in going to Tahiti from Raiatea, as Pritchard said the Tongans did in returning from Fiji.[43] Like winds were used in the trips from Anaa to Tahiti and back, and Tuwarri told Beechey that on his ill-starred journey to Tahiti they misjudged the seasonal winds and were driven back by two successive westerlies. But in the trips between Tahiti and the Tuamotus the most convenient course was to the Tuamotuan islands to the north-east, which were suitably placed for sailing across the prevailing trade wind.[44] These islands make a screen which offered a good target to the navigators, as did the Tahitian islands themselves on the other leg.

The only really satisfactory courses were those across the trade winds in both directions. Thus Pritchard, speaking of the voyages between Tonga and Samoa which were still being made when he was living in Western Polynesia in the middle of the nineteenth century, said that 'the relative positions of the groups generally favoured with a fair wind the voyages either way'.[45] The same conditions applied in the case of the journeys between Atiu and Rarotonga, and Rotuma and the Ellice Islands. If trips were made between Rimatara and Rurutu, the same type of sailing would apply there also, which supports the view that such voyages were made on occasion.

The Pacific Islands vessels, particularly the double canoes, sailed best with the wind on the beam or the quarter. It might therefore be expected that experienced voyagers who were lost at sea would sail across the wind rather than abandon themselves to the drift of the wind and the set of the current. To call the incidents 'drift voyages' is therefore an inadequate description. The distinction is far from academic. The presumption that many voyagers would sail across the wind, which was ordinarily from the east or west, would mean that they would tend to run out of the central areas. This would be particularly significant in the case of the peopling of the peripheral groups and islands.

We come now to the Western Caroline Islanders, who

matched the achievement of the Fijians and the Polynesians, and for the same reason, namely that they lived in an archipelago in which blew reasonably predictable winds.

Cantova was told by the accidental voyagers whom he met in Guam in 1721 that sweet potatoes were introduced into the Carolines by a party of accidental voyagers who were blown from Yap to the Philippines and in due course got back again to the Carolines.[46] The missionaries in the Philippines had given them the sweet potatoes and some iron. This is less than evidence of pre-European two-way contact, much less of deliberate original colonization. The missionaries at that time knew the broad location of the westernmost islands of the Carolines and could direct the returning voyagers. As we have seen, Zuniga, a later missionary in the Philippines, could not believe that the Carolines had been peopled from the Philippines, and recorded that European ships were often driven back, or failed to find the islands they were seeking, even with instrumental navigation. On the other hand the Carolines were accidentally discovered by a Portuguese ship which in 1526 was blown north of the Moluccas. Some of the westernmost Caroline Islands had dark fuzzy strains in the population which were reminiscent of Papuans to some of the early visitors. These are pointers to the possibility of accidental settlement of the Carolines from the Moluccas-New Guinea area.

Whether or not the Carolines and Marianas, which form screens of islands some 300 miles apart at their nearest points, were in contact in pre-European times, may be an open question. The accidental voyagers who were borne to Guam from the Carolines in 1721, comprising people from many Western Caroline Islands, showed little sign of knowing the Marianas. The Marianas vessels, like those of the Palaus in the extreme west of the Carolines, lacked some of the more advanced features of the central Caroline vessels,[47] creating the impression that they retained a more conservative type of vessel in their fringe areas, which was not modified by frequent contacts. No note of deliberate contacts can be found in the earlier records, although de Freycinet gathered accounts of accidental voyages from various parts of the Carolines to the Marianas in the two centuries before the early nineteenth.[48] The first recorded journey from the Carolines to the Marianas which has any suggestion of intent about it was in 1788, when some Caroline Islanders, led by a chief named Luito, appeared in the Marianas. The circumstances are in doubt, because the European visitors who heard about it from the Spaniards in the Marianas thirty years later differ markedly. According to Kotzebue and de Freycinet, there were two expeditions by Luito, all the canoes on the second visit being lost while returning to the Carolines.[49] Both Kotzebue's and de Freycinet's accounts agree in saying that Luito and his companions set off with intent to find islands known from tradition. Kotzebue states that these traditions were derived from deliberate contacts in pre-European times. Since, however, Cantova and others from the Marianas had lived among the Western Caroline Islanders in the previous generation,[50] the source of the traditions need go no farther back than that. Arago, one of de Freycinet's company, says that contact was supposed to have been established as the result of an accidental voyage, the time being not very remote.[51]

Another possible field of doubt in the range of the Micronesian voyaging arises over the question of whether the Western Caroline Islanders on occasion went to the Ponape area on two-way visits. In late historical times a number of German ethnologists made field studies of the Micronesian cultures including the voyaging, and collected the evidence of previous residents and observers.[52] This evidence is a mixture of firm statements of actual voyages, traditional stories of long voyages in former times, and reconstructions from indirect information, including knowledge of the names of distant islands by various islanders. The error of thinking that knowledge of such names was evidence that the islanders had been there was exposed by Anderson in 1777.[53] By the same token the incorporation of such traditional names in the folklore was inevitable in Micronesia as it was everywhere else. Kotzebue and de Freycinet give accounts of no fewer than twelve accidental voyages over the farther gaps in Micronesia, and the evidence of the later Europeans shows that these continued perennially. The more objective later ethnologists jibbed at the more extravagant of the reconstructions of their predecessors. On the other hand they showed a consensus in accepting that the Western Caroline Islanders were in touch with the Ponape area in historical times. This contrasts with Cantova's and Chamisso's evidence, including the information of the Spanish official who in 1804 visited the Carolines and instituted trading visits by the Caroline pilots to Guam, and who dealt with these pilots till 1817. This evidence shows a distinction between the islands known to the Western Caroline Islanders from accidental contacts, including Ponape, the Marshalls and the Philippines, and the islands known from deliberate visits, including the Western Caroline Islands as far east as the Truk area.[54] Nevertheless, this earlier evidence is not conclusively against the thought that on occasion the Western Caroline Islanders visited the Eastern Caroline area both in early times and late, for the gaps of 220 miles were within the proved range of their voyaging. Questions of whether the Western Caroline Islanders visited the Marianas and the Ponape area in pre-European times are all that the sphere of reasonable doubt within the recorded evidence of Pacific voyaging comes down to.

On the voyages within the Western Caroline archipelago there is much evidence from the European explorers. All the islands can be reached without covering gaps of more than 170 miles. Some of the direct passages which were negotiated involved gaps of up to 360 miles.[55] The use of single praus with outriggers, which were economical to produce and adequate for the Caroline sailing season when the winds were steady, enabled the use of large numbers of sea-going praus in the strikes across the larger gaps. Thus in Kotzebue's day, when the Caroline trading fleet was going up to Guam, the use of eighteen canoes was common.[56] The fact that the political organization was well-developed, with suzerains over quite considerable numbers of islands, as Cantova's evidence shows was the case as early as 1721,[57] enabled intensive development of trade without the constant derangement of hostile attack. The central islands of the archipelago were the cradle of the Caroline maritime enterprise, no doubt because they were near to one another, and the screens of islands round them gave them defence in depth in their passages.

The Micronesian prau reached its most advanced form in the Western Caroline Islands and in the Marshalls. The Marshalls prau was identical in all main respects with the Caroline vessel, although with further distinctive developments in the outrigger attachments. The Gilbertese and Marianas praus were of the same general Micronesian type, although lacking some features of the more advanced vessels of the Caroline area. The vessels in Ponape and the other Eastern Caroline islands showed degenerate forms of the same basic Micronesian designs.[58]

The prau was the product of a series of remarkable adaptations to sailing by a prevailing wind. The outrigger was always to windward. The triangular lateen sail was therefore made fast to either prow of the vessel according to direction, the rake of the mast being altered accordingly by being slewed round in a socket. The change could be done in less than a minute on the open sea. The sheer flat lee side of the hull resisted the turning movement of the vessel round the outrigger by tending to dig into the water instead of sliding over it. The jutting lee platform acted as a counterpoise to the outrigger and to the similar platform above the outrigger, the thatched cabins on both platforms being for cover and cargo. Some of these craft were 25 to 40 feet long, the hull being made of many pieces of timber bound together with fibre. The art was to hold the sail against the wind so that the outrigger was as far as possible just clear of or skimming the water. When sailing close-hauled, several men went out on the windward platform to trim the vessel. The sail area was reduced in sudden squalls by pulling a line.

According to Kotzebue's and de Freycinet's information, the seasonal south-west monsoon was feared by the Caroline voyagers. They preferred to sail by the steady trade wind from the north-east. The praus were liable to be overset, and both Kotzebue and de Freycinet give pictures of the trouble the crews had in righting them.[59] Like all the Pacific vessels, they did poorly into the wind, being subject to heavy stress for craft composed of pieces of timber bound with fibre. Yet they could come into the wind when necessary. The Caroline praus, as de Freycinet said, were suited to the fact that in the Micronesian areas the winds in the main sailing season were not unduly violent. The ideal development would no doubt have been to have used according to circumstances both double canoes and single outriggers.

No one archipelago in the Pacific combined the best features of the vessels which were developed in all of them. The Western Caroline and Marshalls prau was the finest single canoe with outrigger, while the Fijians had the best double canoe as well as good single canoes with outriggers. Andia's evidence makes it plain that the Tahitians, on their journeys between the nearer islands, used single canoes with outriggers which were highly efficient,[60] but employed double canoes for the longer journeys. The Tongans were among the foremost of the Pacific voyagers, and yet went to Fiji for their best vessels. The superiority of the Fijian canoes may be attributed as much to their better timber as any other cause.

How fast could the Pacific Islands sea-going vessels sail, and how long did they take on their longer journeys? Chamisso considered that the statements of the Micronesian voyagers on the time of their journeys were so much at variance that they had to be treated with reserve.[61] Yet the Pacific-wide evidence shows a broad pattern which is remarkably uniform when interpreted in terms of the local meteorology. Autourou told de Bougainville that the longer journeys of the Tahitians took fifteen days,[62] and Tupia told Cook he had made a voyage to the west taking ten days to get there and thirty days to get back.[63] These statements are understandable where changing winds were relied on for east-west and west-east passages. The evidence of Morrison, the *Bounty* mutineer, shows that the same sort of thing could apply even on the trips between Tahiti and the Tuamotus, for he tells in his journal of how the Tahitians came down to Maitia with a north wind and waited for the wind to change in order to run on the north-east leg to the Tuamotus[64] – a course giving the best margin of safety against set and drift. The Tongans told Cook they took three days to go to Fiji and two days to Samoa,[65] which accords with Cook's test of a double canoe in a 'gentle gale' at seven knots.[66] Vason, who lived with the Tongans some time later, went with some Tongan voyagers over the sixty or seventy miles from the Haabai Group to Tongatabu, at a speed of six or seven knots, leaving at daybreak and arriving in the evening. The Spaniards in Guam told Kotzebue that the Caroline trading vessels covered the 360 miles from West Fayu to Guam in three days,[68] averaging about five knots. The conclusion may be reached that if the wind held the longer off-shore voyages were accomplished in two or three days.

Studies of the methods of the Micronesian voyagers in historical times show clearly the character and achievement of the navigation. The Caroline and Marshall Islanders had built up a precise knowledge of the currents, landmarks, meteorology and star courses on every journey to every island within their contact areas, and handed on the knowledge by instruction to the younger pilots.[69] The pilots were a favoured class. It is plain that such data could not have been known in advance of the time of first discovery, and that they were built up over a period of time after settlement. The knowledge had to be sustained by continued voyaging and instruction, because a general theory and practice, such as is given by plotting courses by latitude and longitude, was not available. Had the maritime arts not been sustained, the bottom would have dropped out of the off-shore voyaging, as it did on the isolated islands.

Unknown set and drift were the fundamental limiting factors on precise navigation before courses could be plotted on the principle of intersecting lines of latitude and longitude. On the open sea the set of an unknown current means that the whole body of water round the vessel is being displaced with the vessel in a manner unknown to the navigator. If the vessel happens to be going with the current, the navigator will under-estimate the distance traversed, while if he is going against it he will over-state it. When going diagonally across it, the vessel will be displaced with the current even though the alignment of the vessel is in the desired direction throughout, so that the actual course will differ radically from what the navigator thinks it is. All the same effects will be produced by unknown drift or lee-way as the result of under-estimating the strength or constancy of the wind. In storms or bad visibility these effects become magnified at a time when such guidance as can be obtained from the heavenly bodies is lost, and when resistance to the wind without auxiliary power may become increasingly difficult. On the other hand, even though the weather may be clear, if a vessel comes under the influence of an unknown cross-current in a calm, and is carried to leeward of its course, it will be under the necessity of making back into the wind if and when it rises, and if and when the fact that the vessel is to leeward of its destination is known. These effects applied to the voyages of the early Spaniards in the Pacific, despite the fact that they could judge lines of latitude by quadrants with reasonable accuracy provided the Pole Star or the sun was visible, and could keep on an approximate course with compasses in bad visibility. What they lacked was a way of determining longitude with any accuracy. Nobody knows for certain today what islands they discovered in the North Pacific.[70] The fact that these uncertainties could exist, despite the possession of quadrants, compasses and large sailing ships by the European explorers, is a sufficient commentary in itself on the hypothesis of deliberate navigation over long distances by primitive voyagers who did not have these aids. The reconstructionists who have been committing flotillas of Maori and Hawaiian and Gilbertese colonists, complete with wives and families, to the unknown cross-currents and winds of the vast Pacific expanses for the past eighty years have been guilty of a reckless sacrifice of human lives.

Some light on the difficulties of deliberate discovery of islands and the maintenance of contact with them in the days before instruments may be derived from the perplexity of Captain Hudson of the United States Exploring Expedition's ship *Peacock* in 1840. He located Washington Island in the mid-Pacific and then looked for the other islands which had been reported in the vicinity. After a week's search, during which Palmyra, Fanning, and Christmas evaded him, Hudson concluded that no other island but Washington was to be found. On another occasion Captain Wilkes, the commander of the Expedition, left Hull Island in the Phoenix Group to look for Sydney Island, about sixty miles to the east. After a day land was discovered to the north-west. It was Hull Island.[71]

Nor can the notion of deliberate settlement across the longer gaps be salvaged by supposing that accidental voyagers might have crossed them in the first place and followed this up with deliberate settlement, although this no doubt happened occasionally within the contact areas. The supposition that it might have applied between the contact areas which were so obviously the product of a long period of testing and local knowledge pre-supposes deliberate navigation at a time when the courses and geography were little known. If that had happened by intent in earlier times, then these areas would have merged in a common contact area as the knowledge of the courses and local conditions between the contact areas improved. Neither Micronesia nor Fiji nor Polynesia nor Madagascar was settled by early miracles of deliberate navigation which no less miraculously stopped short in later times with complete unanimity from one end of the Pacific to the other, and which never occurred at all in the case of the rest of the world's islands.

The actual voyaging of the Pacific Islanders was spectacular enough in itself. The notion that fleets of brown-skinned colonists pushed into and through these islands in the first place, impelled by a mysterious urge, is purely mythical, is belied by the evidence, and flies in the face of the well-known facts of the evolution of human cultures everywhere, and the retention of those arts which were to the advantage of the community, as long voyaging would have been both for trade and political dominion.

Is there any other area in the world beside the Pacific where comparatively isolated islands might have gone through a process of accidental settlement followed up by the building of an area of deliberate contact? No reference has so far been made to the Vikings, except for an oblique sneer at Leif Ericcson, or rather those that think that the simple folk-tales of the Norse must be made to reflect history. Those who believe, solely on the evidence of four Scandinavian sagas[72] which were written several centuries after the events they relate, which are full of typical folklore including fairylike beings in far lands, and the later of which were obviously derived from the earlier, that Bjarni, Leif Ericcson, and others went to America and back, are entitled to believe it if they can. Others may prefer to think that Vinland, the Land of Perpetual Summer, was put by a kind of nostalgia by the story-tellers in the western ocean because there was nowhere else to put it, like the Islands of the Blest of the ancients, and the Avalon and St Brendan's Island of the Celts. The fervent belief of Icelandic and Norwegian patriots, aided and abetted by their kin in America and Angle-land [sic] who bathe in the reflected glory, that America was an early Nordic stamping ground, obviously deprives the Celts of the right of prior discovery. The Celts may no less fervently claim that Avalon was America and St Brendan's Island Long Island, if not indeed Manhattan. The only thing either theory lacks is evidence. The tales of early Viking visits to America have been supposed to have been supported by similar tales from Polynesia and vice versa, but they are broken reeds. The fact that the ice was probably farther north in earlier times[73] cannot alone sustain the Nordic voyagers on their probes into the western ocean, for there was no ice in Polynesia, nor between

Portugal and Madeira. Some evidence is required before America and Scandinavia must necessarily be regarded as an early area of deliberate voyaging.

Coming a little nearer the home of the Norse, as of the Celts, we find it claimed, again on the evidence of sagas written long after the event, that Iceland was discovered and settled by Nordic voyagers in or about the ninth century, and that the discovery and settlement of Greenland from Iceland was achieved in somewhat similar fashion a short time thereafter, the discoveries not necessarily being by deliberate exploration.

That Scandinavian settlements existed on the south coast of Greenland is proved by the archaeological evidence of burials and ruins there.[74] If the ice was in fact farther north until somewhere round the fourteenth century – and there seems to be an impressive amount of scientific testimony to it – then one would think it likely that the settlement of Greenland occurred in a warmer phase and ended with the colder. There is no difficulty about the belief that the colonization of Greenland was by deliberate settlement following accidental discovery from Iceland, for the distance separating the two islands is under 200 miles at the nearest point.

Coming to Iceland, one finds more rather than less difficulty about the evidence. The people of Iceland are of mixed Scandinavian and Celtic origin. The Scandinavians were the predominant people and wrote the sagas and poetic histories. The Icelandic saga of the coming of the Norse says that Irishmen were there before them. Now there has been some suggestion to the effect that the Scandinavians discovered Iceland by deliberate exploration. How then did the Celts get there? Heaven forbid that it should be concluded that the Irish got there by accident, while the Scandinavians showed greater ingenuity and deliberately found the island by exploration. One might also wonder that the Scots should have stood idly by while the Scandinavians performed these feats, since in later times the Scots are reported to have discovered lands to the south of them under the influence of economic incentive.

It is a matter of history that the Scandinavians were coming across the North Sea to the north of Scotland and Ireland somewhere round the eighth century. It is also a matter of history that the Celts were there before them. Island areas such as those of northern Ireland and the north of Scotland invariably lead to the development of local cruising and so of accidental voyages. There are good grounds for believing that both the Celts and the Scandinavians came upon Iceland in the first place by accident, that the Celts were there first because they were first established in the nearer islands, and that any distinction between the Celts and the Norse in all these islands has been meaningless for at least 500 years owing to merging.

The ghosts of 200,000 ancient voyagers who sank beneath the waves in the dispersal of mankind to the world's farther islands cannot speak. Nor did any of those who survived write books about their migrations. Some of their descendants, however, spoke with a crisper eloquence. Let the last word remain with Cantova's friends from Faraulep; Tupia; Puhoro; the Tongans, Fijians, and Tahitians that Cook, Andia, and Anderson met; the much-travelled Kau Moala who had been to Rotuma; Kadu[75] who spent many months trying to find his home; Luito who sailed to death via the Marianas; Tuwarri the Tuamotuan exile; and the chiefs of Atiu who sailed for Rarotonga with no islands beyond until New Zealand. These are the true authorities on Pacific voyaging who proved in practice what could be done and what could not.

# Sources

*The publications and manuscripts referred to herein are listed in the
Bibliography which follows, and are identified by the name of the author,
together with the date of publication where more than one work by the same
author is listed.*

## CHAPTER ONE *(pages 11–31)*

1. For Cook's and Anderson's
   evidence from the third voyage, Cook, 1784, vol. 1, pp.
   167–224, vol. 2, pp. 1–178.
   (The italics in quoted passages are not in the original
   texts.)
2. Carrington, p. 59; de Brosses,
   vol. 2, pp. 443–5.
3. Cook, 1784, vol. 1, pp. 367–
   79.
4. Martin, vol. 1, p. 323; Dillon,
   vol. 1, p. 295, vol. 2, pp. 103,
   78–79, vol. 1, p. 294; Wilkes,
   vol. 5, p. 43; Hale, pp. 153–
   67.
5. Cook, 1784, vol. 2, pp. 175–8,
   142–3.
6. For Cook's evidence from
   Tupia and other Tahitians in
   1769, Cook, 1893, pp. 119–21,
   229–30.
7. Forster, pp. 511–25.
8. For Tiaio and Ahuahu, Gill,
   1876B, pp. 29, 16.
9. Banks's Journal (unabridged
   manuscript) under date 13

   Aug. 1769; Ellis, W., 1831,
   vol. 3, 393.
10. For review and endorsement
    of reconstructions of Tahitian
    voyages, Lesson, A., vol. 4,
    pp. 6–32.
11. Hale, pp. 122–3; Lesson, A.,
    vol. 4, pp. 16–17.
12. Williams, J., pp. 197–8.
13. Williams, J., p. 468.
14. Gill, 1915, p. 145.
15. Williams, J., pp. 38–40.
16. Wilson, J., p. xliv; Ellis, W.,
    1831, vol. 3, pp. 381–4.
17. Gill, 1876A, p. 22.
18. Corney, vol. 2, pp. 284–7, vol.
    1, p. 354; Morrison, pp.
    200–1.
19. Corney, vol. 2, p. 300.
20. Corney, vol. 2, pp. 309–13.
21. Turner, 1861, p. 270.
22. De Bougainville, pp. 278–80.
23. De Bougainville, pp. 268–9.
24. Ellis, W., 1831, vol. 3, p. 375.
25. Fornander; Smith.
26. See Chapter Three.

## CHAPTER TWO *(pages 32–56)*

1. Cook, 1784, vol. 1, p. 376.
2. De Brosses, vol. 1, pp. 102–4.
3. For discoveries of Atlantic and
   Indian Ocean islands, *Encyclo-
   paedia Britannica* or other standard works of reference.

4. Hornell, 1936, pp. 265–73,
   126–43, 79–92.
5. Williams, J., p. 507.
6. Statements of Pacific meteorology and currents in this
   book are based on information

in United Kingdom Admiralty, 1931–46.

7. Burney, vol. 1, pp. 269–71.
8. Makemson, pp. 45–7, 14.
9. Gatty, pp. 68–9, 71, 85.
10. Cook, 1784, vol. 2, pp. 142–3; Ellis, W., 1827, p. 442; Williams, J., p. 507; Pritchard, p. 403.
11. Corney, vol. 2, pp. 284–7.
12. For simplified statement of basic navigational astronomy, United Kingdom Admiralty, 1952, pp. 710–5.
13. Kotzebue, vol. 3, p. 194; de Freycinet, vol. 2, pp. 102–5.
14. De Freycinet, vol. 2, pp. 102–3.
15. Forster, pp. 510–1.
16. Williams, J., pp. 96–7.
17. Beechey, vol. 1, p. 169.
18. United Kingdom Admiralty, 1952, p. 713 and Fig. 409.
19. United Kingdom Admiralty, 1952, p. 634.
20. United Kingdom Admiralty, 1952, p. 715.

21. Buck, 1949, p. 49.
22. For suggestions concerning search, Smith, 1910, p. 188.
23. Williams, J., p. 76.
24. Gill, 1915, pp. 144–5.
25. De Freycinet, vol. 2, pp. 81–2.
26. For numerous accounts of such partings, Burney.
27. De Freycinet, vol. 2, p. 132.
28. Burney, vol. 1, pp. 232–3, 151–8.
29. Martin, vol. 2, pp. 48–50.
30. Ellis, W., vol. 1, pp. 164–5.
31. Rodman, pp. 82–5.
32. Stokes.
33. De Bovis, p. 19; Polynesian Society. For discussion of sunken land theories, Lesson, A., vol. 1, pp. 386–428.
34. White, T.; Smith, 1907.
35. Kotzebue, vol. 3, p. 98.
36. Martin, vol. 1, pp. 73–6, 317–47.
37. Dillon, vol. 2, pp. 102–3, 111, 133, vol. 1, p. 295.

## CHAPTER THREE (*pages 57–78*)

1. Arbitrary figure based on scaling down of estimates of early visitors to Polynesian groups.
2. Prout, p. 13; Williams, J., pp. 143–51, 76.
3. Turner, 1861, p. 490.
4. For Williams's notes on Manihiki-Rakahanga, Williams, J., pp. 466–8.
5. Gill, 1915, p. 145.
6. Williams, J., pp. 410–1.
7. Williams, J., pp. 506–7.
8. For discussion of provisioning factor, Buck, 1938A, p. 61.
9. Williams, J., pp. 38–40.
10. Williams, J., p. 507.

11. Dillon, vol. 1, pp. 271–3.
12. Ellis, W., 1831, vol. 3, p. 374; Moerenhout, vol. 2, pp. 331–2.
13. Ellis, W., 1827, p. 442, 1831, vol. 1, pp. 125–7.
14. Williams, J., pp. 504–7.
15. Dibble, pp. 16–17.
16. Turner, 1861, pp. 359–60.
17. Turner, 1861, pp. 391–2.
18. Beechey, vol. 1, pp. 168–72.
19. Lang, pp. vii, 4–8.
20. Gill, 1876A.
21. For Gill's accounts of accidental voyages, Gill, 1876A, p. 22.
22. Pritchard, preface.

23. Pritchard, pp. 402–3.
24. For tropical cyclones in Pacific, Visher.
25. Lang, pp. 9–10.
26. For Gilbertese incidents: Sabatier, pp. 25–6; Ellis, A., pp. 145–9.
27. Maude, p. 81.
28. For fuller discussion, see Chapter Six.
29. Lang, p. 14.
30. Porter, vol. 2, pp. 54–5.
31. Lucett, vol. 1, pp. 177–8.
32. Turner, 1884, p. 275.
33. Burrows, pp. 48–9.
34. Firth, 1939, pp. 42, 48.
35. Elbert. For modern linguistic techniques using basic vocabulary comparisons: Swadesh; Greenberg.
36. Williams, J., p. 192.
37. Cook, 1893, pp. 190–1.
38. New Zealand Press Association report, 9 Sept. 1953.
39. Hale, p. 148.
40. Shortland, 1856, p. 27.
41. Makemson, p. 7.
42. Malo, p. 24.
43. Porter, vol. 2, pp. 54–5, 135–6.
44. For Ellis's accounts of voyages, Ellis, W., 1831, vol. 3, pp. 390, 393, 396–7, 400, 371, 376, vol. 1, p. 170, 1827, p. 442.

## CHAPTER FOUR (*pages 79–100*)

1. For early European voyages in Pacific, Burney, vol. 1.
2. De Brosses, vol. 2, pp. 443–6.
3. Cantova, pp. 188–220.
4. Zuniga, vol. 1, p. 33.
5. Kotzebue, vol. 2, pp. 144–6, end-chart, vol. 3, pp. 118–9, 177–80, end-charts.
6. Nevermann, p. 217.
7. Wilkes, vol. 5, pp. 43, 37–108; Hale, pp. 90–1, 161–6.
8. Wilkes, vol. 5, pp. 37–108; Hale, pp. 69–103.
9. Wilkes, vol. 5, p. 43; Hale, pp. 161–7.
10. Kotzebue, vol. 2, pp. 122–3.
11. De Freycinet, vol. 2, pp. 81, 84, 86, 87.
12. Kotzebue, vol. 3, pp. 126–7.
13. Kotzebue, vol. 3, p. 98.
14. Kotzebue, vol. 3, pp. 114–5; Hornell, 1936, pp. 374–5.
15. Dumont d'Urville, vol. 1, pp. viii–ix.
16. Hornell, 1936, p. 28; Spoehr, p. 460.
17. Dibble, p. 17.
18. Heyerdahl, 1950.
19. Hornell, 1945, p. 183.
20. For differing views on American and Polynesian cultural relationships: Lang; Lesson, A., vol. 1, pp. 448–516; Dixon, 1933; Heyerdahl, 1952; Heine-Geldern.
21. For review of early forms of American theory, Lesson A., vol. 1, pp. 429–48.
22. Lang, p. 98 *et seq.*
23. Dixon, 1932; Heine-Geldern, pp. 343–55.
24. Seemann, p. 319; de Candolle, pp. 24, 56.
25. Porter, vol. 2, p. 53.
26. Hillebrand, p. 314; Buck, 1938A, p. 309.
27. For Polynesian accidental voyages, see Chapter Three.
28. Kotzebue, vol. 2, pp. 411–32; Hale, pp. 362–4, 474–8, 445–68, 427–34; Lesson, A., vol. 1, pp. iv–v, 308, 311–14, 375–6;

Turner, 1861, facing page 536; Elbert.

29. Elbert.
30. Best, p. 24.
31. For suggestion of Micronesian route, Buck, 1938A, pp. 41–5, 58–63; for statement that it is generally accepted view, Skinner, pp. 42–3.
32. Markham, vol. 1, pp. 51, 142–3, 227.
33. Anderson, pp. 130, 149.
34. For Gill's evidence in this and following paragraph, Gill, 1876A, pp. 242, 249–50, 260–70, 22–6. Cf. Powell.
35. Buck, 1938A, pp. 48–9.
36. Lesson and Garnot, p. 72.
37. Buck, 1938A, pp. 47–8.
38. Cook, 1784, vol. 1, p. 374.

39. Brown, G., p. 436.
40. Buck, 1938A, p. 48.
41. For borrowing by Tongans of bow for war from Fijians, Martin, vol. 1, pp. 72–3.
42. Brown, J. M., pp. 246–8.
43. Buck, 1938A, pp. 46–7.
44. Cf. Boyd.
45. Cook, 1784, vol. 1, pp. 225–421; Williams, J., pp. 478–500.
46. Piddington, pp. 336–41.
47. Graydon, pp. 332–6. Cf. Boyd, pp. 227, 278.
48. Kotzebue, vol. 2, pp. 411–32; Südsee-Expedition.
49. Burney, vol. 1, pp. 89–90, 101, 109–10.
50. Spoehr, p. 460; Emory, 1953.

## CHAPTER FIVE (*pages 101–127*)

1. Cantova, pp. 222–7; de Brosses, vol. 2, p. 452.
2. Kotzebue, vol. 3, pp. 118–9, 177–80.
3. Codrington, p. 11.
4. Wilkes, vol. 5, pp. 37–108, Hale, pp. 90–1.
5. Pritchard, p. 403; Gill, 1876A, pp. 25–6.
6. Buck, 1938A, pp. 59, 63, 284, 303.
7. Buck, 1938A, pp. 286–7.
8. Wilkes, vol. 5, p. 45.
9. Fornander, vol. 1, preface, pp. 1–26.
10. Fornander, vol. 1, p. 19.
11. Markham, vol. 2, p. 497.
12. Hawkesworth, vol. 3, pp. 473–4.
13. Forster, p. 524.
14. Hale, pp. 122–3; Gill, 1876A, pp. 23, 25, 167.
15. Henry, pp. 399–400.

16. Williams, J., pp. 192, 359.
17. Williams, J., pp. 193–5.
18. Williams, J., pp. 196, 509.
19. Gill, 1876A, p. 23.
20. Williams, J., pp. 408, 424.
21. Stair, pp. 72–3.
22. Gill, 1876B, pp. 16–7, 1876A, p. 25.
23. Fornander, vol. 1, pp. 22–5; Smith, 1910, pp. 61–2.
24. Turner, 1884, pp. 230–1.
25. Fornander, vol. 1, pp. 22–4.
26. Fornander, vol. 1, p. 203.
27. For identification of Maori Hawaiki with Tahitian islands: Smith, 1910, p. 259; Buck, 1949, p. 37.
28. Smith, 1910, pp. 66, 68.
29. Porter, vol. 2, p. 137.
30. For Marquesan lists, Smith, 1910, pp. 115–19.
31. Fornander, vol. 1, pp. 22–3, 180.

SOURCES

32. For review of varying interpretations, Buck, 1938A, pp. 248–52.

33. Fornander, vol. 1, pp. x, xi.
34. Grey, 1855, p. x.
35. Ellis, W., 1827, p. 419.
36. Cook, 1784, vol. 1, pp. 370–1.
37. Corney, vol. 2, pp. 292–4.
38. Métraux, pp. 33–4.
39. Smith, 1913, p. 199; Williams, H. W., pp. 111–2.
40. Stair, pp. 271–89.
41. For inquiries in Rarotonga, Smith, 1910, pp. 272–87.
42. Grey, 1855, p. 132.
43. Williams, H. W., pp. 110–1; Bennett.
44. Prout, pp. 48–9.
45. Smith, 1910, p. 31.
46. Smith, 1910, pp. 24–45.
47. Buck, 1949, pp. 37–8.
48. Buck, 1938A, p. 253.
49. Hawkesworth, vol. 3, pp. 473–4.
50. Smith, 1910, pp. 263, 44, 76, 70.

51. Colenso, p. 59; Grey, 1855, pp. xi–xiii, 1928.
52. Smith, 1913, pp. 119–20.
53. Smith, 1918, p. 226.
54. For account of finding of Rarotonga, Williams, J., pp. 52, 55–7, 62–3, 65, 76, 96–100, 103.
55. Gill, 1876B, pp. 74–5, 1915, pp. 145–50.
56. Grey, 1855, p. 134.
57. Gill, 1876B, p. 16.
58. Buck, 1932B, p. 19.
59. For suggested reconstruction from Atia-te-varinga, Smith, 1910, pp. 76–9.
60. Gill, 1876B, pp. 3, 5, 21.
61. Fornander, vol. 1, p. xvi.
62. Tyerman and Bennet, vol. 2, p. 31; Williams, J., p. 506; Polack, vol. 1, pp. 17–18.
63. Gill, 1876B, pp. 142–9.
64. Cook, 1784, vol. 2, pp. 180–9, 191.
65. Cook, 1784, vol. 2, p. 75.
66. Buck, 1938A.

CHAPTER SIX (*pages 128–143*)

1. Ellis, W., vol. 1; Martin; Shortland, 1856, p. 27.
2. Buck, 1938A, pp. 310–1.
3. King, pp. 26–9.
4. Gill, 1876B, p. 135.
5. Bligh, p. 147.
6. Buck, 1938B, pp. 194–5.
7. Williams, J., p. 297.
8. Williams, J., pp. 151–2.
9. Martin, vol. 1, p. 265.
10. Raeside; Cook, 1893, pp. 121–2.
11. For opinions of this type: Smith, 1910, pp. 186–7; Buck, 1938A, pp. 138, 306; Heyerdahl, 1950, pp. 103–4.
12. Hillebrand, p. 314; Buck, 1938A, p. 309.

13. Williams, J., p. 492; Buck, 1938A, p. 309.
14. For development of cultivated plants, de Candolle.
15. De Candolle, pp. 73–4, 307; MacDaniels, p. 3; Rock, pp. 115–6.
16. Cf. Porter, vol. 2, pp. 54–5.
17. Moerenhout, vol. 1, p. 54.
18. Moerenhout, vol. 1, pp. 380–1.
19. Williams, J., p. 492.
20. Buck, 1950, p. 31.
21. Heyerdahl, 1950, p. 104.
22. Merrill, pp. 205–6.
23. Brown, F. B. H., p. 7.
24. For distribution of sweet potato, Dixon, 1932.
25. Turner, 1861, p. 192.

26. For *feʻi* and seedless banana in Tahiti and Hawaii, Mac-Daniels, pp. 3–4, 12, 51.
27. Duff, p. 156.
28. Duff, p. 80.
29. Duff, pp. 163–7; Hale, p. 148.
30. Duff, pp. 12, 228–33.

31. Buck, 1949, pp. 314–6.
32. Métraux, pp. 331–41, 392–411, 419.
33. De Bougainville, pp. 278–80.
34. Piddington, pp. 224–5; Handy, pp. 22–3.

## CHAPTER SEVEN (*pages 144–162*)

1. For archaeology of mid-Pacific equatorial atolls; Emory, 1934; Buck, 1938A, pp. 140–2; Duff, pp. 127, 203.
2. Christophersen.
3. For ethnology of northern Cooks: Buck, 1932A and B; Beaglehole.
4. Buck, 1932B, pp. 11–13; Duff, p. 3; Williams, J., pp. 466–8.
5. Moerenhout, vol. 1, p. 206.
6. Hale, pp. 155, 166.
7. Turner, 1884, p. 275; Gill, 1876A, p. 22; Pritchard, p. 405.
8. For cultural affinities of Pukapuka, Beaglehole, pp. 413–5.
9. For ethnology of Tokelaus: Hale, pp. 150–5; Macgregor, 1937.
10. Dillon, vol. 2, p. 79; Turner, 1861, p. 270.
11. Cook, 1784, vol. 1, pp. 368–9; Burrows, p. 171.
12. For stories of Tokelau contacts, Macgregor, 1937, pp. 26–8.
13. Elbert, p. 159.
14. Williams, J., pp. 197–8, 468; Ellis, W., 1831, vol. 1, pp. 125–7; Dillon, vol. 2, pp. 103, 135; Cook, 1784, vol. 1, pp. 200–2.
15. Macgregor, 1933, p. 43; Bryan, pp. 70, 73, 82; Emory, 1939.
16. Maude.
17. Hale, pp. 90–1.

18. Kotzebue, vol. 2, pp. 144–6, end-chart, vol. 3, pp. 118–9, 177–80, end-charts.
19. Wilkes, vol. 5, pp. 37–108; Hale, pp. 69–103.
20. Porter, vol. 2, pp. 54–5, 135–6.
21. For general account of mid-Pacific atolls, Bryan.
22. Métraux, p. 35.
23. For cultural affinities of Easter Island, Métraux, pp. 412–20; for linguistic relationships, Elbert, pp. 159, 166.
24. Métraux, p. 417.
25. Métraux, pp. 13, 19, 153–4.
26. For archaeology of Pitcairn and reconstructions therefrom: Lavachery; Buck, 1938A, pp. 216–21; Duff, pp. 142–3.
27. Laval, p. 15n.
28. Buck, 1938A, p. 218; Moerenhout, vol. 1, pp. 54, 380–1.
29. Dillon, vol. 2, pp. 111–2.
30. Moerenhout, vol. 1, p. 138.
31. Moerenhout, vol. 2, pp. 331–2.
32. Aitken, p. 165; Moerenhout, vol. 2, p. 333; Wilson, J., p. xliv; Ellis, W., vol. 3, pp. 380–1.
33. Moerenhout, vol. 1, p. 152, vol. 2, pp. 346–8.
34. Smith, 1893; McCarthy.
35. Buck, 1938A, pp. 44–5.
36. Turner, 1861, pp. 391–2.
37. Markham, vol. 2, pp. 493–4.

## CHAPTER EIGHT (*pages 163–185*)

1. For archaeology of New Zealand, Duff.
2. For moa-hunter sites, Duff, pp. 254–89.
3. Duff, pp. 79–137, 234, 258–9.
4. Duff, pp. 10–1.
5. Holland, p. 2.
6. Spoehr, p. 460.
7. Duff, pp. 11, 80; Gifford, p. 128.
8. Elbert, pp. 159, 166.
9. Cook, 1893, p. 191.
10. Hawkesworth, vol. 3, pp. 473–4.
11. Marsden, p. 219.
12. Polack, vol. 1, pp. 17–18.
13. Williams, J., p. 506.
14. Hale, pp. 146–7.
15. Shortland, 1856, p. 28.
16. Tyerman and Bennet, vol. 2, p. 31.
17. Buck, 1949, pp. 4–64.
18. Thomson, vol. 1, pp. 59–68.
19. Colenso, pp. 48, 59.
20. White, J., vol. 1, pp. iv–vi.
21. White, J., vol. 2, p. 189, vol. 4, pp. 3–26.
22. Smith, 1913, pp. 189–91; Best, pp. 22–3.
23. Williams, H. W.
24. Buck, 1949, p. 11.
25. Buck, 1938A, pp. 75, 250–2.
26. Buck, 1949, pp. 4–64, 1938A *passim*.
27. Ngata, pp. 337–346.
28. Wilson, J. A., p. 7.
29. For early account of tribal histories, canoe traditions and genealogies, Shortland, 1856, Ch. 1.
30. Buck, 1938A, pp. 176–8.
31. Shortland, 1851, p. 102.
32. Smith, 1910, pp. 257–87. Cf. Wilson, J. A., p. 13.
33. Buck, 1949, pp. 36–8, 1938A, p. 78.
34. Ramsden, p. 43.
35. See Chapter V.
36. Maretu.
37. Smith, 1910, pp. 70, 76, 44; Gill, 1876B, p. 167, 1876A, p. 25; Buck, 1944, p. 295.
38. Andersen, pp. 259–60.
39. Elbert, p. 166.
40. Duff, pp. 78, 192, 285–8.
41. Duff, pp. 18, 28, 31.
42. Buck, 1938A, p. 60.
43. Williams, J., p. 498.
44. Jones, pp. 303–5.
45. Raeside.
46. Cf. Duff, pp. 7–8, 16–22.
47. Duff, pp. 7, 31; Skinner and Phillipps, pp. 169–71.
48. Shand, pp. 52–5.
49. Prout, p. 48.
50. Colenso, p. 59.
51. Stowell; Lawlor, pp. 172–7.
52. Grey, 1928.
53. Banks, 1896, p. 212.

## CHAPTER NINE (*pages 186–212*)

1. Shand, p. 10.
2. Hornell, 1936, p. 401.
3. Kotzebue, vol. 3, p. 139.
4. Elbert, p. 148; Hornell, 1936, pp. 395–8; Kotzebue, vol. 3, pp. 98, 126, 193.
5. Krämer, 1938, p. 87.
6. Kotzebue, vol. 3, p. 179.
7. Kotzebue, vol. 2, pp. 144–6, end-chart.
8. Cook, 1784, vol. 1, pp. 209–11.

9. Williams, J., pp. 17–18.
10. Bligh, p. 147; Williams, J., p. 68.
11. Gill, 1876A, p. 15.
12. Gill, 1876A, pp. 102–3.
13. Ellis, W., 1831, vol. 3, p. 390.
14. Morrison, pp. 68, 124.
15. Hornell, 1936, pp. 398–408.
16. Eilers, 1934, p. 385.
17. Cantova, p. 220.
18. Kotzebue, vol. 3, pp. 126–30, 139.
19. Lesson, A., vol. 1, p. 325.
20. Sabatier, pp. 26–7.
21. Dillon, vol. 2, p. 103.
22. Hale, p. 165.
23. Dillon, vol. 2, p. 112, vol. 1, pp. 294–5.
24. Cook, 1784, vol. 1, p. 376.
25. Williams, J., pp. 153–4.
26. Williams, J., pp. 96–7, 275–6; Gill, 1876A, pp. 175–6; Hornell, 1936, pp. 170–5.
27. For archaeology of Nihoa and Necker, Emory, 1928.
28. King, pp. 32–3.
29. Lesson, A., vol. 4, pp. 6–32.
30. Markham, vol. 1, p. 227, vol. 2, pp. 488–98.
31. Codrington, p. 6.
32. Dillon, vol. 2, p. 138; Firth, 1954, pp. 89–92.
33. Markham, 1, pp. 39, 142–3; Amherst and Thomson.
34. Macgregor, 1933, pp. 40–1.
35. Kotzebue, vol. 2, pp. 144–5.
36. Nevermann, pp. 221–30.
37. Cook, 1784, vol. 1, pp. 368–9.
38. Martin, 1, pp. 73–6, 317–47.
39. For Rotuma incidents, Dillon, vol. 1, pp. 294–5, vol. 2, pp. 97, 102–3.
40. Pritchard, p. 390.
41. Dillon, vol. 2, p. 78.
42. Dillon, vol. 2, pp. 78–9; Hornell, 1936, pp. 319–27.
43. Cook, 1784, vol. 2, pp. 142–3; Pritchard, p. 403.
44. Beechey, vol. 1, pp. 168–72; Morrison, p. 201.
45. Pritchard, p. 390.
46. Cantova, pp. 215–6.
47. Hornell, 1936, p. 419.
48. De Freycinet, vol. 2, pp. 81, 84, 86, 87.
49. Kotzebue, vol. 2, pp. 240–1, vol. 3, pp. 111–2; de Freycinet, vol. 2, p. 84.
50. De Freycinet, vol. 2, p. 83.
51. Arago, Part 2, p. 11.
52. Südsee-Expedition, sections on navigation.
53. Cook, 1784, vol. 2, pp. 177–8.
54. Cantova, pp. 215–220; Kotzebue, vol. 3, pp. 184, 126–39.
55. Kotzebue, 3, pp. 122–3, 135.
56. Kotzebue, vol. 2, p. 242.
57. Cantova, pp. 210–15.
58. De Freycinet, vol. 2, pp. 123–32; Hornell, 1936, pp. 361–71, 374–84.
59. Kotzebue, vol. 2, p. 243; de Freycinet, vol. 2, pp. 102, 131.
60. Corney, vol. 2, pp. 282–3.
61. Kotzebue, 3, pp. 130, 134, 137.
62. De Bougainville, pp. 268–9.
63. Cook, 1893, p. 121.
64. Morrison, p. 201.
65. Cook, 1784, vol. 1, p. 376.
66. Cook, 1784, vol. 1, p. 376.
67. Vason, p. 145.
68. Kotzebue, vol. 2, pp. 242–3. Cf. de Freycinet, vol. 2, p. 132.
69. De Freycinet, vol. 2, pp. 102–5; Nevermann, pp. 215–6.
70. Burney, vol. 1.
71. Wilkes, vol. 5, p. 4, vol. 3, p. 370.
72. Cf. Leach, pp. 282–9, 277, 129.
73. Cf. Raeside, p. 169.
74. Cf. Stefansson, pp. 77–143.
75. Kotzebue, vol. 2, pp. 122–3.

# Bibliography

AITKEN, A. 1930. 'Ethnology of Tubuai.' *Bishop Museum Bulletin 70*.

AMHERST, Lord, and THOMSON, B. 1891. *The Discovery of the Solomon Islands*, 2 vols. Hakluyt Society. Second series, vols. 7, 8.

ANDERSEN, J. C. 1952. 'Maori Place-names.' *Polynesian Society Memoir*. Vol. 20.

ANDERSON, J. 1826. *Mission to the East Coast of Sumatra*. Edinburgh, Blackwood.

ARAGO, J. E. V. 1823. *Narrative of a Voyage Round the World*. London, Treuttel.

ARMSTRONG, E. S. 1900. *The History of the Melanesian Mission*. London, Isbister.

BANKS, J. 1896. *Journal ... edited by Sir Joseph D. Hooker*. London, Macmillan.

BANKS, J. MS. Journal. Unabridged manuscript. Copy, Turnbull Library.

BEAGLEHOLE, E. and P. 1938. 'Ethnology of Pukapuka.' *Bishop Museum Bulletin, 150*.

BEECHEY, F. W. 1831. *Narrative of a Voyage*. 2 vols. London, Colburn.

BENNETT, H. D. 1937. 'Maori Traditions.' *Wellington Evening Post*, Aug. 31.

BEST, E. 1924. 'The Maori as he Was.' Wellington, Dominion Museum. *New Zealand Board of Science and Art Manual No. 4.*

BLIGH, W. 1792. *A Voyage to the South Sea*. London, Nicol.

BOUGAINVILLE, L. A. DE. 1772. *A Voyage Round the World*. London, Nourse.

BOVIS, E. DE. 1909. *État de la société taïtienne*. Papeete, Imprimerie du Gouvernement. Reprint from *Revue Coloniale*, 1855.

BOYD, W. C. 1951. *Genetics and the Races of Man*. Oxford, Blackwell Scientific Publications.

BROSSES, C. DE. 1756. *Histoire des Navigations aux Terres Australes*. 2 vols. Paris, Durand.

BROWN, F. B. H. 1935. 'Flora of South-eastern Polynesia. III. Dicotyledons.' *Bishop Museum Bulletin 130*.

BROWN, G. 1910. *Melanesians and Polynesians*. London, Macmillan.

BROWN, J. M. 1907. *Maori and Polynesian*. London, Hutchinson.

BRYAN, E. H. 1941. *American Polynesia*. Honolulu, Tongg.

BUCK, P. H. 1932A. 'Ethnology of Tongareva.' *Bishop Museum Bulletin 92*.

BUCK, P. H. 1932B. 'Ethnology of Manihiki and Rakahanga.' *Bishop Museum Bulletin 99*.

BUCK, P. H. 1938A. *Vikings of the Sunrise*. Philadelphia, Lippincott.

BUCK, P. H. 1938B. 'Ethnology of Mangareva.' *Bishop Museum Bulletin 157*.

# BIBLIOGRAPHY

BUCK, P. H. 1949. *The Coming of the Maori*. Wellington, Whitcombe and Tombs.

BUCK, P. H. 1950. 'Material Culture of Kapingamarangi.' *Bishop Museum Bulletin 200.*

BURNEY, J. 1803–17. *A Chronological History of the Discoveries in the South Sea or Pacific Ocean.* 5 vols. London, Nicol.

BURROWS, E. G. 1937. 'Ethnology of Uvea.' *Bishop Museum Bulletin 145.*

CANDOLLE, A. DE. 1909. *Origin of Cultivated Plants*. London, Kegan Paul.

CANTOVA, J. A. 1770. In *Choix de lettres édifiantes et curieuses écrites des missions étrangères par quelques missionnaires de la compagnie de Jésus.* Pp. 188–247. Paris, LeClerc.

CARRINGTON, H. 1939. *Life of Captain Cook*. London, Sidgwick and Jackson.

CHRISTOPHERSEN, E. 1927. 'Vegetation of Pacific Equatorial Islands.' *Bishop Museum Bulletin 44.*

CODRINGTON, R. H. 1891. *The Melanesians*. Oxford, Clarendon Press.

COLENSO, W. 1868. 'The Maori Races of New Zealand.' *New Zealand Institute, Transactions and Proceedings.* Vol. 1 Essays.

COOK, J. 1784. *A Voyage to the Pacific Ocean*. Vols. 1, 2. London, Nicol and Cadell.

COOK, J. 1893. *Captain Cook's Journal during his First Voyage ... edited by W. J. L. Wharton*. London, Stock.

CORNEY, B. G. 1913–18. *The Quest and Occupation of Tahiti.* 3 vols. Hakluyt Society. Second series, vols. 32, 36, 43.

DIBBLE, S. 1839. *History of the Sandwich Islands*. New York, Taylor and Dodd.

DILLON, P. 1829. *Narrative ... of a Voyage in the South Seas.* 2 vols. London, Hurst Chance.

DIXON, R. B. 1932. 'The Problem of the Sweet Potato in Polynesia.' *American Anthropologist*, Vol. 34, pp. 40–66.

DIXON, R. B. 1933. 'Contacts with South America Across the South Pacific.' In *The American Aborigines, ed. Jenness D.* Toronto, pp. 313–53.

DUFF, R. 1950. 'The Moa-hunter Period of Maori Culture'. Wellington, Department of Internal Affairs. *Canterbury Museum Bulletin 1.*

DUMONT D'URVILLE, J. S. C. 1853. *Voyage Autour du Monde.* 2 vols., Paris, Furne.

EILERS, A. 1934. *Ergebnisse der Südsee-Expedition 1908–10* (Part 2B, Vol. 8). *Inseln um Ponape*. Hamburg, Friederichsen, de Gruyter.

ELBERT, S. H. 1953. 'Internal Relationships of Polynesian Languages and Dialects.' *Southwestern Journal of Anthropology*. Vol. 9, pp. 147–73.

ELLIS, A. 1946. *Mid-Pacific Outposts*. Auckland, Brown and Stewart.

ELLIS, W. 1827. *Narrative of a Tour through Hawaii*. London, Fisher and Jackson.

ELLIS, W. 1831. *Polynesian Researches*. 4 vols. London, Fisher and Jackson.

# BIBLIOGRAPHY

EMORY, K. P. 1928. 'Archaeology of Nihoa and Necker Islands.' *Bishop Museum Bulletin 53.*

EMORY, K. P. 1934. 'Archaeology of the Pacific Equatorial Islands.' *Bishop Museum Bulletin 123.*

EMORY, K. P. 1939. 'Archaeology of the Phoenix Islands.' Hawaiian Academy of Science. Proceedings, Fourteenth Annual Meeting, 1938–9. *Bishop Museum Special Publication 34.*

EMORY, K. P. 1953. 'A Program for Polynesian Archeology.' *American Anthropologist.* Vol. 55, pp. 752–5.

FIRTH, R. W. 1939. *Primitive Polynesian Economy.* London, Routledge.

FIRTH, R. W. 1954. 'Anuta and Tikopia: symbiotic elements in social organisation.' *Polynesian Society Journal.* Vol. 63, pp. 87–131.

FORNANDER, A. 1878–85. *An Account of the Polynesian Race.* 3 vols. London, Trubner.

FORSTER, J. R. 1778. *Observations made During a Voyage Round the World.* London, Robinson.

FREYCINET, L. C. DE. 1824–44. *Voyage Autour du Monde.* 8 vols. Paris, Pillet.

GATTY, H. 1943. *The Raft Book.* New York, Grady Press.

GIFFORD, E. W. 1951. 'Anthropological Problems in Fiji.' *Polynesian Society Journal.* Vol. 60, pp. 122–9.

GILL, W. W. 1876A. *Life in the Southern Isles.* London, Religious Tract Society.

GILL, W. W. 1876B. *Myths and Songs of the South Pacific.* London, King.

GILL, W. W. 1915. 'The Origin of the Island Manihiki.' *Polynesian Society Journal.* Vol. 24, pp. 144–51.

GRAYDON, J. J. 1952. 'Blood Groups of the Polynesians.' *Mankind.* Vol. 4, pp. 329–39.

GREENBERG, J. H. 1953. 'Historical Linguistics and Unwritten Languages.' In *Anthropology Today.* International symposium on anthropology. Chicago University Press.

GREY, G. 1855. *Polynesian Mythology and Ancient Traditional History of the New Zealand Race.* London, Murray.

GREY, G. 1928. 'Polynesian Migrations. Coming of the Maoris.' *Auckland Star,* 3 Nov.

HALE, H. 1846. *United States Exploring Expedition during the Years 1838, 1839, 1840, 1841, 1842 ... Ethnography and Philology.* Philadelphia, Lea and Blanchard.

HANDY, E. S. C. 1930. 'The Problem of Polynesian Origins.' *Bishop Museum Occasional Papers.* Vol. IX, No. 8.

HAWKESWORTH, J. 1773. *An Account of the Voyages ... by Commodore Byron, Captain Wallis, Captain Carteret, and Captain Cook.* 3 vols. London, Strahan and Cadell.

HEINE-GELDERN, R. 1952. 'Some Problems of Migration in the Pacific.' *Kultur und Sprache.* Ed. W. Koppers. Wiener Beiträge zur Kulturgeschichte und Linguistik. IX. 1952. Pp. 313–62.

HENRY, T. 1928. 'Ancient Tahiti.' *Bishop Museum Bulletin 48.*

# BIBLIOGRAPHY

HEYERDAHL, T. 1950. *The Kon-Tiki Expedition*. London, George Allen and Unwin.

HEYERDAHL, T. 1952. *American Indians in the Pacific*. London, George Allen and Unwin.

HILLEBRAND, W. 1888. *Flora of the Hawaiian Islands*. New York, Westermann.

HOLLAND, S. G. 1953. 'Western Samoa.' *New Zealand Department of External Affairs Publication No. 128*.

HORNELL, J. 1936. 'Canoes of Oceania.' Vol. 1. *Bishop Museum Special Publication 27*.

HORNELL, J. 1945. 'Was there pre-Columbian Contact between the Peoples of Oceania and America?' *Polynesian Society Journal*. Vol. 54, pp. 167–91.

JONES, F. WOOD-. 1912. *Coral and Atolls*. London, Lovell Reeve.

KING, J. 1784. *A Voyage to the Pacific Ocean*. Vol. 3. London, Nicol and Cadell.

KOTZEBUE, O. VON. 1821. *Voyage of Discovery in the South Sea*. London, Longman.

KRAMER, A. 1938. *Ergebnisse der Südsee-Expedition 1908–10* (Part 2B, Vol. 11) *Ralik-Ratak (Marshall Inseln)*. (First half.) Hamburg, Freiderichsen, de Gruyter.

LANG, J. D. 1877. *Origins and Migrations of the Polynesian Nation*. Sydney, Robertson.

LAVACHERY, H. 1936. 'Contributions a l'étude de l'archéologie de l'île de Pitcairn.' *Société des Américanistes de Belgique Bulletin 19*.

LAVAL, H. 1938. *Mangareva*. Braine-le-Comte, Maison des Pères des Sacrés-Cœurs.

LAWLOR, P. A. 1954. *Books and Bookmen*. Wellington, Whitcombe and Tombs.

LEACH, H. G. 1946. *Pageant of Old Scandinavia*. Princeton University Press.

LESSON, A. 1880–4. *Les Polynésiens*. 4 vols. Paris, Leroux.

LESSON, R. P., and GARNOT, —. 1826. 'Zoologie' (vol. 1—first part). In Duperrey, R. J., *Voyage Autour du Monde*. Paris, Bertrand.

LUCETT, E. 1851. *Rovings in the Pacific*. 2 vols. London, Longman.

McCARTHY, F. D. 1934. 'Norfolk Island.' *Polynesian Society Journal*. Vol. 43, pp. 267–70.

MACDANIELS, L. H. 1947. 'A Study of the *fe'i* Banana and its Distribution with Reference to Polynesian Migrations.' *Bishop Museum Bulletin 190*.

MACGREGOR, G. 1933. 'Anthropological Work of the Templeton Crocker Expedition.' *Bishop Museum Annual Report for 1933*, pp. 38–43, *Bulletin 124*.

MACGREGOR, G. 1937. 'Ethnology of Tokelau Islands.' *Bishop Museum Bulletin 146*.

MAKEMSON, M. W. 1941. *The Morning Star Rises*. New Haven, Yale University Press.

# BIBLIOGRAPHY

MALO, D. 1903. *Hawaiian Antiquities.* Honolulu, Hawaiian Gazette Co.

MARETU. MS. Autobiography. Manuscript in the Polynesian Society Library.

MARKHAM, C. 1904. *The Voyages of Pedro Fernandez de Quiros, 1595 to 1606.* 2 vols. Hakluyt Society. Second series, vols. 14, 15.

MARSDEN, S. 1932. *The Letters and Journals of Samuel Marsden, 1765–1838, edited by J. R. Elder.* Dunedin, Coulls Somerville Wilkie.

MARTIN, J. 1817. *An Account of the Natives of the Tonga Islands.* 2 vols. London, Constable.

MAUDE, H. E. 1952. 'The Colonization of the Phoenix Islands.' *Polynesian Society Journal.* Vol. 61, pp. 62–89.

MERRILL, E. D. 1945. *Plant Life of the Pacific World.* New York, Macmillan.

METRAUX, A. 1940. 'Ethnology of Easter Island.' *Bishop Museum Bulletin 160.*

MOERENHOUT, J. A. 1837. *Voyages aux îles du Grand Océan.* 2 vols. Paris, Bertrand.

MORRISON, J. 1935. *The Journal of James Morrison.* Great Britain, Golden Cockerel Press.

NEVERMANN, H. 1938. *Ergebnisse der Südsee-Expedition, 1908–10* (Part 2B, vol. 11) *Ralik-Ratak (Marshall Inseln).* (Second half.) Hamburg, Freiderichsen, de Gruyter.

NGATA, A. P. 1950. 'The Io Cult – Early Migration – Puzzle of the Canoes.' *Polynesian Society Journal.* Vol. 59, pp. 335–46.

PIDDINGTON, R. 1939. Part 2 of Williamson, R. W., and Piddington, R., *Essays in Polynesian Ethnology.* Pp. 199–353. Cambridge University Press.

POLACK, J. S. 1840. *Manners and Customs of the New Zealanders.* 2 vols. London, Madden.

POLYNESIAN SOCIETY. 1924. 'The Polynesians as Navigators.' *Polynesian Society Journal.* Vol. 33, note on pp. 221–2.

PORTER, D. 1815. *Journal of a Cruise made to the Pacific Ocean.* 2 vols. Philadelphia, Bradford and Inskeep.

POWELL, G. 1953. 'The Indonesian Element in Melanesian.' *Polynesian Society Journal.* Vol. 62, pp. 73–9.

PRITCHARD, W. T. 1866. *Polynesian Reminiscences.* London, Chapman and Hall.

PROUT, E. 1843. *Memoirs of the Life of the Rev. John Williams.* London, Snow.

QUATREFAGES, J. L. A. DE. 1866. *Les Polynésiens et leur Migrations.* Paris, Bertrand.

RAESIDE, J. D. 1948. 'Some Post-Glacial Climatic Changes in Canterbury.' *Royal Society of New Zealand Transactions and Proceedings.* Vol. 77, Part 1, pp. 153–71.

RAMSDEN, E. 1951. *Rangiatea.* Wellington, Reed.

ROCK, J. F. 1913. *The Indigenous Trees of the Hawaiian Islands.* Honolulu.

# BIBLIOGRAPHY

RODMAN, H. 1928. 'The Sacred Calabash.' *Polynesian Society Journal.* Vol. 37, pp. 75–85.

SABATIER, E. *c.* 1939. *Sous l'équateur du Pacifique: les Iles Gilbert.* Paris, Editions Dillen.

SEEMANN, B. 1852–7. *The Botany of the Voyage of H.M.S. 'Herald'.* London. Lovell Reeve.

SHAND, A. 1911. 'The Moriori People of the Chatham Islands,' *Polynesian Society Memoir.* Vol. 2.

SHORTLAND, E. 1815. *The Southern Districts of New Zealand.* London, Longman.

SHORTLAND, E. 1856. *Traditions and Superstitions of the New Zealanders.* London, Longman.

SKINNER, H. D. 1951. 'Some Aspects of the History of Polynesian Material Culture.' *Polynesian Society Journal.* Vol. 60, pp. 40–6.

SKINNER, H. D., and PHILLIPPS, W. J. 1953. 'Necklaces, Pendants and Amulets from the Chatham Islands and New Zealand.' *Polynesian Society Journal.* Vol. 62, pp. 169–83.

SMITH, S. P. 1893. Note 28. *Polynesian Society Journal.* Vol. 2, p. 126.

SMITH, S. P. 1907. Note. *Polynesian Society Journal.* Vol. 16, p. 93.

SMITH, S. P. 1910. *Hawaiki.* Wellington, Whitcombe and Tombs.

SMITH, S. P. 1913. 'Lore of the Whare-wananga.' Part 2, Chs. III–V. *Polynesian Society Journal.* Vol. 22, pp. 118–33, 189–218.

SMITH, S. P. 1918. 'Guiding Stars in Navigation.' *Polynesian Society Journal.* Vol. 27, p. 226.

SPOEHR, A. 1952. 'Time Perspective in Micronesia and Polynesia.' *Southwestern Journal of Anthropology.* Vol. 8, pp. 457–65.

STAIR, J. B. 1897. *Old Samoa.* London, Religious Tract Society.

STEFANSSON, V. 1943. *Greenland.* London, Harrap.

STOKES, J. F. G. 1928. Note. *Polynesian Society Journal.* Vol. 37, pp. 85–7.

STOWELL, H. 1925. 'Maori Migrations.' *New Zealand Herald,* 20 June–18 July.

STOWELL, H. 1926. 'The Ancient Maori. III. Canoe Migrations.' *Christchurch Weekly Press.* 7 Oct.

SÜDSEE-EXPEDITION 1908–10, ed. Thilenius, A. 1932–8. *Ergebnisse der Südsee-Expedition 1908–10. II. Ethnographie: B. Micronesien.* Vols. 5–11. Hamburg, Freiderichsen, de Gruyter.

SWADESH, M. 1952. 'Lexico-statistic Dating of Prehistoric Ethnic Contacts.' *American Philosophical Society Proceedings.* Vol. 96, pp. 452–63.

THOMSON, A. S. 1859. *Story of New Zealand.* 2 vols. London, Murray.

TURNER, G. 1861. *Nineteen Years in Polynesia.* London. Snow.

TURNER, G. 1884. *Samoa.* London, Macmillan.

TYERMAN, D., and BENNET, G. 1831. *Journal of Voyages and Travels.* 2 vols. London, Westley and Davis.

UNITED KINGDOM ADMIRALTY. 1931–46. *Pacific Islands Pilot.* 3 vols. Hydrographic Department, Admiralty.

# BIBLIOGRAPHY

United Kingdom Admiralty. 1952. *Manual of Seamanship*. Vol. 2. London, H.M. Stationery Office.

Vason, G. 1815. *An Authentic Narrative of Four Years' Residence at Tongatabu*. London. Longman.

Visher, S. S. 1925. 'Tropical Cyclones of the Pacific.' *Bishop Museum Bulletin 20.*

Webber, J. 1808. *Views in the South Seas*. London, Boydell.

White, J. 1887–91. *Ancient History of the Maori*. 6 vols. Wellington, Government Printer.

White, T. 1907. 'On the Use of Birds in Navigation.' *Polynesian Society Journal*. Vol. 16, pp. 92–3.

Wilkes, C. 1845. *Narrative of the United States Exploring Expedition during the Years 1838, 1839, 1840, 1841 and 1842*. 5 vols. Philadelphia, Lea and Blanchard.

Williams, H. W. 1937. 'The Maruiwi Myth.' *Polynesian Society Journal*. Vol. 46, pp. 105–22.

Williams, J. 1837. *A Narrative of Missionary Enterprises in the South Sea Islands*. London, Snow.

Wilson, J. 1799. *A Missionary Voyage to the Southern Pacific Ocean*. London, Chapman.

Wilson, J. A. 1894. *Sketches of Maori Life and History*. Auckland, Champtaloup and Cooper.

Zuniga, M. de 1814. *An Historical View of the Philippine Islands ... translated by John Maver*. London, Black and Parry.

# Index

Bau, 198
Bauro, 196
Beaglehole, E. and P., 218 (Ch. 7:3, 8), 221
Beechey, F. W., 44, 64–5, 75, 89, 201, 214 (Ch. 2:17; Ch. 3:18), 220 (Ch. 9:44), 221
Belotu, 103, 104, 197
Bennet, G., 217 (Ch. 5:62), 219 (Ch. 8:16), 226
Bennett, H. D., 217 (Ch. 5:43), 221
Bermuda, 36
Beru, 103
Best, E., 216 (Ch. 4:30), 219 (Ch. 8:22), 221
Betel-nut, 93, 94
Birds, 52, 192
Bjarni, 210
Black Sea, 33
Bligh, W., 130, 189, 217 (Ch. 6:5), 220 (Ch. 9:10), 221
Blood group, 98, 223 (Graydon)
Bogha, 188
Bokak, 188
Bonin, 84
Borabora, 76
Bougainville, de, 20, 21, 22, 27, 28, 42, 56, 141, 206, 213 (Ch. 1:22, 23), 218 (Ch. 6:33), 220 (Ch. 9:62), 221
*Bounty*, 27, 130, 135, 156, 189, 190, 207
Bovis, de, 214 (Ch. 2:33), 221
Bow and arrow, 93
Boyd, W. C., 216 (Ch. 4:44, 47), 221
Breadfruit, 77, 95, 133, 134, 135, 136, 153, 156, 157
Brendan, 34
Brosses, de, 15, 213 (Ch. 1:2; Ch. 2:2), 215 (Ch. 4:2), 216, (Ch. 5:1), 221
Brown, B. F. H., 217 (Ch. 6:23)
Brown, George, 93, 216 (Ch. 4:39), 221
Bryan, E. H., 218 (Ch. 7:15), 221

Buck, 113, 120, 126, 168, 170, 171, 175, 214 (Ch. 2:21; Ch. 3:8), 215 (Ch. 4:26), 216 (Ch. 4:31, 35, 37, 40, 43; Ch. 5:6, 7, 27), 217 (Ch. 5:32, 47, 48, 58, 66; Ch. 6:2, 6, 11, 12, 13, 20), 218 (Ch. 6:31; Ch. 7:1, 3, 4, 26, 28, 35), 219 (Ch. 8:17, 24, 25, 26, 30, 33, 37, 42), 221, 222
Bulutu, 103, 104, 109
Burattu, 103
Burney, J., 214 (Ch. 2:7, 26, 28), 215 (Ch. 4:1), 216 (Ch. 4:49), 220 (Ch. 9:70), 222
Burotu, 197
Burrows, E. G., 215 (Ch. 3:33), 218 (Ch. 7:11), 222
Buru, 103, 104, 197

Calabash, 50–1, 226 (Rodman)
California, 85
Canaries, 35
Candolle, de, 215 (Ch. 4:24), 217 (Ch. 6:14, 15)
Cantova, 80, 81, 82, 101, 202, 203, 204, 212, 215 (Ch. 4:3), 216 (Ch. 5:1), 220 (Ch. 9:17, 46, 54, 57), 222
Cape Verde Islands, 36
Caribbean, 38
Caroline Islands, accidental voyages, 15, 52, 53, 79–82, 83; canoes of, 80, 81, 83, 204–7; discovery of, 202; extent of voyaging, 79–82, 187, 190–1, 107, 202–5, 207; geographical relationships of, 79, 81, 82, 90, 162; introduction of sweet potato, 202; maritime achievement, 53–4, 83, 84, 197–8, 201–7; navigation methods, 43, 46, 47, 49, 202–7; settlement of, 30, 84, 202. *See also* Ponape; Truk; West Fayu; Yap
Carrington, H., 213 (Ch. 1:2), 222
Carthaginians, 35–6
Caucasus, 109

Manahune, 170, 174

Mangaia, Mangaian, 12, 23, 25, 26, 27, 67, 72, 78, 117, 120, 125, 130, 131, 139, 186, 189. *See also* Ahuahu

Mangareva, 28, 63, 131, 135, 152, 154, 155, 156, 157, 160, 221 (Buck, 1938B), 224 (Laval)

Manicolo, 196

Manihi, 150

Manihiki, Manihikian, 26, 30, 48, 52, 58–61, 62, 66, 71, 119, 120, 144, 149–50, 151, 152, 192, 214 (Ch. 3:4), 221 (Buck, 1932B), 223 (Gill, 1915)

Manila, 79

Mannicolo, 19

Manua, 24, 61, 66, 73, 96, 105, 114

Maori, carving art of, 140; extent of voyaging, 41, 46, 167–8, 183–4, 186; language, 73, 149, 165, 177; movements to New Zealand, 41, 46, 143, 165–85; prehistory of, in New Zealand, 163–85; relationships with Chathams, 41, 74–5, 182–3; sailing directions, 46; story of accidental arrivals, 74; traditions, 46–7, 104, 107, 109–15, 119, 120, 122, 127, 221 (Andersen, J. C.; Bennett; Best; Brown, J. M.), 222 (Buck, 1949), 226 (Stowell, 1926), 227 (White, J.; Wilson, J. A.); tribal divisions of, 171–4. *See also* New Zealand.

Mapuagua, 63

Mareiu, 176, 189, 219 (Ch. 8:36), 225

Marianas, 43, 79, 81, 83, 84, 202, 203, 204, 205, 212

Mariner, W., 19, 42, 49–50, 54, 55, 56, 132, 198. *See also* Martin.

Markham, C., 216 (Ch. 4:32; Ch. 5:11), 218 (Ch. 7:37), 220 (Ch. 9:30, 33), 225

Marquesas Islands, extent of voyaging, 12, 30, 75, 76, 195–6; food plants and exiles from, 70, 71, 77; geographical relationships of, 12, 75, 76, 145, 149, 154, 195, 196; harpooning in, 140; knowledge of other islands, 83; linguistic and cultural affinities of, 75, 96, 140–3, 147–8, 154, 163–70, 172, 173–8, 181, 182, 184–5; mention of, in Forster's and Tupia's data, 25, 195, 196; traditional homelands, 107–8, 114, 122, 165; warfare in, 172

Marsden, S., 166–7, 219 (Ch. 8:11), 225

Marshall Islands, accidental voyages, 53, 82–3, 188; extent of voyaging, 82, 153, 188, 197; geographical relationships of, 75, 79–80, 82, 83, 153, 187–8, 197; headgear, 93; maritime achievement, 54, 205–7

Martin, J., 213 (Ch. 1:4), 214 (Ch. 2:29, 36), 216 (Ch. 4:41), 217 (Ch. 6:1, 9), 220 (Ch. 9:38), 225. *See also* Mariner.

Maruiwi, 170, 174

Mataki-te-rangi, 157

Mauke, 131, 176, 177, 188, 189, 192, 194

Maude, H. E., 215 (Ch. 3:27), 218 (Ch. 7:16), 225

Maui, 113, 116

Mauritius, 36, 49

Mediterranean, 33

Melanesia, Melanesian, 56, 89, 90, 126, 170, 221 (Armstrong; Brown), 225 (Powell). *See also* Fiji; New Guinea; New Hebrides; Santa Cruz; Solomons.

Mendana, 91, 197

Merrill, E. D., 217 (Ch. 6:22), 225

Meteorology, 15, 20, 25, 26, 30, 32, 33, 35, 36, 37, 38, 39–42, 46–54, 55, 56, 59, 60, 63–7, 69,